Lecture Notes in Computer Science 15014

Founding Editors

Gerhard Goos
Juris Hartmanis

Editorial Board Members

The series Lecture Notes in Computer Science (LNCS), including its subseries Lecture Notes in Artificial Intelligence (LNAI) and Lecture Notes in Bioinformatics (LNBI), has established itself as a medium for the publication of new developments in computer science and information technology research, teaching, and education.

LNCS enjoys close cooperation with the computer science R & D community, the series counts many renowned academics among its volume editors and paper authors, and collaborates with prestigious societies. Its mission is to serve this international community by providing an invaluable service, mainly focused on the publication of conference and workshop proceedings and postproceedings. LNCS commenced publication in 1973.

David Duenas-Cid · Peter Roenne ·
Melanie Volkamer · Jurlind Budurushi ·
Michelle Blom · Adrià Rodríguez-Pérez ·
Iuliia Spycher-Krivonosova ·
Jordi Castellà Roca · Jordi Barrat Esteve
Editors

Electronic Voting

9th International Joint Conference, E-Vote-ID 2024
Tarragona, Spain, October 2–4, 2024
Proceedings

 Springer

Editors
David Duenas-Cid
Kozminski University
Warsaw, Poland

Peter Roenne
University of Luxembourg
Esch-sur-Alzette, Luxembourg

Melanie Volkamer
Karlsruhe Institute of Technology
Karlsruhe, Germany

Jurlind Budurushi
Baden-Wuerttemberg Cooperative State
University
Karlsruhe, Germany

Michelle Blom
University of Melbourne
Melbourne, VIC, Australia

Adrià Rodríguez-Pérez
Universitat Pompeu Fabra
Barcelona, Spain

Iuliia Spycher-Krivonosova
University of Bern
Bern, Switzerland

Jordi Castellà Roca
Universitat Rovira i Virgili
Tarragona, Spain

Jordi Barrat Esteve
Universitat Rovira i Virgili
Tarragona, Spain

ISSN 0302-9743   ISSN 1611-3349 (electronic)
Lecture Notes in Computer Science
ISBN 978-3-031-72243-1   ISBN 978-3-031-72244-8 (eBook)
https://doi.org/10.1007/978-3-031-72244-8

This work was supported by KASTEL Security Research Lab.

This Springer imprint is published by the registered company Springer Nature Switzerland AG
The registered company address is: Gewerbestrasse 11, 6330 Cham, Switzerland

If disposing of this product, please recycle the paper.

Preface

This volume contains a selection of papers presented at E-Vote-ID 2024, the Ninth International Joint Conference on Electronic Voting, held on October 2–4, 2024. This is the first time the conference was held on the Mediterranean coast in Tarragona (Spain). The conference venue, in the fishermen's harbor of Tarragona, represents Catalan and Mediterranean cultures' singularity, bringing a new spirit to the conference and contributing to diversifying the venues where E-Vote-ID was held.

The E-Vote-ID Conference resulted from merging EVOTE and Vote-ID and counting up to 20 years since the first E-Vote conference in Austria. Since that conference in 2004, over 1800 experts have attended the venue, including scholars, practitioners, representatives of various authorities, electoral managers, vendors, and PhD students. The conference collected the most relevant debates on the development of Electronic Voting and Electoral Technologies, from aspects relating to security and usability through to practical experiences and applications of voting systems, also including legal, social, or political aspects, amongst others, turning out to be an important global reference point concerning these issues.

This year, as in previous editions, the conference consisted of:

- Security, Usability, and Technical Issues Track;
- Governance of E-Voting Track;
- Election and Practical Experiences Track;
- PhD Colloquium;
- Poster and Demo Session.

E-VOTE-ID 2024 received 36 submissions for consideration in the first two tracks (Technical and Governance Tracks), each being reviewed by 3 to 5 program committee members using a double-blind review process. As a result, 10 papers were accepted for this volume, representing 36% of the submitted proposals. The selected papers cover a wide range of topics connected with electronic voting, including experiences and revisions of the actual uses of E-voting systems and corresponding processes in elections.

We would also like to thank the local organizers, Prof. Jordi Castellà, Prof. Jordi Barrat, and the Fundació Universitat Rovira i Virgili, for their excellent collaboration in preparing the conference. We would like to extend our gratitude to the Port de Tarragona for their invaluable support and for allowing the use of their installations for the conference. The gratitude also goes to the KASTEL Security Research Labs for granting Open Access to these proceedings. Finally, we would like to thank and appreciate the international program members for their hard work in reviewing, discussing, and shepherding papers. They ensured, once again, the excellence of this proceedings with their knowledge and experience.

October 2024

David Duenas-Cid
Peter Roenne
Melanie Volkamer
Jurlind Budurushi
Michelle Blom
Adrià Rodríguez-Pérez
Iuliia Spycher-Krivonosova
Jordi Castellà Roca
Jordi Barrat Esteve

Organization

General Chairs

David Duenas-Cid   Kozminski University, Poland
Peter Roenne   University of Luxembourg, Luxembourg
Melanie Volkamer   Karlsruhe Institute of Technology, Germany

Local Chairs

Jordi Barrat i Esteve   Universitat Rovira i Virgili, Catalonia
Jordi Castellà i Roca   Universitat Rovira i Virgili, Catalonia

Track Chairs on Security, Usability and Technical Issues

Jurlind Budurushi   Baden-Wuerttemberg Cooperative State University, Germany
Michelle Blom   University of Melbourne, Australia

Track Chairs on Governance Issues

Adrià Rodríguez-Pérez   Universitat Pompeu Fabra, Catalonia
Iuliia Spycher-Krivonosova   University of Bern, Switzerland

Program Committee

Marta Aranyossy   Corvinus University of Budapest, Hungary
Roberto Araujo   Universidade Federal do Pará, Brazil
Bernhard Beckert   Karlsruhe Institute of Technology, Germany
Josh Benaloh   Microsoft, USA
Matthew Bernhard   Voting Works, USA
Jeremy Clark   Concordia Institute for Information Systems Engineering, Canada
César Collazos   Universidad del Cauca, Colombia

Contents

Belenios with Cast-as-Intended: Towards a Usable Interface

Véronique Cortier[1]([✉]), Pierrick Gaudry[1], Anselme Goetschmann[1], and Sophie Lemonnier[1,2]

[1] Loria – Université de Lorraine, CNRS, Inria, France
veronique.cortier@loria.fr
[2] Université de Lorraine, PErSEUs, 57000 Metz, France

Abstract. In this work we consider Belenios-CaI, a protocol offering a cast-as-intended mechanism and building upon Belenios, a voting system used in about 7000 elections to date. We modify the design of Belenios-Cai from the user perspective without changing its core cryptographic mechanism. The goal is to increase its usability by letting the voter simply check whether two symbols are equal or different.

We conducted a user-study among 165 participants in a research center to evaluate the usability of our implementation of Belenios-CaI. Since the cast-as-intended mechanism assumes that voters make some random choices, we also evaluate whether the choices made by voters are sufficiently "random" to provide verifiability and whether it could affect their privacy. The study shows that, for our population, Belenios-CaI is considered as usable with the random choices of the voters seeming sufficient for verifiability and privacy.

1 Introduction

E-voting aims at two main security properties, namely vote privacy and verifiability; the latter is often split in several sub-properties:

- cast-as-intended: the ballot cast by the voter contains their intended vote;
- recorded-as-cast: the ballot recorded in the ballot box corresponds to the one cast by the voter;
- tallied-as-recorded: the result corresponds to the ballots recorded in the ballot box;
- eligibility: ballots recorded in the ballot box only come from legitimate voters.

In this paper, we focus on cast-as-intended, which aims at protecting against a malicious voting device that could try to modify the vote of a voter, e.g. when encrypting it. Specifically, we consider the recently proposed Belenios-CaI system [5], which builds upon Belenios [6], a system now in production for 8 years and

This work was partially supported by the French National Research Agency under the France 2030 programme with the reference ANR-22-PECY-0006 and ANR Chair IA ASAP (ANR-20-CHIA-0024), with support from the region Grand Est, France

D. Duenas-Cid et al. (Eds.): E-Vote-ID 2024, LNCS 15014, pp. 1–19, 2025.
https://doi.org/10.1007/978-3-031-72244-8_1

with more than 700,000 voters in total. In Belenios-CaI, voters audit their ballot by checking a control value. Instead of the sole encryption $\mathsf{enc}(v)$ of the voter's vote v, the ballot consists of three encryptions $\mathsf{enc}(v), \mathsf{enc}(a), \mathsf{enc}(b)$ and a zero-knowledge proof that $v + a = b$ modulo c, where c is some constant greater than the number of voting options. The voting device displays the ballot and the values v, a, b, c. The voter should check that $v + a = b$ modulo c and randomly challenge their voting device to open either $\mathsf{enc}(a)$ or $\mathsf{enc}(b)$. The voting device has to provide the corresponding randomness and the correctness of the encryption is then discharged to auditors: the voter simply checks that either a or b appears next to their ballot on the public bulletin board and the auditors check that the randomness corresponds to the audited encryption. An interesting feature of Belenios-CaI is that the voter does not need any second device nor additional secure channel to receive extra material. However, Belenios-CaI presents usability issues. First of all, voters need to compute arithmetic operations (modular addition). Moreover the audit of the ballot involves several verifications that must be performed by the voter, which seems cumbersome.

Our contributions. We propose an encoding of addition to ease the voter's journey. Namely, we consider addition modulo 2 only, and encode addition by asking voters to tell whether two symbols are identical or different, which is a much simpler task. We design and implement a voter interface that guides the voter to perform the checks for each voting choice. We also extend the current implementation of Belenios to support the new ballot format and verification. This yields the first implementation of Belenios-CaI. The code is open-source and covers all parts of the elections (server and voting client).

In order to check the usability of Belenios-CaI with our approach, we conducted an experiment with 165 participants, which were randomly assigned either Belenios-CaI or the original Belenios. The goal was to study whether Belenios-CaI introduces a reasonable overhead of complexity w.r.t. Belenios, a system that is used on an everyday basis. Moreover, in Belenios-CaI, voters must choose to open either $\mathsf{enc}(a)$ or $\mathsf{enc}(b)$ "at random", a difficult task for voters, who are not perfect random generators. Hence we study whether the bias in the randomness could affect verifiability but also privacy. More precisely, we investigate three research questions.

Q1 - Usability *Is Belenios-CaI usable?*
We aim at understanding (i) whether voters still manage to vote with Belenios-CaI and (ii) how the additional step affects perceived usability w.r.t. Belenios.

Q2 - Secrecy *Is the secrecy of the vote degraded by the control pattern?*
Belenios-CaI exposes additional information on the public bulletin board under the form of a control pattern selected by the voter (the selection of a or b for each voting choice). Although there is by design no correlation between the voting choice and the control pattern of a ballot, it is possible that the voter's control pattern selection is influenced by their choice of voting option. This would represent an

important leakage since it can compromise the secrecy of the vote.

Q3 - Verifiability *Is the randomness provided by the voters sufficient to provide cast-as-intended verifiability?*
We aim at determining whether the random selection performed by voters is sufficient to prevent an adversary controlling voting clients from manipulating an election with a very low probability of being detected.

Our experiment shows that Belenios-CaI remains reasonably usable compared to Belenios and provide sufficient guarantees w.r.t. cast-as-intended. Moreover, our statistical analysis did not detect any meaningful correlation between votes and control patterns, indicating that Belenios-CaI does not threaten vote privacy. It is important to note, however, that our experiment was conducted in a research center in computer science, where most participants are researchers, PhD students or engineers. As future work, it would be necessary to conduct a wider experiment on the general population in order to determine whether the bias of our population could affect the conclusion of the study.

Related work. Several cast-as-intended mechanisms have been proposed, as summarized in Table 1. A natural approach is to use a second device checking that the voting device has correctly encrypted the voter's intended vote. This is the approach followed by Estonia [9] where the voting device exports in a QR-code the randomness used for encrypting the vote. The Polyas system [15] refines this approach to provide a better receipt-freeness resistance. The Benaloh's challenge [3] follows the same idea except that the audited ballot is never the one that is cast, again to mitigate vote-buying attacks. While the Benaloh's challenge does not require explicitly a second device, it needs an independent party that can check the correctness of the encryption. Another approach is to use *return codes*, as proposed in Switzerland [8,18]. Voters receive a voting sheet where each voting choice is associated to a return code (specific to each voter). Once a voter casts a vote, their voting device displays a code that must match the one written on their voting sheet (for their voting choice). This approach relies on a secure postal channel to distribute voting sheets and on a heavy infrastructure (several independent online servers). In order to avoid a second device and keep the infrastructure simple, some systems (e.g. Select [11], Selene [17], Hyperion [16]) introduce a *tracker* that appears on the public bulletin board, next to the voter's vote, allowing them to check that their vote has been counted. One important advantage of this approach is its simplicity w.r.t. voters: they *see* their vote. However, in case of a vote manipulation, voters can only detect it once the election is over and tallied, which renders dispute-resolution even more complex.

User studies have already been conducted on other cast-as-intended mechanisms. In particular, Marky *et al.* [14] show that the Benaloh's challenge is very difficult to conduct for voters. In a recent study, Hilt *et al.* [10] investigate how

Table 1. Comparison of cast-as-intended mechanisms

| | Audit using randomness of ballot | | | Return codes | Trackers | Belenios-CaI |
	Estonia [9]	Polyas [15]	Benaloh [3]	[8,18]	[11,16,17]	
Single device				✓	✓	✓
Verify and go	✓	✓	✓	✓		✓
Cast ballot is audited	✓	✓		✓	✓	✓
Single online server		✓	✓		✓	✓

voters react to vote manipulations for systems that provide cast-as-intended through a second device while Volkamer *et al.* [19] study whether code-voting and QR-codes may respectively increase security and usability. Marky *et al.* [13] study voter's perception when physical printed audit trails are used in parallel with online voting. Of course, no user study was applied to Belenios-CaI yet, due to its recent design.

2   Context

2.1   Overview of Belenios-CaI

We provide a brief overview of Belenios-CaI, that was introduced in [5] as a variant of Belenios. We refer to this article for the precise description and security analysis. We assume here that the reader is familiar with Helios-like e-voting systems. As in Belenios, the actors are the voters, a voting server, some decryption trustees, a credential authority (a.k.a. registrar), and a public bulletin board, with external auditors. In Belenios-CaI, the roles of the decryption trustees and the credential authority are unchanged, so we will not talk about them further.

For a given question, there is a set of possible answers (the candidates), and each of them can be selected, possibly with a limit on selections. The ballot is a set of micro-ballots, one for each answer, that encodes the selected / not-selected choice of the voter. Each micro-ballot takes the following form:

$$\mathsf{bal} = (\mathsf{enc}(v), \mathsf{enc}(a), \mathsf{enc}(b), \pi),$$

where v has a value of 0 or 1, which encodes the choice of the voter, a and b are random integers chosen by the voting device such that $b \equiv v + a \bmod 10$, and π is a zero-knowledge proof that the three plaintexts hidden in the three ciphertexts are indeed integers that verify these arithmetic properties.

Once the ballot is sent to the server by the voting device, the voter receives from the server (on a channel not controlled by the voting device) a tracking number that also serves as a commitment on the ballot. This number can no longer be changed, because the voter will look for it on the public bulletin board.

Then, the audit phase starts. The voting device shows the a and b values to the voter, who must check that the modular equality $b \equiv v + a \bmod 10$ indeed holds. A key point, here, is that this operation must be done by the voter themself, and not by their voting device. Then, the voter picks one of the two values a and b at random, and the voting device sends to the server the randomness that was used to

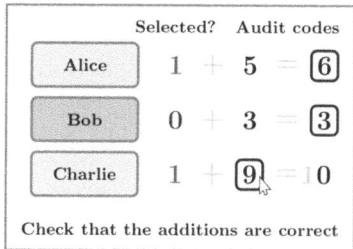

Fig. 1. Original Belenios-CaI audit phase (picture from [5]). The voter checks an addition modulo 10, and randomly selects one of the a or b value for each line.

encrypt this value, so that the server can open the ciphertext. It then publishes on the board the tracking number, the ballot, the revealed randomness, and the corresponding a or b decrypted value. The voter visits the board (possibly with another device), and checks that everything is as expected. In addition to their usual tasks, the auditors must check that the revealed randomness indeed opens the ciphertext to the value a or b published by the server on the board.

In a typical setting, there are several micro-ballots, and therefore there is one (a, b) pair for each possible answer. In [5], it is suggested to present them as in Fig. 1, with all the data corresponding to one micro-ballot put on a single line, thus forming a table. Using additions modulo any number at least 2 instead of 10 is possible, and yields the same theoretical security.

2.2 Terminology Used in the Present Study

In our paper, we will use slightly different names for the various elements in the audit phase of the voter's journey:

- The **control values** are the values a and b, such that the **vote** v verifies $b \equiv v + a \mod 10$. These were called audit codes in [5].
- The **mask** is the random choice made by the voter of which control value will be revealed. This is just one bit per line (whether the blue box is on the left or on the right, in Fig. 1).
- The **control pattern** is the combination of the mask and of the control values that must be revealed. On Fig. 1, this is the set of blue boxes, with their positions in the table, and the values inside them. The control pattern is the data that is visible on the public bulletin board at the end of the voter's journey and that they should compare to what their device showed to them.

3 User Interface Design

As first contribution, we present the design of a user interface for Belenios-CaI.

3.1   Challenges

Non-trivial Process. Belenioscai requires the voter to perform a verification and a random selection for each voting item. The risk is that most of the voters would not actually verify what is asked but just validate when possible, to complete the process faster. This risk is exacerbated by the fact that voters perform this task online and anonymously [12]. Since this would compromise the verifiability of the cast-as-intended property, the system should enforce the verification.

Table 2. Possible values for v, a and b modulo 2: on the left, the two cases where the voter did not select the answer, and on the right, the two cases where they did.
In the first two columns, 0 is represented by *crossed* and 1 by *checked*. In the third, 0 corresponds to *thumb-up* and 1 to *thumb-down*. (Symbols taken from Google Fonts [1].)

v	$+$	a	$=$	$b \bmod 2$	v	$+$	a	$=$	$b \bmod 2$
☒		☒		👍	☑		☒		👎
0		0		0	1		0		1
☒		☑		👎	☑		☑		👍
0		1		1	1		1		0

More generally, we aim at designing an interface that guides voters linearly through simple tasks.

Arithmetical Operations. Further, the system should be usable by anyone and we should not assume technical knowledge of the voter. In particular, the voter cannot be relied on to perform arithmetical operations. Since Belenios-CaI depends on the computation of a modular addition for each voting option, a workaround had to be found.

Voter Randomness. Another critical aspect of the protocol is the randomness provided by the voter during the selection of a mask. Although a slightly biased randomness is sufficient for verifiability as explained in Sect. 4.3, it should not be influenced by the intention of the voter to preserve vote secrecy.

3.2   Design Choices

Compute Instead of Verify. In order to bring the voter to do the verification required by Belenios-CaI, we ask them to perform the computation instead of just verifying it. This forces the voter to examine each line and select one of the answers. If they make a mistake, a warning indicates the issue.

Modulo 2 with Symbols. The computation modulo 10 can be performed more intuitively using a simple trick: by choosing $m = 2$, computing $v + a \mod m$ is equivalent to answering the question "Is v identical to a?" and mapping "yes" to $b = 0$ and "no" to $b = 1$.

In order to make the task clearer and the resulting pattern easier to visualize, we replaced the numbers with symbols. A first pair of symbols was needed to represent whether a voting option is chosen or not. We used checkboxes as illustrated in Table 2, which we will denote as *checked* and *crossed* in the following. Since the value of a is compared with v, their domain have to be the same. The symbols for b were selected to represent "yes" and "no", denoted as *thumb-up* and *thumb-down*.

Hide Vote During Selection. Since voters have to select random control values, independently of their voting option, the voting option and choice are hidden during this step of the audit phase, as illustrated in Fig. 2.

3.3   Audit Flow

Steps. In order to make the flow as simple and linear as possible, the interface lets the voter perform the necessary operations in four steps as depicted in Fig. 2. More details about this process can be found in Fig. 1 of the intial paper [5].

1. (*check*) The relationship between v, a and b is verified by answering the question "Are the two symbols identical?" for each line, *i.e.*, for each voting item.
2. (*select*) The voter randomly picks one of the control values, for each line.
3. (*save*) The control pattern resulting from the selection is saved by the voter in the form of a PDF file.
4. (*ballot box*) After casting the ballot, the voter verifies that the control pattern corresponding to their ballot is identical to the one in the *save* step.

Note that the first two steps include an action for each voting item, therefore the voting time increases significantly for an election with a larger number of candidates.

Layout. Since the goal of the audit phase is to prevent a malicious voting client from manipulating the cast ballot by making any tampering visible, the interface should have a stable layout with components moving as little as possible. Thus, the grid structure with one row per voting item and three columns (for v, a and b) remains unchanged across the three steps.

During the *select* step, the voter should pick one control value or the other independently of whether the line in question corresponds to an option voted for, therefore the first column, containing v, is grayed out (see Fig. 2b). In the *save* step, the masking of the chosen voting option is kept to prevent a voter from taking a screenshot of their vote along with the control pattern, thus producing a receipt with their vote in clear. Nevertheless, the name of the voting item has to be displayed to avoid a malicious voting client from swapping two items in the interface without being detected.

3.4 Prototype

We implemented a fully functional and publicly available prototype[1] of our design based on the existing Belenios project. Next to implementing the user interface of the audit phase as outlined in this section, other adaptations were made to Belenios while developing the prototype.

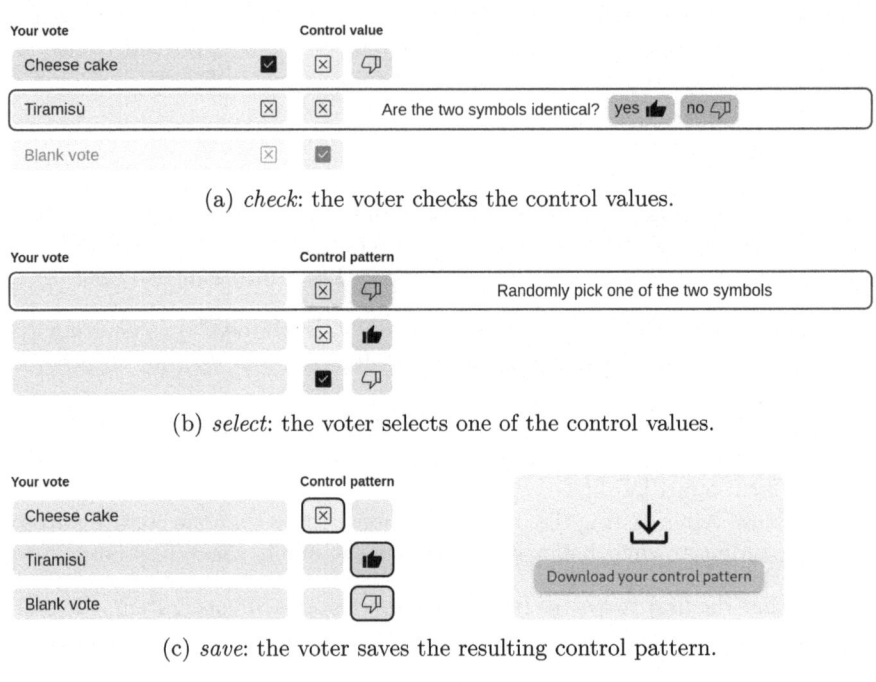

(a) *check*: the voter checks the control values.

(b) *select*: the voter selects one of the control values.

(c) *save*: the voter saves the resulting control pattern.

(d) *ballot box*: the voter verifies their control pattern in the ballot box.

Fig. 2. Four steps of the audit phase.

---

[1] https://gitlab.inria.fr/agoetsch/belenios-cai.

- The zero-knowledge proofs needed by Belenios-CaI were added to the ballot data structure. They ensure, *e.g.*, that the relationship $v+a \equiv b \mod 2$ holds for the encryption of each voting item.
- To improve the usability of the system, the instruction to copy and save the ballot tracking number manually was replaced by the download of a PDF document containing the tracking number. The control pattern can be downloaded in a similar way. The voter should check that the downloaded documents match what is displayed by the voting client.
- The static ballot box page was improved to include a search function, only displaying the ballots with a tracking number including characters entered by the user. The control pattern was also added along its ballot.

4   Experimental Setting

4.1   Participants

We organized an experiment inviting the employees working in our French computer science research center (Loria and Inria), to vote using Belenios. We discuss the potential biases and their effect in Sect. 6.

The median age of the 129 participants who completed the experiment and fully filled the survey is 40 years old, 32% of them identified as a woman and 67% as a man. More details can be found in the extended version of this paper [7]. 11%, denoted as "admin staff", are not working in the field of computer science, while the other participants are researchers in computer science (permanent, postdoc or PhD students).

Participants had to vote using either our prototype Belenios-CaI (denoted by cai) or the original software Belenios-base (denoted by base). The assignment to a group was made by alternating cai and base when participants connected to the voting system (i.e. in a round-robin manner).

4.2   Methods

The experiment was conducted online and lasted for a week.

Participants Task. Participants were contacted by email. They were proposed to first vote online for their favorite dessert among 5 choices from the local canteen. This voting question, asked with the consent of the pastry chef, satisfied both requirements of low impact (no focus on the integrity in this context), and of high motivation (to incentivize more participants). The invitation message included a short description of the data collected for the experiment, together with a link to a web page with a more detailed data management policy. Participants were told that the experiment was aiming at evaluating usability but they were not told that two versions were running.

When connecting to the voting system, participants are asked for their personal credential (included in the invitation email). Then they select their voting choice. After reviewing their choice, the participants authenticate themselves using a short code received by email. Lastly, if they are assigned Belenios-CaI, they have to audit their encrypted ballot as described in Sect. 3.3. If assigned to Belenios-base, they are directed immediately to the "success" page.

Then they were asked to answer a survey. This survey was mentioned in the invitation email and voters were reminded about the survey once they had voted.

Tools. In order to understand the behavior of the participants and identify obstacles in their journey, the voting system was modified to record the time spent on each step of the process as well as the number of mistakes made in the process and the number of clicks on specific elements of the interface. It was also modified in order to assign either Belenios-CaI and Belenios-base in a round-robin manner.

Since the election organized for the experiment had no impact and the results were not used, this version sacrifices privacy to understand the behavior of voters. In particular, the private decryption key was owned by our voting server in order to later decrypt the individual ballots. This was needed to measure the correlation between audit patterns and the voting choice. To keep the experiment anonymous, participants were identified with their voting credential only, letting us link data from the voting system with their vote and the survey results without keeping track of their vote identifiers (email address).

Survey. Available in French or English and hosted on a local instance of LimeSurvey, the survey was split in three sections. The first one contained personal questions about the participant, the second the questions to obtain a System Usability Score (SUS) [4] and the third some further questions about the voting process. SUS takes the form of a 10-question survey on a 5-level Likert scale and results in a usability score on a scale of 0–100. We selected SUS for its simplicity and robustness [2].

4.3   Data Collection and Analysis

Since the research questions address different aspects of the practicality of Belenios-CaI, we describe separately the data collected to address them.

Q1 Usability. Our goal is to measure if the addition of an audit phase in Belenios-CaI negatively impacts its usability compared to Belenios-base. We consider three main aspects to compare the usability of Belenios-CaI w.r.t. Belenios-base:

- effectiveness: we first record the success rate of the cai and base groups, i.e. whether a voter manages to cast her ballot;
- satisfaction: we compute the SUS scores of both groups resulting from the survey;

– efficiency: we record the time spent on each voting step and the number of mis-clicks to understand where the voters struggled during the process. To focus on the voting interface we denote *normalized voting time* the time spent in the voting booth without the authentication step, where the voter has to enter a validation code sent by email.

In each case, we compare the measure (success rate, SUS score, or voting time) between cai and base, to see if they differ significantly. For this, we compute the mean value and the standard error, and check if the intervals overlap.

Q2 Secrecy. In order to investigate whether the control pattern reveals some information about the vote (Q2), ballots were individually decrypted at the end of the experiment and paired with their corresponding control pattern.

We investigate three possible correlations; for each of them, we performed a Chi-squared independence test:

– Do voters prefer to select the right control value (b) on items they voted for?
– Do voters select a more easily when the symbol is *checked* on non-voted items?
– Do voters select more easily a positive symbol (*thumb-up* or *checked*) on items they voted for?

Note that in our interface, the symbols of control values for a voted item are always either both positive or both negative (see the right part of Table 2), thus we do not expect a revealing behavior on voted items.

Q3 Verifiability. The main desired property of the system is the verifiability of cast-as-intended: a ballot should contain the vote intended by the voter, and any manipulation attempt by an adversary controlling voting clients should be detected with high probability. Since Belenios-CaI relies on the randomness provided by the voters to ensure this property, we evaluate whether the data collected during our experiment supports this hypothesis. The set of observed control masks was the only data needed to perform this analysis.

If one mask was significantly more frequent, e.g. if voters would select control values on the right in 99% of cases, an adversary could modify a ballot without being detected with high probability by adapting the control values on the left.

Strategy of an Adversary. To modify a voting item without being detected, an adversary has to adapt the control value which will not be selected by the voter during the *select* step. In the case of an election where voters choose one among k options, modifying a ballot only requires changing 2 voting items, the one chosen by the voter and the one chosen by the adversary. Therefore, the adversary needs to predict the left-or-right selection on these 2 lines.

Adversary Success Rate. Assuming that the adversary knows the distribution of control masks, they know in particular the distribution of the sub-mask composed of the 2 lines they need to modify D. We call *peak* the most frequent sub-mask and $p = D(peak)$ its frequency. Since the adversary succeeds when the voter selects the predicted mask, their success rate when attempting to modify the same two lines of m ballots is $p_{adv} = p^m$.

For example, let us consider an attacker attempting to manipulate the ballots of $m = 10$ voters who are voting for the first candidate by creating ballots for the second candidate instead. Further, we assume that the sub-mask distribution for the first two voting items is $D(0,0) = 0.1$, $D(0,1) = 0.1$, $D(1,0) = 0.7$, $D(1,1) = 0.1$. In this case we have $peak = 1,0$ and $p = 0.7$, which yields $p_{adv} = p^m = 0.7^{10} = 0.028$.

We observe that the success rate of the adversary decreases exponentially with the number of ballots they attempt to manipulate, which indicates that Belenios-CaI is effective mostly in large elections, since in that case an adversary needs to modify proportionally more ballots to impact the result.

Assessing Observed Distribution. Given the actual distribution of masks observed during our experiment, we compute the pair of voting items with the highest maximal frequency, which indicates the most important weakness in terms of security. We call this observed peak in the mask distribution p_{obs}. To evaluate whether the experiment provides enough evidence that the frequency of *peak* is at most a chosen acceptable value p_{acc}, we perform a statistical test where the null hypothesis H_0 is defined as "$p \geq p_{acc}$", in order to determine whether H_0 can be rejected with a significance level $\alpha = 0.01$. We consider the number of occurrences of the *peak* mask and model its distribution as a binomially distributed random variable $X \sim B(n, p_{acc})$, where n is the size of the group of our experiment.

5   Results

5.1   Participants' Group

An invitation email was sent to 880 employees. It contained a link to the voting system, a personal voting credential, a link to the survey and information about data privacy in the experiment. Among them, 178 started voting and 165 could cast a ballot, as illustrated in Fig. 3. 138 participants completed the survey, but 6 of them did not enter their voting credentials when asked, which prevented us from linking their answer to their ballot. This leaves 129 participants who successfully voted and completed the survey.

Groups. A group of participants (cai) was assigned to the Belenios-CaI system while the other part (base) used the original system without cast-as-intended. The base group contains 71 participants while cai only 58. The difference is due to a weakness of our round-robin assignment: when a person connected to the

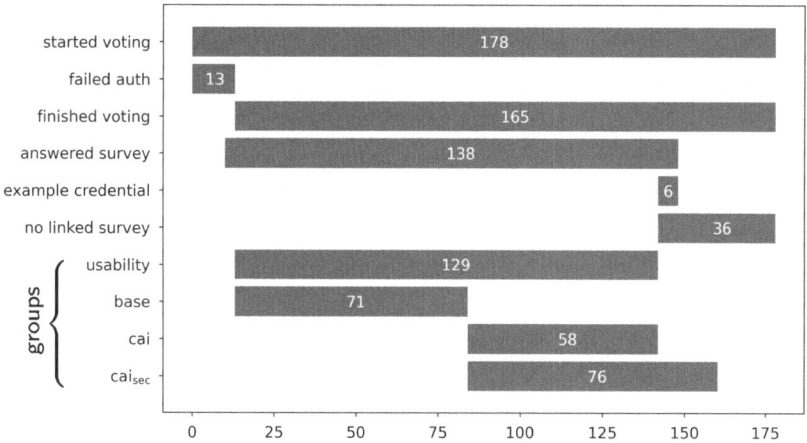

Fig. 3. Number of participants in the different groups. Some participants could not authenticate during the voting process. Among the ones who filled the survey, some used the credential given as example, which prevented us from linking their survey answer to their vote. The usability group was used to address Q1, with cai denoting the participants assigned to Belenios-CaI and base the ones assigned to Belenios-base. The group cai_sec denotes the participants assigned to Belenios-CaI even if they did not answer the survey. It is used to address the security-oriented questions Q2 and Q3.

voting system and was assigned to cai but did not complete their vote, their participation was not recorded as exploitable but resulted in two consecutive participants assigned to base.

To address the first research question Q1, we used the data of the participants in base and cai, forming the usability group. In the case of Q2 and Q3, since these research questions address security properties of Belenios-CaI and are not related to the survey, we considered all participants who used the Belenios-CaI system, also including those who did not fill the survey. We designate this group as cai_sec, consisting of 76 participants (see Fig. 3).

5.2 Q1 Usability

Success Rate. First, we observe that all of the 76 participants which were assigned to group cai and managed to authenticate could successfully conclude the audit phase and cast their ballot. This indicates that the usability of the audit step was sufficient to let every participant complete it. More details about the number of voters and their progress can be found in [7].

SUS Score. The SUS score seems to differ between the cai and the base groups, with a higher score for base (mean value of 78.45, std. error of 1.61) than for cai (mean of 72.07, std. error of 1.82), hence the intervals do not overlap. Figure 4a illustrates in a more qualitative way this difference, showing the

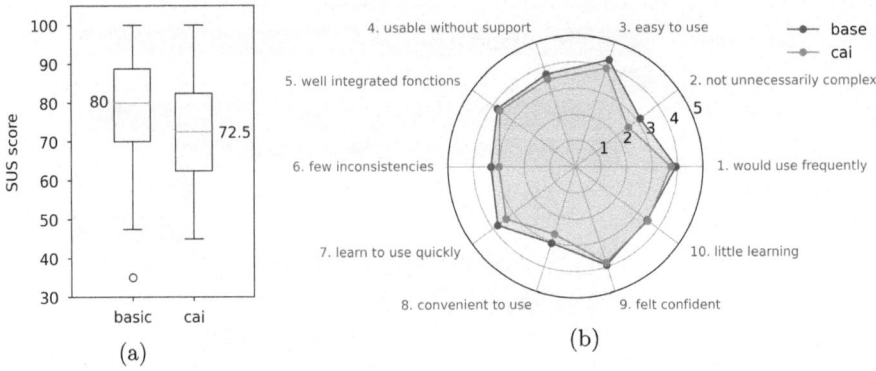

Fig. 4. On the left, comparison between SUS scores of **base** and **cai** groups. On the right the score of each question displayed separately; for the "negative" questions 2, 4, 6, 8, 10, we displayed the reverted score, so that on this picture, higher is always better.

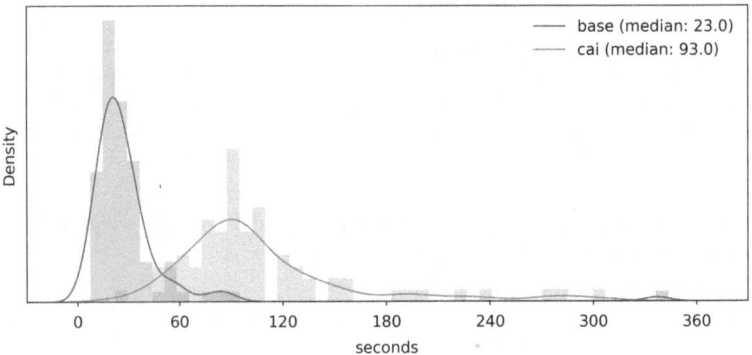

Fig. 5. Normalized voting time distribution of **base** and **cai** groups.

median and the quartiles in both cases. We observe that the median score of both groups can be classified as "good" according to [2]. Figure 4b displays the average score to each of the questions in the SUS survey for both groups, showing that the difference is distributed over the different aspects measured by SUS.

Voting Time. Similarly, the *normalized voting time* (see Sect. 4.3) of cai is higher than base. The mean value for cai is 113.2 sec. (std. error 8.16) and for base it is 29.9 sec. (std. error of 3.86). Figure 5 complements this data with the median values and the shape of the distributions in both cases.

The difference between the voting times of both groups is explained integrally by the time on the audit phase (median: 71 s). Although this additional time is important, the overall voting time remains under 2 min, a time still acceptable to complete a voting process.

5.3   Q2 Secrecy

The control patterns selected by the voters are published in the ballot box next to their ballot tracker. Thus, any dependence between a vote and its corresponding control pattern is a threat to vote secrecy. We investigate here whether the data collected during our experiment contains evidence of such a dependence.

Data. Each vote is composed of one item per possible voting option; each item is a triple (v, a, b), where only one of a and b is displayed on the board. This results in a total of 380 items $(= 5 \cdot |\mathsf{cai_{sec}}|$, for the 5 voting options of each ballot and a population $|\mathsf{cai_{sec}}| = 76$). As detailed in Sect. 3, v and a are represented in the voter interface as *checked* or *crossed* (for 1 and 0, respectively), and b takes the shape of *thumb-up* or *thumb-down*. Note that we consider each item of the ballots separately, distinguishing between 76 *voted items* (corresponding to the chosen option) and 304 *non-voted items*.

Independence Tests. We performed the three hypothesis tests listed in Sect. 4.3. The results of the Pearson's χ^2 tests are displayed in Table 3, for three pairs of variables that should be independent, otherwise an attacker could deduce some information on the vote and break privacy. In all cases, the test indicates independence.

5.4   Q3 - Verifiability

We start by aggregating the observed control masks, *i.e.*, the left-right selection in the control patterns. The mask with the highest frequency is $1, 1, 1, 1, 1$, present in 10 out of $|\mathsf{cai_{sec}}| = 76$ ballots, *i.e.*, in 13.2% of cases. This observation suggests that the distribution is not too skewed and that cast-as-intended can

Table 3. Results of Pearson's χ^2 independence tests, for three pairs of variables, where correlation could lead to a privacy leak. For each line, the number of choices for each variable is 2, therefore the degree of freedom is 1, and the reference value for χ^2 at a significance level of 0.05 is 3.84. Any computed value less than 3.84 means that the variables are independent.
In the third line, we define $positive = a \cdot \overline{mask} + \overline{b} \cdot mask$, which has value 1 when the selected control value is *checked* or *thumb-up* and 0 otherwise.

Question	Variables	χ^2	indep.?
Do voters prefer to select the right control value (b) on items she voted for?	$v, mask$	0.024	yes
Do voters select a more easily when the symbol is *checked* on non-voted items?	$mask, a$	0.049	yes
Do voters select more easily a positive symbol (thumb-up or check mark) on items she voted for?	$v, positive$	0.52	yes

be ensured. For completeness, the distribution of control masks observed in our experiment can be found in the extended version of this paper [7].

We follow the method proposed in Sect. 4.3 to assess the observed distribution and decide whether this leads to an acceptable advantage for an attacker. Among the $\binom{5}{2} = 10$ combinations, it turns out to be the first two voting items with $peak = 0, 0$ give the highest frequency and $p_{obs} = \frac{31}{76} = 0.41$. This value is the result of our experiment with a sample size of $|\mathsf{cai}_{sec}| = 76$.

This 0.41 value is well below what we decided to be an acceptable value $p_{acc} = 0.7$. For the sake of completeness, we computed the probability that we observed a peak at 0.41, if the real distribution includes a peak with 0.7. This probability is $1.25 \cdot 10^{-7}$ (details are given in [7]) and confirms that, based on our observation, an adversary will gain only an acceptable advantage regarding the verifiability property.

5.5 Feedback Given in the Free Text Questions

In the third part of the survey, participants were given the opportunity to provide comments on various aspects and we thank them for their suggestions.

Regarding security, many participants say they trust the system, but they also acknowledge that this is mostly due to the fact that they know the authors of this experiment and trust their expertise. They do not understand how the various steps in the voter's journey have an impact on the security. Some participants are more skeptical and seem to be reluctant against Internet voting in general.

Feedback about usability is mostly positive, in the sense that many participants consider that the number of steps is high but that this is acceptable if justified for security. However, many also mention that not understanding the precise reasons for these steps generates some frustration. Among the difficulties mentioned by the participants, going back and forth between the mailbox and the browser is mentioned several times as a problem. Some also say that they managed to use the system but that they believe it might be difficult for others (elders, in particular). Some remarks were specifically related to the cast-as-intended functionality, and one participant explicitly mentioned the hesitation when having to randomly choose the mask.

More generally, feedback from participants confirms that Belenios-CaI does not seem to be hindering the voting system, but it does offer some ideas for improving the user experience and acceptance of the online voting system.

6   Discussion

Considering the cost of ensuring cast-as-intended in perceived usability and in voting time, we observe that it might not be worth the additional security in the case of small scale elections since a few modifications may still happen with realistic probability. However, for large elections, the protection against malicious voting clients can make the traded usability acceptable. Indeed, it is unlikely that an attacker can modify sufficiently many votes without being detected.

Limitations. The recruitment of participants was performed in the research center where the authors work. Therefore, most participants had at least a Master in Computer Science. They may have a different understanding of how to "randomly" select the control values, as compared to the general population. Furthermore, although participation was anonymous, the fact that many participants know the authors of the study might have introduced a bias in the responses to the survey. But since we are interested in the comparison between Belenios and Belenios-CaI and not in a system alone, the possible bias should be equivalent for both systems and not affect the difference in perceived usability.

The main goal of the study was to determine whether Belenios-CaI is an acceptable evolution of Belenios. It does not evaluate whether the underlying cast-as-intended mechanism is more usable than others such as Benaloh's challenge [3] or return codes [8,18].

Future Work. The analysis regarding secrecy and verifiability performed in Sect. 5.3 only provides insight about settings similar to our experiment. To make stronger statements concerning the impact of voter-generated randomness on vote privacy, a study on a larger population sample, more representative of the general population, would be necessary.

Another interesting aspect would be the evaluation of verification efficiency, *i.e.*, whether Belenios-CaI allows voters to detect a manipulation, and a comparison with other systems providing cast-as-intended verifiability.

Acknowledgments. We are very grateful to Stéphane Glondu for his help with Belenios implementation.

References

1. Google Fonts: Material icons (2024). https://fonts.google.com/icons
2. Bangor, A., Kortum, P.T., Miller, J.T.: An empirical evaluation of the system usability scale. Int. J. Hum. Comput. Interact. **24**(6), 574–594 (2008). https://doi.org/10.1080/10447310802205776
3. Benaloh, J.: Simple verifiable elections. In: Electronic Voting Technology Workshop, USENIX (2006)
4. Brooke, J.: SUS: a quick and dirty usability scale. In: Usability Evaluation in Industry. CRC Press, pp. 207–212 (1996). https://doi.org/10.1201/9781498710411

5. Cortier, V., Debant, A., Gaudry, P., Glondu, S.: Belenios with cast as intended. In: Essex, A., et al. (eds.) Financial Cryptography and Data Security, pp. 3–18. Springer, Cham (2024). https://doi.org/10.1007/978-3-031-48806-1_1
6. Cortier, V., Gaudry, P., Glondu, S.: Belenios: a simple private and verifiable electronic voting system. In: Guttman, J.D., Landwehr, C.E., Meseguer, J., Pavlovic, D. (eds.) Foundations of Security, Protocols, and Equational Reasoning. LNCS, vol. 11565, pp. 214–238. Springer, Cham (2019). https://doi.org/10.1007/978-3-030-19052-1_14
7. Cortier, V., Gaudry, P., Goetschmann, A., Lemonnier, S.: Belenios with cast-as-intended: towards a usable interface, Technical report, 04646244, HAL (2024). https://inria.hal.science/hal-04646244
8. Haenni, R., Koenig, R.E., Locher, P., Dubuis, E.: CHVote protocol specification, Cryptology ePrint Archive (2017). https://eprint.iacr.org/2017/325
9. Heiberg, S., Martens, T., Vinkel, P., Willemson, J.: Improving the verifiability of the Estonian internet voting scheme. In: Krimmer, R., et al. (eds.) E-Vote-ID 2016. LNCS, vol. 10141, pp. 92–107. Springer, Cham (2017). https://doi.org/10.1007/978-3-319-52240-1_6
10. Hilt, T., Berens, B., Truderung, T., Udovychenko, M., Neumann, S., Volkamer, M.: Systematic user evaluation of a second device based cast-as-intended verifiability approach. In: VOTING (FC workshop), Springer (2024)
11. Küsters, R., Müller, J., Scapin, E., Truderung, T.: sElect: a lightweight verifiable remote voting system. In: CSF. IEEE (2016)https://doi.org/10.1109/CSF.2016.31
12. Lelkes, Y., Krosnick, J.A., Marx, D., Judd, C.M., Park, B.: Complete anonymity compromises the accuracy of self-reports. J. Exp. Soc. Psychol. **48**(6), 1291–1299 (2012). https://doi.org/10.1016/j.jesp.2012.07.002
13. Marky, K., Gerber, N., Krumb, H., Khamis, M., Mühlhäuser, M.: Investigating voter perceptions of printed physical audit trails for online voting. In: SP. IEEE (2024). https://doi.org/10.1109/SP54263.2024.00136
14. Marky, K., Kulyk, O., Renaud, K., Volkamer, M.: What Did I Really Vote For? On the Usability of Verifiable E-Voting Schemes. In: CHI, ACM (2018),https://doi.org/10.1145/3173574.3173750
15. Müller, J., Truderung, T.: CAISED: a protocol for cast-as-intended verifiability with a second device. In: Volkamer, M., et al. (eds.) Electronic Voting. E-Vote-ID 2023. LNCS, vol. 14230. Springer, Cham (2023). https://doi.org/10.1007/978-3-031-43756-4_8
16. Ryan, P., Roenne, P., Rastikian, S.: Hyperion: an enhanced version of the Selene end-to-end verifiable voting scheme. In: EvoteID (2021)
17. Ryan, P.Y.A., Rønne, P.B., Iovino, V.: Selene: voting with transparent verifiability and coercion-mitigation. In: Clark, J., Meiklejohn, S., Ryan, P.Y.A., Wallach, D., Brenner, M., Rohloff, K. (eds.) FC 2016. LNCS, vol. 9604, pp. 176–192. Springer, Heidelberg (2016). https://doi.org/10.1007/978-3-662-53357-4_12
18. Swiss Post: Swiss post voting system: system specification, version 1.1.1., Technical report, Swiss Post (2022)
19. Volkamer, M., Kulyk, O., Ludwig, J., Fuhrberg, N.: Increasing security without decreasing usability: a comparison of various verifiable voting systems. In: SOUPS, USENIX (2022)

Threshold Receipt-Free Single-Pass eVoting

Thi Van Thao Doan[1]([✉]), Olivier Pereira[1,2], and Thomas Peters[1]

[1] Université catholique de Louvain, ICTEAM - Crypto Group,
1348 Louvain-la-Neuve, Belgium
{thi.doan,olivier.pereira,thomas.peters}@uclouvain.be
[2] Microsoft Research, Redmond, WA, USA

Abstract. In 2001, Hirt proposed a receipt-free voting scheme, which prevents malicious voters from proving to anybody how they voted, under the assumption of the availability of a helping server that is trusted for receipt-freeness, and only for that property. This appealing design led to a number of subsequent works that made this approach non-interactive and more efficient. Still, in all of these works, receipt-freeness depends on the honesty of one single server.

In order to remove this single point of failure, we design a new model in which multiple helping servers are available and propose a new security definition called *threshold receipt-freeness*. Our definition requires that receipt-freeness should be guaranteed even if some of the helping servers happen to be fully malicious and ensures that voters can express their votes even if the corrupted servers choose the content of their local view of the ballots.

Eventually, we propose a generic construction of a single-pass verifiable voting system achieving threshold receipt freenes with a mixnet-based tallying process. Our ballot submission process relies on the recently designed traceable receipt-free encryption primitive.

1 Introduction

Electronic voting (eVoting) systems allow voters to generate ballots containing their vote intent, and submit these ballots to an electronic server. When all the ballots have been recorded, the talliers compute the result of the election and, hopefully, provide information allowing to check the validity of the tallying process. This verification mechanism ensures voters that their individual ballots have been faithfully recorded and counted in the tally. However, the information supporting verifiability can often be leveraged by malicious observers to demand voters to convincingly demonstrate how they voted, e.g., by disclosing all the random coins used to produce their ballots. eVoting systems preventing this kind of attacks are called receipt-free.

© The Author(s) 2025
D. Duenas-Cid et al. (Eds.): E-Vote-ID 2024, LNCS 15014, pp. 20–36, 2025.
https://doi.org/10.1007/978-3-031-72244-8_2

1.1 Receipt-Freeness

Since the introduction of Receipt-Freeness (RF) by Benaloh and Tuinstra [1], there has been a large amount of work targeting a well-balanced combination of receipt-freeness and verifiability. One such approach requires the use of fully trusted devices during the election [10,12]. Hirt [9] refined this approach by proposing a scheme in which every voter must have their encrypted vote re-randomized by a ballot processing server, which must be trusted for receipt-freeness. The re-randomized ballot is then posted on a public bulletin board. Since the randomness contained in that ballot is no longer known by the voters, the voters cannot prove how they voted. This results in receipt-freeness. The ballot processing server of Hirt [9] serves as an observer [5] establishing receipt-freeness, but cannot violate the privacy of the votes or the correctness of the tally. However, the server must interact with the voter to confirm the correctness of the randomization, and the observer and the voter must jointly generate a proof of the validity of the randomized ballot.

To avoid such interactions between parties, the more recent line of work [3,4,7,8] has designed mechanisms that make it possible to achieve non-interactive receipt-freeness. A voter generates a signed encrypted vote in a manner that allows the ciphertext and signature to be re-randomized by any individual, knowing neither the signing key nor the encrypted message, but the re-randomized signature will only be valid as long as the plaintext has not been modified. This creates a single-pass voting system [2] in which the ballot is sent from the voter, processed by a ballot processing server, and then posted on the bulletin board.

An encryption primitive designed to capture the desired form of non-interactive receipt-freeness was named traceable receipt-free encryption (TREnc) by Devillez et al. [6], who propose a mechanism realizing this primitive based on the signature of randomizable ciphertext with a one-time linearly homomorphic signature scheme, a primitive proposed by Libert et al. [11].

Yet, it is worth noting that even though the ballot processing server is not trusted for ballot privacy and election integrity, all of the aforementioned proposals rely on the assumption that the ballot processing server to which the voter submits his vote is trusted for RF, i.e., it does not collaborate with any vote-seller or coercer. This maintains a single point of failure. For instance, if the random coins utilized for re-randomizing ballots are transmitted to malicious voters, then the voters can demonstrate how they voted to any third party.

1.2 Our Contributions

We design an approach that removes the single point of failure of the existing receipt-free voting solutions. We first extend the traditional voting models to account for the involvement of *multiple* ballot processing servers. More precisely, the voting algorithm creates a ballot that can be split into n ballot pieces. Each ballot piece is processed in parallel by a ballot processing server before being gathered at a single place, usually a public bulletin board. Second, based on this enlarged syntax, we propose a security notion of *threshold receipt freeness*, and define a related correctness security notion. These security definitions capture the property that the voting system will accurately record the voter intent, while guaranteeing receipt-freeness as long as the number of malicious servers remains below the chosen threshold.

More precisely, we enhance the security model by introducing two thresholds: (1) the threshold for receipt-freeness (t_{rf}), which sets the maximum number of malicious ballot processing servers that the system can tolerate without compromising RF; and (2) the threshold for correctness (t_{corr}), which specifies the maximum number of ballot pieces that can be missing (intentionally or not) while still allowing the ballot to be processed in the tally. To reflect the fact that voters must be able to cast their intentions vote as in the single ballot processing model when $t_{rf} = 0$, our threshold RF notions is defined in two steps. The first step ensures that as long as at most t_{rf} ballot processing servers fix the content of any voter's incoming ballot pieces, the voter can still cast a ballot containing any vote intent. The second step is a natural RF extension of the indistinguishable notion due to Devillez et al. [6].

Eventually, as a feasibility result, we build a generic voting system from a linear secret sharing scheme and a TREnc. In a nutshell, the voter simply relies on a t-out-of-n threshold secret sharing to split the vote in n pieces, and on a TREnc to encrypt all these pieces independently. As long as an homomorphic part of the TREnc ciphertexts can be stripped from the published randomized ballot pieces, the recombination of the vote can be made on the bulletin board during the tally before executing a mixnet. We show that this construction is threshold RF up to $t_{rf} = t - 1$ malicious servers and threshold correct up to $t_{corr} = n - t$ missing ballot pieces.

Roadmap. The remainder of this paper is organized as follows. The background is provided in Sect. 2. In Sect. 3, we extend the traditional model of voting systems to the context of multiple ballot processing servers, and define out notions of threshold receipt-freeness and correctness. Section 4 describes our generic construction, and we demonstrate the security of this construction in Sect. 5. We conclude in Sect. 6.

2   Background on Traceable Receipt-Free Encryption

We start by reminding the notion of Traceable Receipt-Free Encryption (TREnc), a public key encryption primitive supporting the receipt-free submission of secret ballots [6].

Definition 1. (TREnc) A *TREnc* is a public key encryption (Gen, Enc, Dec) that is augmented with a 5-tuple of algorithms (LGen, LEnc, Trace, Rand, Ver):

LGen(pk): The link generation algorithm takes as input a public encryption key pk in the range of Gen and outputs a link key lk.

LEnc(pk, lk, m): The linked encryption algorithm takes as input a pair of public/link keys (pk, lk) and a message m, outputs a ciphertext.

Trace(pk, c) : The tracing algorithm takes as input a public key pk, a ciphertext c and outputs a trace τ. We call τ the trace of c.

Rand(pk, c): The randomization algorithm takes as input a public key pk and a ciphertext c, outputs another ciphertext.

Ver(pk, c): The verification algorithm takes as input a public key pk, a ciphertext c and outputs 1 if the ciphertext is valid, 0 otherwise.

Definition 2. (TREnccorrectness) A TREnc scheme is required to satisfy the following correctness requirements:

Encryption compatibility: For every pk in the range of Gen and message m, the distributions of Enc(pk, m) and LEnc(pk, LGen(pk), m) are identical;

Link traceability: For every pk in the range of Gen, every lk in the range of LGen(pk), the encryptions of every pair of messages (m_0, m_1) trace to the same trace, that is, Trace(pk, LEnc(pk, lk, m_0)) = Trace(pk, LEnc(pk, lk, m_1)), always;

Publicly Traceable Randomization: For every pk in the range of Gen, every message m and every c in the range of Enc(pk, m), we have that Dec(sk, c) = Dec(sk, Rand(pk, c)) and Trace(pk, c) = Trace(pk, Rand(pk, c));

Honest verifiability: For every pk in the range of Gen and every messages m, it holds that Ver(pk, Enc(pk, m)) = 1.

A voter encrypts his vote m by picking a link key lk using LGen and computing LEnc to generate a ciphertext c, which is then submitted to a ballot processing server. The server runs Rand to produce a re-randomized ciphertext c', which is included in the tally as long as Ver(pk, c') = 1. The correctness ensures that the voter's intent is accurately reflected in the resulting ciphertext. The voter can also store the trace of the ciphertext Trace(pk, c), which is equal to Trace(pk, c'), and confirms that it has been correctly recorded on the public bulletin board.

The *traceability* notion ensures that no corrupt authority would be able to modify a ciphertext in a way that modifies the plaintext without modifying the trace at the same time. Moreover, the trace cannot serve as a receipt for an encrypted message, since the trace and the message are independent, as guaranteed by the link traceability correctness. The traceability guarantees that, if the voter only produced a single ciphertext with a given trace, then any other ciphertext with the same trace will be an encryption of the same plaintext.

Definition 3. (Traceability) A TREnc is *traceable* if for every PPT adversary $\mathcal{A} = (\mathcal{A}_1, \mathcal{A}_2)$, the experiment $\mathsf{Exp}_{\mathcal{A}}^{trace}(\lambda)$ defined in Fig. 1 (right) returns 1 with a probability negligible in λ.

While the traceability relates to a model in which the voter is honest but the ballot processing server might be corrupted, the *traceable-CCA* notion (TCCA) focuses on protecting the privacy of the vote against a malicious voter. This is achieved through an indistinguishable experiment that guarantees that any malicious ballots computed with an identical trace cannot be recognized after randomization. This essentially guarantees the absence of a vote receipt.

Definition 4. (TCCA) A TREnc is TCCA secure if for every PPT adversary $\mathcal{A} = (\mathcal{A}_1, \mathcal{A}_2)$ the experiment $\mathsf{Exp}_{\mathcal{A}}^{TCCA}(\lambda)$ defined in Fig. 1 (left) returns 1 with a probability negligibly close in λ to $\frac{1}{2}$.

$\mathsf{Exp}_{\mathcal{A}}^{\mathsf{tcca}}(\lambda)$

$(\mathsf{pk}, \mathsf{sk}) \leftarrow\!\!{\scriptstyle\$}\ \mathsf{Gen}(1^{\lambda})$
$(c_0, c_1, \mathsf{st}) \leftarrow\!\!{\scriptstyle\$}\ \mathcal{A}_1^{\mathsf{Dec}(\cdot)}(\mathsf{pk})$
$b \leftarrow\!\!{\scriptstyle\$}\ \{0, 1\}$
if $\mathsf{Trace}(\mathsf{pk}, c_0) \neq \mathsf{Trace}(\mathsf{pk}, c_1)$ or
$\mathsf{Ver}(\mathsf{pk}, c_0) = 0$ or $\mathsf{Ver}(\mathsf{pk}, c_1) = 0$ **then return** b
$c^* \leftarrow\!\!{\scriptstyle\$}\ \mathsf{Rand}(\mathsf{pk}, c_b)$
$b' \leftarrow\!\!{\scriptstyle\$}\ \mathcal{A}_2^{\mathsf{Dec}^*(\cdot)}(c^*, \mathsf{st})$
return $b' = b$

$\mathsf{Exp}_{\mathcal{A}}^{\mathsf{trace}}(\lambda)$

$(\mathsf{pk}, \mathsf{sk}) \leftarrow\!\!{\scriptstyle\$}\ \mathsf{Gen}(1^{\lambda})$
$(m, \mathsf{st}) \leftarrow\!\!{\scriptstyle\$}\ \mathcal{A}_1(\mathsf{pk}, \mathsf{sk})$
$c \leftarrow\!\!{\scriptstyle\$}\ \mathsf{Enc}(\mathsf{pk}, m)$
$c^* \leftarrow\!\!{\scriptstyle\$}\ \mathcal{A}_2(c, \mathsf{st})$
if $\mathsf{Trace}(\mathsf{pk}, c) = \mathsf{Trace}(\mathsf{pk}, c^*)$ and
$\mathsf{Ver}(\mathsf{pk}, c^*) = 1$ and $\mathsf{Dec}(\mathsf{sk}, c^*) \neq m$
then return 1
else return 0

Fig. 1. Security experiments. In the case of TCCA, $\mathcal{A}_2$ has access to an oracle $\mathsf{Dec}^*(\cdot)$ which, on input c, returns $\mathsf{Dec}(c)$ if $\mathsf{Trace}(\mathsf{pk}, c) \neq \mathsf{Trace}(\mathsf{pk}, c^*)$ and $\bot$ otherwise.

Homomorphic Part. In this paper we assume that it is easy to strip an homomorphic part of any TREnc ciphertext that carries the encrypted vote and allows decryption. The constructions of [6] satisfy this condition.

3   Voting Scheme with Multiple Ballot Processing Severs

We adapt the general e-voting definition of [6] to cope with multiple ballot processing servers, and formalize threshold receipt-freeness and correctness.

3.1   Definitions and Notations

The election adminstrator (EA) is in charge of generating the keys of the system by running SetupElection. Given the public parameter of the system, voters can cast their intentions through Vote which creates a ballot $\mathsf{b} = \{\mathsf{b}_i\}_{i=1}^n$. Each ballot piece b_i is processed by the i-th ballot processing server which simply runs the algorithm ProcessBallot. The other algorithms are unchanged.

Definition 5. (Voting System) A voting system equipped with n ballot processing servers is a tuple of PPT algorithms (SetupElection, Vote, ProcessBallot, TraceBallot, Valid, Append, Publish, VerifyVote, Tally, VerifyResult) associated to a result function $\rho_m : \mathbb{V}^m \cup \{\bot\} \rightarrow \mathbb{R}$ where $\mathbb{V}$ is the set of valid votes and $\mathbb{R}$ is the result space such that:

> SetupElection(1^{λ}): on input security parameter 1^{λ}, generate the public and secret keys (pk, sk) of the election. Below, pk is an implicit input.
> Vote(id, v): when receiving a voter id and a vote v, output a ballot $\mathsf{b} = \{\mathsf{b}_i\}_{i=1}^n$ and auxiliary data aux. Given aux, running Vote(id, v, aux) allows computing ballots that can be related (in our case, ciphertexts with the same traces). Vote(id, v; ρ) denotes the deterministic computation of the algorithm given random coin ρ.
> ProcessBallot(b_i): on input a ballot share b_i, output an updated ballot share b_i'.

TraceBallot(b): on input ballot b, outputs a tag τ. The tag is the information that a voter can use to trace his ballot, using VerifyVote.

Valid(BB, b): on input ballot box BB and ballot b, outputs 0 or 1. The algorithm outputs 1 if and only if the ballot is valid.

Append(BB, b): on input ballot box BB and ballot b, appends b to BB if Valid(BB, b) = 1.

Publish(BB): on input ballot box BB, outputs the public view PBB of BB, which is the one that is used to verify the election. Depending on the context, it may be used to remove some voter credentials for instance.

VerifyVote(PBB, τ): on input public ballot box PBB and tag τ, outputs 0 or 1. This algorithm is used by voters to check if their ballot has been processed and recorded properly.

Tally(BB, sk): on input ballot box BB and private key of the election sk, outputs the tally r and a proof Π that the tally is correct w.r.t. the result function ρ_m.

VerifyResult(PBB, r, Π): on input public ballot box PBB, result of the tally r and proof of the tally Π, outputs 0 or 1. The algorithm outputs 1 only if Π is a valid proof that r is the correct election result.

When voters cast their votes, they record the tracking code computed from TraceBallot to trace their processed ballots on the public bulletin board PBB. Processed ballot shares that originate from the same voter are gathered and pushed to the ballot box BB, using Append. Recombined processed ballots are made publicly available on PBB by running Publish. Voters can verify that their ballots have been correctly recorded on PBB by relying on VerifyVote and their tracking codes. Other algorithms are as usual. If we write ProcessBallot(b) = $\{ProcessBallot(b_i)\}_{i=1}^{n}$, it is easy to see that our syntax is indeed a generalization of [6] which corresponds to the particular case of $n = 1$.

3.2 Threshold Receipt-Freeness

We formalize receipt-freeness in the multi-ballot processing model. Intuitively, the receipt-free threshold t_{rf} is the maximum number of malicious ballot processing servers tolerated by the system to guarantee receipt freeness.

Definition 6 (Threshold receipt-freeness). A voting system $\mathcal{V}$ with n ballot processing severs has receipt-freeness with threshold $t_{rf} \leq n$ if

1. There exists an algorithm Deceive such that, for every PPT adversary $\mathcal{A}$, $\Pr[\mathsf{Exp}_{\mathcal{A},\mathcal{V},t_{rf}}^{\mathsf{deceive}}(\lambda) = 1]$ negligible in λ. (The experiment is defined in Fig. 2.)
2. There exist algorithms SimSetupElection and SimProof such that, for every PPT adversary $\mathcal{A}$, the following advantage is negligible in λ

$$\mathsf{Adv}_{\mathcal{A},\mathcal{V}}^{\mathsf{rf},t_{rf}}(1^\lambda) = \left| \Pr\left[\mathsf{Exp}_{\mathcal{A},\mathcal{V}}^{\mathsf{rf},t_{rf},0}(\lambda) = 1\right] - \Pr\left[\mathsf{Exp}_{\mathcal{A},\mathcal{V}}^{\mathsf{rf},t_{rf},1}(\lambda) = 1\right] \right|,$$

where the experiment $\mathsf{Exp}_{\mathcal{A},\mathcal{V}}^{\mathsf{rf},t_{rf},\beta}(\lambda)$ is defined in Fig. 3.

$$\mathsf{Exp}_{\mathcal{A},\mathcal{V}}^{\mathsf{deceive},\mathsf{t_{rf}}}(\lambda)$$

$(\mathsf{pk}, \mathsf{sk}) \leftarrow_{\$} \mathsf{SetupElection}(1^\lambda)$
$(v_0, v_1, \rho, I) \leftarrow_{\$} \mathcal{A}(\mathsf{pk})$
if $I \not\subset [n]$ or $|I| > \mathsf{t_{rf}}$ **then return** 0
$b_0 \leftarrow \mathsf{Vote}(\mathsf{id}, v_0, \rho)$
$b_1 \leftarrow \mathsf{Deceive}(\mathsf{id}, v_0, v_1, \rho, I)$
if $\{b_0^i\}_{i \in I} \neq \{b_1^i\}_{i \in I}$ or $b_1 \notin \mathsf{Vote}(\mathsf{id}, v_1)$
or $\mathsf{TraceBallot}(b_0) \neq \mathsf{TraceBallot}(b_1)$
then return 1
return 0

Fig. 2. Deceive experiment.

The Experiment. $\mathsf{Exp}_{\mathcal{A},\mathcal{V},\mathsf{t_{rf}}}^{\mathsf{deceive}}(\lambda)$. The setup of the election creates the public and secret keys $(\mathsf{pk}, \mathsf{sk})$ and pk is given to $\mathcal{A}$. Then $\mathcal{A}$ chooses at most $\mathsf{t_{rf}}$ indexes of the corrupt ballot processing servers I. It also chooses the votes v_0, v_1 and the random coin ρ in the hope that ρ is a receipt ensuring that the computed ballot b contains v_0. However, $\mathcal{A}$ only sees the at most $\mathsf{t_{rf}}$ ballot pieces $(b_i)_{i \in I}$ and the public tracking codes for which the Deceive algorithm allows computing the complement ballot pieces so that b is a valid vote for v_1. (See Fig. 2.)

The Experiment. $\mathsf{Exp}_{\mathcal{A},\mathcal{V}}^{\mathsf{rf},\mathsf{t_{rf}},\beta}(\lambda)$. The experiment given in Fig. 3 is parameterized by a bit β, and the adversary has access to the following oracles:

- $\mathcal{O}$init: Is called a single time and generates the secret and public keys for the election. The public key is shared with the adversary. When $\beta = 1$, depending on the computational model, a simulated setup may be performed. This setup provides trapdoor information that can be used to produce a simulated tally correctness proof. Two empty ballot boxes BB_0 and BB_1 are initialized. The adversary will only have access to $\mathsf{Publish}(\mathsf{BB}_\beta)$ that is updated throughout the experiment.
- $\mathcal{O}$receiptLR: Allows the adversary to cast valid ballots and query the honest ballot processing servers to process their respective ballot pieces so that, on input $(\mathsf{id}, \mathsf{B}_0, \mathsf{B}_1, \mathsf{B}_2)$ for voter id, the oracle runs ProcessBallot on both sets B_0 and B_1 of valid ballot pieces if they share the same traces for the same index and gets B_0' and B_1'. As long as $|\mathsf{B}_0 \cup \mathsf{B}_2| = |\mathsf{B}_1 \cup \mathsf{B}_2| \leq n$ and $|\mathsf{B}_2| \leq \mathsf{t_{rf}}$, $b_0 = \mathsf{B}_0'||\mathsf{B}_2$ is appended to BB_0 and $b_1 = \mathsf{B}_1'||\mathsf{B}_2$ is appended to BB_1. Up to reordering, we can always assume that the first servers are honest. B_2 represents the ballot pieces for which the malicious vote seller and the corrupt servers together know their whole content.
- $\mathcal{O}$board: Returns the view $\mathsf{Publish}(\mathsf{BB}_\beta)$ of the public bulletin board.
- $\mathcal{O}$tally: Allows the adversary to see the result of the election obtained by tallying valid BB_0, as well as a proof of correctness of the tally. If $\beta = 1$, this proof is simulated with respect to the content derived from BB_1.

The adversary first calls $\mathcal{O}$init. Following this, it can call the oracles $\mathcal{O}$receiptLR and $\mathcal{O}$board in any order and any number of times. Finally, the

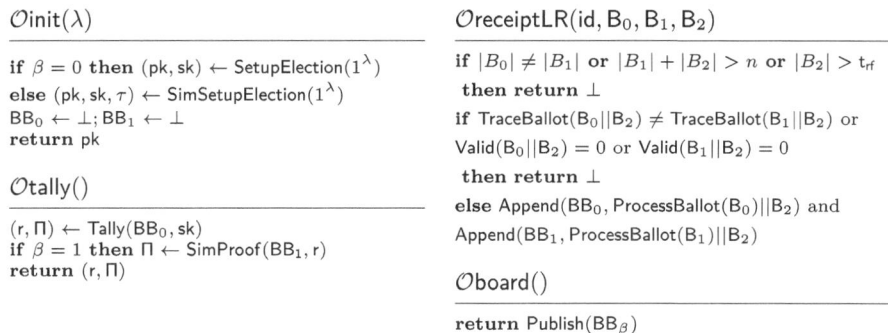

Fig. 3. Threshold receipt freeness oracles from experiment $\mathsf{Exp}_{\mathcal{A},\mathcal{V}}^{\mathsf{rf},\mathsf{t_{rf}},\beta}(\lambda)$, for $\beta = 0, 1$.

adversary calls the oracle $\mathcal{O}\mathsf{tally}$ to receive the (simulated) result of the election. It must then return its guess of the bit β, which is the output of the experiment. If $n = 1$ and $\mathsf{t_{rf}} = 0$, we get back the receipt freeness definition of [6].

3.3 Threshold Correctness

We formalize correctness in the multi-ballot processing model. Intuitively, the correctness threshold $\mathsf{t_{corr}}$ is the maximum number of ballot pieces of any ballot that could not reach the bulletin board while still allowing to include the corresponding underlying voter's intention in the tally.

Definition 7 (Threshold correctness). A voting system $\mathcal{V}$ with n ballot processing servers satisfies correctness with threshold $\mathsf{t_{corr}} < n$ if for every PPT adversary $\mathcal{A}$, $\Pr[\mathsf{Exp}_{\mathcal{A},\mathcal{V}}^{\mathsf{corr},\mathsf{t_{corr}}}(\lambda) = 1]$ is negligible in λ. (The experiment is defined in Fig. 4.)

The Experiment. $\mathsf{Exp}_{\mathcal{A},\mathcal{V}}^{\mathsf{corr},\mathsf{t_{corr}}}(\lambda)$. The experiment is given in Fig. 4, and the adversary is given access to the following oracles:

- $\mathcal{O}\mathsf{init}$: Generates and returns both the secret and public keys of the election.
- $\mathcal{O}\mathsf{vote}$: Takes a potential vote v for a user id, honestly produces and outputs a ballot b using Vote. The tracking code $\mathsf{TraceBallotb}$ is stored in the list $\mathcal{L}$. This represents ballots and tracing information from honest voters.
- $\mathcal{O}\mathsf{append}$: Allows the adversary to select two valid ballots b_0 and b_1 of at least $n - \mathsf{t_{corr}}$ valid ballot pieces as if there were potentially maliciously processed from honest ballots output by $\mathcal{O}\mathsf{vote}$. That is, both ballots must have their respective sets of tracking codes included in a single set of codes from $\mathcal{L}$. Both ballots are then respectively appended to BB_0 and BB_1. It represents maliciously processed ballot pieces that use the same tracing information as honest ballots but for which the adversary tries to change the content of the votes and blocks at most $\mathsf{t_{corr}}$ pieces of them.
- $\mathcal{O}\mathsf{cast}$: Allows the adversary to cast a malicious valid ballot b in BB_0 and BB_1.

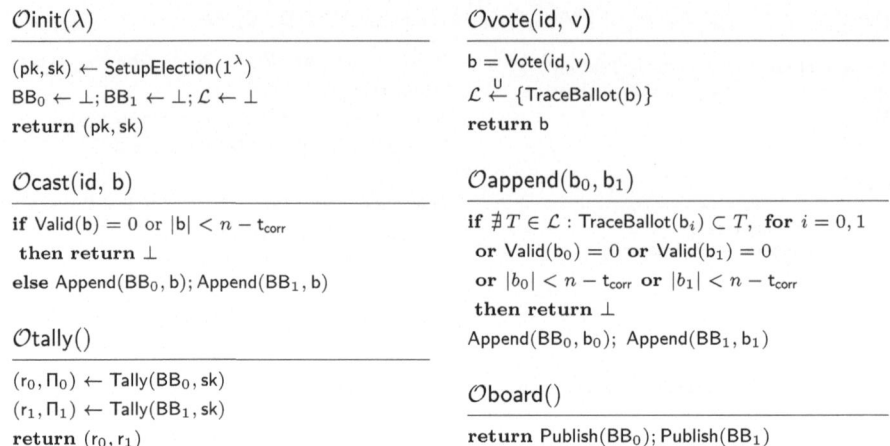

Fig. 4. Threshold correctness experiment $\mathsf{Exp}_{\mathcal{A},\mathcal{V}}^{\mathsf{corr},\mathsf{t_{corr}}}(\lambda)$ which outputs 1 only if $\mathsf{r}_0 \neq \mathsf{r}_1$.

– $\mathcal{O}$board: Returns the views $\mathsf{Publish}(\mathsf{BB}_0)$ and $\mathsf{Publish}(\mathsf{BB}_1)$ of the public bulletin boards.
– $\mathcal{O}$tally: Allows the adversary to get the results of the election obtained by honestly tallying BB_0 and BB_1.

The adversary $\mathcal{A}$ initiates the experiment by invoking the oracle $\mathcal{O}$init, and the experiment terminates when it calls $\mathcal{O}$tally. The output of the experiment is a bit that is equal to 1 only if the adversary managed to compute valid ballots providing distinct outcomes from both ballot boxes. To attempt creating such ballots, the adversary can query all the other oracles many times in many orders.

Remarks. We leave it open to define a stronger threshold correctness notion where the adversary would remain unable to modify the result of the election by selecting distinct ballot pieces from a maliciously generated ballot. Here malicious ballots are equally processed on both ballot boxes. In our construction, this is not an issue as we implicitly define the vote as the one contained in the recombination of all the stripped ciphertexts included in the ballot pieces of each voter. The recombined ciphertexts are then tallied based on a mixnet. Achieving the stronger notion in a construction with an homomorphic tally requires designing new malleable proofs that can be adapted through all the randomness used by the n servers. Indeed, if the vote v is represented with a bit, the randomizable shared proof that $v(1-v) = 0$ is hardly adaptable locally by the n servers as their adaptation must depend on the others' randomizing factors.

4 Our Construction Based on **TREnc**

Our voting system is based on a TREnc. As recalled in Sect. 1, a TREnc consists of various algorithms including Gen, Enc, Trace, Rand, Ver, and Dec in particular.

SetupElection (λ)

$(\mathsf{pk}, \mathsf{sk}) \leftarrow \mathsf{TREnc.Gen}(1^\lambda)$
return pk

Vote(id, v[, aux])

$M = \mathsf{Share}(\mathsf{pk}, t, \mathsf{v}) = \{x_1, \dots, x_n\}$
if aux is empty **for** $i = 1$ to n **do**
    $\mathsf{lk}_i \leftarrow\$ \mathsf{TREnc.LGen}(\mathsf{pk})$
else $\{\mathsf{lk}_i\}_{i=1}^n \leftarrow$ aux
for $i = 1$ to n **do**
    $b_i \leftarrow \mathsf{TREnc.LEnc}(\mathsf{pk}, \mathsf{lk}_i, x_i)$
return $b = \{b_i\}_{i=1}^n$, aux $= \mathsf{lk} = \{\mathsf{lk}_i\}_{i=1}^n$

TraceBallot(b)

return $\{\mathsf{TREnc.Trace}(b_i)\}_{i=1}^{|b|}$

ProcessBallot(b_i)

return $\mathsf{TREnc.Rand}(\mathsf{pk}, b_i)$

Valid(BB, b)

if $\exists b' \in$ BB : TraceBallot$(b') =$ TraceBallot(b)
then return $\perp$
$k = 0$
for $i = 1$ to $|b|$ **do**
    if TREnc.Ver$(b_i) = 1$
        $k \leftarrow k + 1$
if $k \geq t$ **then return** 1 **else return** 0

VerifyVote(PBB, τ)

if $\exists b \in$ PBB : Valid(b) $\wedge \tau ==$ TraceBallot(b)
then return 1 **else return** 0

Fig. 5. Instantiation of our voting scheme.

We will use these algorithms to demonstrate how to design a voting system that can provide the properties of threshold receipt-freeness and correctness as previously described in Sects. 3.2 and 3.3.

The message (or the vote) v is divided into n message shares using a t-out-of-n threshold secret sharing scheme, originally proposed by Shamir [13], where at least t message pieces must be combined to reconstruct the message. Moreover, any $t-1$ pieces remain independent of v. To generate the ballot b, the voter encrypts each share of his message by calling the Enc function of TREnc, which produces a ballot share b_i. The process is repeated n times for n message shares, resulting in the creation of a full ballot consisting of n ballot shares, i.e., $b = \{b_i\}_{i=1}^n$. Each share is processed by a specific ballot processing server. For instance, server i exclusively receives the ballot share b_i, and does not have access to any other share b_j where $j \neq i$. The instantiation of our voting scheme is illustrated in Fig. 5, where n is the implicit input of all the algorithms.

First, EA runs the SetupElection algorithm to generate the public and secret keys of the election. This is achieved by running the key generation algorithm from TREnc, denoted by TREnc.Gen. The public key pk is published and stored on the PBB, while sk is only known by the talliers (sk can be securely generated in a distributed way in our prime-order groups using standard techniques). For the sake of simplicity, we consider a model with a single tallier.

When a voter wants to cast a vote v, he prepares a ballot using the Vote algorithm. First, the Share is executed to implement the t-out-of-n threshold secret-sharing scheme. This function takes as input the number of ballot processing parties n, the threshold t, and the secret v to output the shares $M = \{x_1, \dots, x_n\}$. Then, it calls the encryption function Enc of TREnc (which includes $\mathsf{LGen}(\mathsf{pk}) = \mathsf{lk}$ and $\mathsf{LEnc}(\mathsf{pk}, \mathsf{lk}, \mathsf{v})$) on each message share x_i to produce a ballot share b_i for $i = 1$ to n. In the end, Vote returns a ballot b and aux $= \mathsf{lk}$.

Each b_i is then submitted to a distinct ballot processing server, while the full trace $\tau = \mathsf{TraceBallot(b)}$ is sent directly to the PBB. We have that $\tau = \{\tau_i\}_{i=1}^{|b|}$ including all traces of available ballot shares in b, where $\tau_i = \mathsf{TREnc.Trace}(b_i)$. When a server receives a b_i, it extracts its trace using $\mathsf{TREnc.Trace}(b_i)$ and verifies that no shares with the same trace were recorded before. If b_i is valid, i.e., $\mathsf{TREnc.Ver}(b_i) = 1$, it will be re-randomized with the help of $\mathsf{ProcessBallot}(b_i) = \mathsf{TREnc.Rand}(b_i)$, while invalid shares are discarded. Although each randomizer processes only one share of each voter at a time, the ProcessBallot algorithm can be executed in parallel for n number of randomizers. The resulting ballot share is then made available on the BB.

The tallying process commences with the gathering of ballot shares from the same ballot. To do this, the tallier compares traces received on BB to the full trace τ posted by each voter on the public board earlier. Subsequently, the validity of each ballot is verified using the function TREnc.Ver on each ballot share. The function $\mathsf{Valid(BB,b)}$ in Fig. 5 returns 1 if there are at least t valid ballot shares of b on the public board, and 0 otherwise. Consequently, the combination algorithm Combine takes as input the homomorphic parts of all valid ballot shares available, which may be at most n, and outputs the combined encryption of the original message v. The resulting (CPA-secure) ciphertext contains the reconstruction of the vote from the encrypted shares. According to the principles of Lagrange polynomial interpolation, the final message remains unaltered even when more than t valid shares are combined.

The Validity of the Vote. The purpose of the Valid function is to ensure that the input of the tally is valid. However, this function does not guarantee that the encrypted vote is within the range of the vote space. To address this issue, a verifiable *mixnet* will be added after the combination process is completed, which disassociates the ballots from their corresponding voters. This anonymization process will be carried out by shuffling the resulting combined encryptions through multiple shuffling centers, after which they will be decrypted individually. Invalid votes are discarded. The tallier returns the result of the election r along with proof of its correctness Π, which can be verified by anyone with VerifyResult. Voters also can verify the presence of their vote on the bulletin board by utilizing $\mathsf{VerifyVote(PBB, \tau)}$ to confirm if any entry in PBB matches τ.

Correlation Between. $\mathsf{t_{rf}}$ and $\mathsf{t_{corr}}$. In accordance with the threshold secret sharing scheme used, the voting system requires that at least t of a ballot's valid shares are available on the BB to reconstruct the ballot. By definition, $\mathsf{t_{corr}} = n - t$. In terms of receipt-freeness, since a b_i is computed as a TREnc ciphertext, first, the TREnc's traceability ensures that as long as the lk remains secret, it is infeasible for anyone to change the message share x_i while keeping the trace τ_i unchanged even with sk. Additionally, knowing the link keys $\mathsf{lk} = \{\mathsf{lk}_i\}_{i=1}^{n}$ allows voting for any voting shares even for fixed traces (that an RF adversary would like to see on PBB) and the secret sharing properties allows computing shares of any vote v even with $t-1$ chosen shares. Moreover, the TCCA security of TREnc guarantees that an honest randomization will erase all malicious information that can be introduced in the ballot, rendering it infeasible for the individual who generated it to prove to anyone that it is the ballot of a particular vote. Consequently, as long as the combination includes at least *one* honestly re-randomized ballot share if $t - 1$ ciphertexts are corrupt, RF is achieved. As a result, the number of allowed malicious randomizers, i.e., process ballot servers should be no greater than $t_{rf} = t - 1$. See Sect. 5.1 for the proof.

Given that $1 \leq t_{corr} \leq n - t$, the proposed voting system offers a solution for scenarios where some randomizers are not functioning properly, whether intentionally or unintentionally. In such cases, incomplete ballots will nevertheless be proceeded to the tally. This ensures that the system can provide flexibility by handling unflavored cases and maintaining the integrity of the election process. In a specific case where a n-out-of-n threshold secret-sharing scheme is employed, $t_{corr} = 0$ and $t_{rf} = n - 1$. That means, provided that all n valid ballot shares arrive on the BB, the system achieves RF even when only one honest randomizing server exists. To the best of our knowledge, this represents the strongest security notion for single-pass RF that has been proposed in the literature to date.

5   Security of the Voting Scheme

In this section, we prove that our generic voting scheme described in the previous section is threshold receipt-free (Sect. 5.1) and threshold correct (Sect. 5.2).

5.1   Threshold Receipt-Freeness

Theorem 1. *If the TREnc used in the voting scheme is TCCA secure and verifiable, and if the proof system used to prove the correctness of the tally is zero-knowledge, our voting scheme has threshold receipt freeness. More precisely, for a t-out-of-n secret sharing of the vote,* $t_{rf} = t - 1$, $\Pr[\mathsf{Exp}^{deceive}_{\mathcal{A},\mathcal{V},t_{rf}}(\lambda) = 1] \leq \varepsilon_{verif}$, *where* ε_{verif} *is the verifiability advantage of any adversary against TREnc, and* $\mathsf{Adv}^{rf,t_{rf}}_{\mathcal{A},\mathcal{V}}(1^\lambda) \leq \varepsilon_{ZK} + q(n - t_{rf})\varepsilon_{tcca}$, *where* ε_{ZK} *is the zero-knowledge advantage of any adversary against the proof system,* ε_{tcca} *is the TCCA advantage of any adversary against TREnc (recalled in Definition 4), and q is the number of queries made to $\mathcal{O}receiptLR$ made by the adversary $\mathcal{A}$.*

Proof. The experiment $\mathsf{Exp}^{deceive,t_{rf}}_{\mathcal{A},\mathcal{V}}(\lambda)$. Given $\rho = \{r_{ss}, r_{enc}\}$, where r_{ss} contains all random coins for the secret sharing scheme Share, i.e., the coefficients of the polynomial f in the Shamir's t-out-of-n threshold scheme, while r_{enc} contains lk and all the random coins in TREnc.LEnc, the Deceive function aborts and outputs 0 if either v_0, v_1, ρ, or I fail to parse correctly. Otherwise,

1. It selects r_{ss} from ρ to output $\{v_0^i\}_{i \in I} = \mathsf{Share}(\mathsf{pk}, n, t, v_0; r_{ss})$, where each v_0^i is an evaluation of a degree-$(t - 1)$ polynomial f at a point i. The adversary will be able to verify if $\{v_0^i\}_{i \in I}$ are in $\{b_0^i\}_{i \in I}$ since these will be processed by dishonest randomizers and with known randomness r_{enc}.

2. To secretly share v_1, it produces another polynomial g of degree $t-1$ such that $g(0) = v_1$. To this end, the evaluation of g at a point i is fixed to be v_0^i for all $i \in I$, thereby providing at most t linear conditions. If $|I| < \mathsf{t_{rf}} = t-1$, add random input-output evaluation pairs to the interpolation to reach the appropriate degree. Subsequently, evaluate g at the point $i \in [n]\backslash I$ to compute v_1^i.

3. To generate $\mathsf{b_1}$, it selects r_{enc} from ρ to run $\mathsf{TREnc.LEnc}$ on message shares $\{v_0^i\}_{i \in I}$ and $\{v_1^i\}_{i \in [n]\backslash I}$, which keeps the traces as $\mathsf{lk} \in r_{enc}$.

Since the Share operation based on the polynomial g is carried out honestly, any combination of t ballot shares in $\mathsf{b_1}$ will result in the decryption of the same encrypted message. Eventually, even if the random coin r_{enc} are maliciously distributed, the TREnc verifiability guarantees that $\mathsf{b_1} \in \mathsf{Vote}(\mathsf{id}, v_1)$.

The experiment $\mathsf{Exp}_{\mathcal{A},\mathcal{V}}^{\mathsf{rf},\mathsf{t_{rf}},\beta}(\lambda)$. To proceed with the $\mathcal{O}\mathsf{receiptLR}$ oracle defined in Fig. 3, an attacker must produce two valid ballots, namely $\mathsf{b_0} = \mathsf{B_0}||\mathsf{B_2}$ and $\mathsf{b_1} = \mathsf{B_1}||\mathsf{B_2}$. The oracle then verifies that both ballots have identical traces. More precisely, the conditions $\mathsf{Valid}(\mathsf{b_0}) = \mathsf{Valid}(\mathsf{b_1}) = 1$ and $\mathsf{TraceBallot}(\mathsf{b_0}) = \mathsf{TraceBallot}(\mathsf{b_1})$ must be met before processing them.

The proof involves a series of indistinguishable games, starting with the experiment $\mathsf{Exp}_{\mathcal{A},\mathcal{V}}^{\mathsf{rf},\mathsf{t_{rf}},0}(\lambda)$ ($\beta = 0$) and ending with $\mathsf{Exp}_{\mathcal{A},\mathcal{V}}^{\mathsf{rf},\mathsf{t_{rf}},1}(\lambda)$ ($\beta = 1$).

$\mathsf{Game}_1(\lambda)$: This is the experiment $\mathsf{Exp}_{\mathcal{A},\mathcal{V}}^{\mathsf{rf},\mathsf{t_{rf}},0}(\lambda)$ given in Fig. 3 with $\beta = 0$. By definition, $\Pr[S_1] = \Pr[\mathsf{Exp}_{\mathcal{A},\mathcal{V}}^{\mathsf{rf},\mathsf{t_{rf}},0}(\lambda) = 1]$.

$\mathsf{Game}_2(\lambda)$: This game is as $\mathsf{Game}\ 1$, with the exception that the keys of the election are generated using $\mathsf{SimSetupElection}$ which still produces the secret key sk of TREnc but also creates the additional trapdoor key to simulate proof for the tally. Moreover, we still honestly run Tally to get the result of the election but we erase the proof and instead run $\mathsf{SetupElection}$ on input the honest result. Since the proof system of the tally is zero-knowledge, we have $|\Pr[S_1] - \Pr[S_2]| \leq \varepsilon_{\mathsf{ZK}}$.

$\mathsf{Game}_3(\lambda)$: This game is as the previous game, except that the decryption is executed on-the-fly using $\mathsf{Dec}(\mathsf{sk}, \cdot)$ of TREnc in each call to $\mathcal{O}\mathsf{receiptLR}$ before the (perfect) randomization in $\mathsf{ProcessBallot}$. The result of the election is then computed from the resulting function. Since the view in $\mathsf{Game}\ 2$ is identical to that of $\mathsf{Game}\ 1$, we have $\Pr[S_2] = \Pr[S_3]$.

$\mathsf{Game}_4(\lambda)$: In this game, we introduce the following modification in the way we answer to the $\mathcal{O}\mathsf{receiptLR}$ queries made by the adversary, by gradually replacing processed ballots from B_0 by those of B_1 in BB_0.

$\mathsf{Game}_{4,1}(\lambda)$: In order to compute B_0', instead of re-randomizing b_0^1, we re-randomize b_1^1. In other words, $\mathsf{B}_0' = (\mathsf{b}_1^{1'}, \mathsf{b}_0^{2'}, \ldots, \mathsf{b}_0^{n-\mathsf{t_{rf}}'})$. The probability that $\mathcal{A}$ distinguishes the difference after this modification is the probability that one is able to distinguish whether the first element of B_0' is the randomization of b_0^1 or b_1^1. Since each ballot share is a valid TREnc ciphertext and that Valid rejects replaying the same traces, the TCCA challenger can call its own TCCA decryption oracle to compute the result as in Game 3 before the challenge phase since the corresponding trace has never been involved in an earlier query in another ballot piece, it follows that $|\Pr[S_3] - \Pr[S_{4,1}]| \leq \varepsilon_{\text{tcca}}$.

$\mathsf{Game}_{4,i}(\lambda)$: Keep doing the same way, we replace each element of B_0' by a corresponding element in B_1'. Hence, $|\Pr[S_{4,i-1}] - \Pr[S_{4,i}]| \leq \varepsilon_{\text{tcca}}$.

At the end of Game 4, we have $\mathsf{B}_0' = (\mathsf{b}_1^{1'}, \ldots, \mathsf{b}_1^{n-\mathsf{t}_{\mathsf{rf}}'})$, which is identical to B_1'. Consequently, for the first query to $\mathcal{O}\mathsf{receiptLR}$ query, we have $|\Pr[S_3] - \Pr[S_4]| \leq (n - \mathsf{t}_{\mathsf{rf}})\varepsilon_{\text{tcca}}$. Then, by an hybrid argument on all the q queries made by the adversary, we get $|\Pr[S_3] - \Pr[S_4]| \leq q(n - \mathsf{t}_{\mathsf{rf}})\varepsilon_{\text{tcca}}$. The view of $\mathcal{A}$ in Game 4 is exactly its view in $\mathsf{Exp}_{\mathcal{A},\mathcal{V}}^{\mathsf{rf},\mathsf{t}_{\mathsf{rf}},1}(\lambda)$. We thus have $\mathsf{Adv}_{\mathcal{A},\mathcal{V}}^{\mathsf{rf},\mathsf{t}_{\mathsf{rf}}}(1^\lambda) \leq \varepsilon_{\mathsf{ZK}} + q(n - \mathsf{t}_{\mathsf{rf}})\varepsilon_{\text{tcca}}$.

$\square$

5.2 Threshold Correctness

Theorem 2. *If the TREnc used in the voting scheme is traceable and verifiable, then the proposed voting scheme has threshold correctness. More precisely, for a t-out-of-n secret sharing of the vote, we have $\mathsf{t}_{\mathsf{corr}} = t - 1$ and for any efficient adversary $\mathcal{A}$, $\Pr[\mathsf{Exp}_{\mathcal{A},\mathcal{V}}^{\mathsf{corr},\mathsf{t}_{\mathsf{corr}}}(\lambda) = 1] \leq qn\varepsilon_{\text{trace}}$, where $\varepsilon_{\text{trace}}$ is the advantage of any adversary against traceability of TREnc (recalled in Definition 3), and q is the number of $\mathcal{O}\mathsf{append}$ queries.*

Proof. In the experiment $\mathsf{Exp}_{\mathcal{A},\mathcal{V}}^{\mathsf{corr},\mathsf{t}_{\mathsf{corr}}}(\lambda)$, to append ballots to BB_1 and BB_0, $\mathcal{A}$ can make $\mathcal{O}\mathsf{cast}$ and $\mathcal{O}\mathsf{append}$ queries.

$\mathcal{O}\mathsf{cast}$ appends the same malicious valid ballot to both bulletin boards. Since the identical ballot is published to both bulletin boards, this will not assist the adversary in winning the game, as it will not result in any difference in the tally results. That is also because the recombination is made deterministically on all the valid pieces.

$\mathcal{O}\mathsf{append}$ records two valid ballots, b_0 and b_1, which are maliciously processed from an honestly generated ballot b, to the bulletin board BB_0 and BB_1 respectively. As defined, $\mathsf{b} = \{\mathsf{b}^i\}_{i=1}^n = \mathsf{Vote}(\mathsf{id}, \mathsf{v})$, $T = \mathsf{TraceBallot}(\mathsf{b})$, and $\mathsf{TraceBallot}(\mathsf{b}_0), \mathsf{TraceBallot}(\mathsf{b}_1) \subset T$. Let us call I_0, I_1 two subset indexes of $[n]$, we denote $\mathsf{b}_0 = \{\mathsf{b}_0^i\}_{i \in I_0}$ and $\mathsf{b}_1 = \{\mathsf{b}_1^i\}_{i \in I_1}$ with $|I_0|, |I_1| \geq n - \mathsf{t}_{\mathsf{corr}}$. As a result, $\mathsf{TraceBallot}(\mathsf{b}_j^i) \in T$ for all $j = 0, 1$ and $i \in I_j$.

First, since each ballot share is a TREnc ciphertext and TREnc is traceable, it is infeasible for anyone to produce another ciphertext that traces to the same trace and would decrypt to a different message. We thus have $\mathsf{Dec}(\mathsf{sk}, \mathsf{Combine}(\{\mathsf{b}_j^i\})) = \mathsf{Dec}(\mathsf{sk}, \mathsf{Combine}(\{\mathsf{b}^i\}))$ for all $j = 0, 1$ and for each $i \in I_j$, except with a negligible probability $\varepsilon_{\text{trace}}$.

Second, since b is generated honestly, a combination of any subgroup of at least $n - \mathsf{t}_{\mathsf{corr}}$ shares returns the same message v. Consequently, it always holds that $\mathsf{Dec}(\mathsf{sk}, \mathsf{Combine}(\{\mathsf{b}^i\}_{i \in I_0})) = \mathsf{Dec}(\mathsf{sk}, \mathsf{Combine}(\{\mathsf{b}^i\}_{i \in I_1}))$.

The first and second points above infer that $\mathsf{Dec}(\mathsf{sk}, \mathsf{Combine}(\{\mathsf{b}_0^i\}_{i \in I_0})) = \mathsf{Dec}(\mathsf{sk}, \mathsf{Combine}(\{\mathsf{b}_1^i\}_{i \in I_1}))$ but with a negligible probability.

It is easy to see that with sk we can always decrypt each ballot pieces and figure it out whether the adversary managed to compute a TREnc ciphertext that reuses a trace but does not contain the original honest voting shares as message. Hence, $\Pr[\mathsf{Exp}_{\mathcal{A},\mathcal{V}}^{\mathsf{corr},\mathsf{t_{corr}}}(\lambda) = 1] \leq qn\varepsilon_{\mathrm{trace}}$ by a standard guessing technique. □

As previously discussed, the current threshold correctness notion does not account for scenarios where an adversary introduces a malicious ballot with distinct ballot pieces. In such cases, different combinations of ballot shares could yield different combined messages. However, since all valid ballot shares on the bulletin board (possibly more than t) are combined, only one message can be reconstructed. As the adversary cannot predict which ballot shares will be available due to any potential non-operational randomizers, it should produce truthful ballots to ensure the resulting vote accurately reflects its intent.

Verifiability. Our voting scheme satisfies both individual and universal verifiability. Individual verifiability is guaranteed through the VerifyVote steps, which allow voters to confirm the accurate recording of their votes and ensure that their preference remains unaltered. Universal verifiability is upheld by the verifiable mixnet, ensuring accurate tally computation and trustworthy final results.

6   Conclusion

We propose the notion threshold receipt-freeness, an extension of receipt-freeness that involves multiple ballot processing servers, removing a single point of failure of previous methodologies. Apart from preventing a malicious voter from providing proof of their vote to any third party, the novel definition allows an honest voter to cast their vote for their preferred candidate, even if some servers are compromised, provided that the adversary cannot vote on their behalf.

Additionally, we develop a generic construction of a single-pass verifiable voting system, based on traceable receipt-free encryption. Given any number n of ballot processing servers and $1 \leq t \leq n$, the resulting system maintains receipt-freeness and correctness as long as only t valid processed ballot pieces reach the bulletin board and even if $t-1$ of them were processed by the malicious servers who may reveal their random coins. Moreover, the trustworthy servers might differ for each voter. Practically, one may setup an election with only 3 servers so that any voter trusts at least any 2 of them, and their intentions will be taken into account if any 2 ciphertexts among the 3 computed are posted on the bulletin board after re-randomization.

Since the ballots are composed of n TREnc ciphertexts, their size is linear in the number of servers. We think that designing ballots of sub-linear size in n would require new techniques. Moreover, we leave it open to design a threshold receipt-free and correct election system compatible with homomorphic tally. Designing randomizable proof in a single-pass that maintains validity of the vote, for instance in an approval voting scenario, through the n servers which do not interact together seems to be challenging.

Acknowledgments. Thomas Peters is a research associate of the Belgian Fund for Scientific Research (F.R.S.-FNRS). This work has been funded in part by the Walloon Region through the project CyberExcellence (convention number 2110186).

References

1. Benaloh, J., Tuinstra, D.: Receipt-free secret ballot elections (extended abstract). In: Proceedings of the Twenty-Sixth Annual ACM Symposium on Theory of Computing, STOC 94, pp. 544–553. ACM (1994)

2. Bernhard, D., Cortier, V., Pereira, O., Smyth, B., Warinschi, B.: Adapting helios for provable ballot privacy. In: Computer Security–ESORICS 2011. LNCS, vol. 6879, pp. 335–354. Springer (2011). https://doi.org/10.1007/978-3-642-23822-2_19

3. Blazy, O., Fuchsbauer, G., Pointcheval, D., Vergnaud, D.: Signatures on randomizable ciphertexts. In: Public Key Cryptography–PKC 2011. LNCS, vol. 6571, pp. 403–422. Springer (2011). https://doi.org/10.1007/978-3-642-19379-8_25

4. Chaidos, P., Cortier, V., Fuchsbauer, G., Galindo, D.: BeleniosRF: a non-interactive receipt-free electronic voting scheme. In: Proceedings of the 2016 ACM SIGSAC Conference on Computer and Communications Security, pp. 1614–1625. ACM (2016)

5. Chaum, D., Pedersen, T.P.: Wallet databases with observers. In: Advances in Cryptology - CRYPTO '92. LNCS, vol. 740, pp. 89–105. Springer, Springer (1992). https://doi.org/10.1007/3-540-48071-4_7

6. Devillez, H., Pereira, O., Peters, T.: Traceable receipt-free encryption. In: Agrawal, S., Lin, D. (eds.) Advances in Cryptology - ASIACRYPT 2022. LNCS, vol. 13793, pp. 273–303. Springer (2022). https://doi.org/10.1007/978-3-031-22969-5_10

7. Devillez, H., Pereira, O., Peters, T., Yang, Q.: Can we cast a ballot as intended and be receipt free? In: 2024 IEEE Symposium on Security and Privacy (SP). IEEE Computer Society (2024)

8. Doan, T.V.T., Pereira, O., Peters, T.: Encryption mechanisms for receipt-free and perfectly private verifiable elections. In: International Conference on Applied Cryptography and Network Security–ACNS 2024. LNCS, vol. 14583, pp. 257–287. Springer (2024). https://doi.org/10.1007/978-3-031-54770-6_11

9. Hirt, M.: Multi party computation: Efficient protocols, general adversaries, and voting. Diss. ETH No. 14376 (2001)

10. Lee, B., Kim, K.: Receipt-free electronic voting through collaboration of voter and honest verifier. In: Japan-Korea Joint Workshop on Information Security and Cryptology (JW-ISC2000), pp. 101–108 (2000)

11. Libert, B., Peters, T., Joye, M., Yung, M.: Linearly homomorphic structure-preserving signatures and their applications. Des. Codes Crypt. **77**(2–3), 441–477 (2015)

12. Magkos, E., Burmester, M., Chrissikopoulos, V.: Receipt-freeness in large-scale elections without untappable channels. In: Towards The E-Society: E-Commerce, E-Business, and E-Government (I3E 2001). IFIP Conference Proceedings, vol. 202, pp. 683–693. Kluwer (2001)

13. Shamir, A.: How to share a secret. Commun. ACM **22**(11), 612–613 (1979)

Improving the Computational Efficiency of Adaptive Audits of IRV Elections

Alexander Ek[1] , Michelle Blom[2] , Philip B. Stark[3] , Peter J. Stuckey[4] ,
and Damjan Vukcevic[1]([⊠])

[1] Department of Econometrics and Business Statistics, Monash University,
Clayton, Australia
damjan.vukcevic@monash.edu
[2] Department of Computing and Information Systems, University of Melbourne,
Parkville, Australia
[3] Department of Statistics, University of California, Berkeley, CA, USA
[4] Department of Data Science and AI, Monash University, Clayton, Australia

Abstract. AWAIRE is one of two extant methods for conducting risk-limiting audits of instant-runoff voting (IRV) elections. In principle AWAIRE can audit IRV contests with any number of candidates, but the original implementation incurred memory and computation costs that grew superexponentially with the number of candidates. This paper improves the algorithmic implementation of AWAIRE in three ways that make it practical to audit IRV contests with 55 candidates, compared to the previous 6 candidates. First, rather than trying from the start to rule out all candidate elimination orders that produce a different winner, the algorithm starts by considering only the final round, testing statistically whether each candidate could have won that round. For those candidates who cannot be ruled out at that stage, it expands to consider earlier and earlier rounds until either it provides strong evidence that the reported winner really won or a full hand count is conducted, revealing who really won. Second, it tests a richer collection of conditions, some of which can rule out many elimination orders at once. Third, it exploits relationships among those conditions, allowing it to abandon testing those that are unlikely to help. We provide real-world examples with up to 36 candidates and synthetic examples with up to 55 candidates, showing how audit sample size depends on the margins and on the tuning parameters. An open-source Python implementation is publicly available.

We thank Vanessa Teague for helpful discussions. This work was supported by the Australian Research Council (Discovery Project DP220101012, OPTIMA ITTC IC200100009) and the US National Science Foundation (SaTC 2228884).

D. Duenas-Cid et al. (Eds.): E-Vote-ID 2024, LNCS 15014, pp. 37–53, 2025.
https://doi.org/10.1007/978-3-031-72244-8_3

1   Introduction

Risk-limiting audits (RLAs) are gaining attention in the world of election security and assurance.[1] An RLA is any procedure with a guaranteed minimum probability of correcting the reported outcome of an election if the reported outcome is wrong, and that never alters a correct outcome.[2] *Outcome* means who or what won, not the vote tallies. The *risk limit* α is the maximum chance that a wrong outcome will not be corrected. RLAs generally involve sampling cast ballot cards at random and manually reading the votes on those cards. RLAs can use a broad variety of sampling designs and can use a variety of information from the voting system to improve efficiency [7–9].

Improving the efficiency of RLAs—i.e., reducing the sample size an RLA requires when the reported outcome is correct—is an active field of research. Efficient RLAs for *instant-runoff voting* (IRV), a common form of ranked-choice voting, were developed relatively recently. IRV is tallied in rounds. The least popular candidate is eliminated in each round until only one candidate remains: the winner. In each round, each ballot's most preferred choice among the remaining candidates is counted as a vote for that candidate. Tabulating an IRV election produces an *elimination order*; the last candidate in the order is the winner.

IRV is used in political contests in several countries: the federal House of Representatives in Australia, along with most analogues at the state-level; the president of India; single-winner contests in Ireland such as the president of Ireland and by-elections to Dáil Éireann (the Irish lower house); and various contest in U.S. states including Alaska, California, Colorado, Maine, and Nevada, and by some political parties for statewide primary elections.

RAIRE [3] and AWAIRE [6] are the only extant methods for conducting RLAs of IRV elections. Both confirm the outcome by ruling out all elimination orders that yield a different winner (*alt-orders*). Both involve constructing 'assertions' which, if true, collectively rule out all alt-orders.[3] These assertions are then checked statistically using tools available in the SHANGRLA framework for RLAs [7,8]. RAIRE is a two-stage approach: generate a sufficient set of assertions before any sampling (offline), then test the assertions by sampling. AWAIRE perform both steps simultaneously (online), using the sample to 'learn' a sufficient set of assertions that can be tested efficiently, while testing them.

Another difference between the two methods is that RAIRE requires *cast vote records* (CVRs, the voting equipment's internal record of the preferences

---

[1] https://www.ifes.org/publications/risk-limiting-audits-guide-global-use,   and https://www.ncsl.org/elections-and-campaigns/risk-limiting-audits (visited 15 May 2024).

[2] The collection of ballot cards from which the audit sample is drawn must be a demonstrably complete and trustworthy record of the validly cast votes; otherwise, no audit procedure can guarantee a nonzero chance of catching and correcting wrong outcomes. See, e.g., Appel & Stark [1].

[3] The assertions used by RAIRE may also rule out some orders that correspond to the reported winner indeed winning, but through an elimination order that differs from the reported order.

expressed on each ballot) to select the set of assertions to minimize expected workload if the CVRs are accurate.[4]

AWAIRE has benefits over RAIRE, leveraging the insight that one can decompose every alt-order into a set of *requirements* that must all be true for the alt-order to be true, and let the sample dictate which requirements to use to reject the alt-order, while, RAIRE pre-commits to a subset of requirements to test. Because of this, AWAIRE can adaptively identify the requirements that are easiest to disprove, even when the CVRs are not accurate; it does not require CVRs, but can use them if they are available; and it is more resilient than RAIRE if the CVRs imply an incorrect elimination order but the reported winner is correct.

Here, we address the main drawback of AWAIRE as presented so far: its computational performance. For contests with k candidates, the original implementation of AWAIRE tracked and tested all $k! - (k-1)!$ alt-orders and their numerous requirements. That limited it to elections with at most 6 candidates, fewer than many real-world IRV elections. We show how to vastly decrease the computational resources AWAIRE needs.

The new implementation tracks a *frontier* of suffixes of alt-orders. Often, the sample allows AWAIRE to reject a suffix that an exponential number of alt-orders share. Otherwise, the new approach extends the suffix, replacing it in the frontier with all suffixes with one more candidate. As the suffixes grow in length, they entail more requirements, which may make them easier to reject. By parsimoniously expanding suffixes, the algorithm never needs to consider very many at a time, and most of the possible requirements may never need to be tested. We also consider forms of requirements that RAIRE uses but that were not used in the original implementation of AWAIRE. As a result, the new version of AWAIRE is computationally tractable for IRV elections with more than 50 candidates.

2   Background

We refer the reader to the original AWAIRE paper [6] for details of the notation and terminology, but we summarize the key objects and ideas here: *alt-orders*, *requirements*, *test supermartingales* (TSMs), *base TSMs*, and *intersection TSMs*.

Let $\mathcal{C}$ denote the set of candidates, $k = |\mathcal{C}|$ the number of candidates, and B the number of *ballot cards*[5] cast in the contest. We identify each ballot card b with an ordering of a subset of candidates, possibly the empty set.

An *alt-order* is a candidate elimination order in which someone other than the reported winner is last—i.e., the reported winner did not win. There are $(k-1)(k-1)! = k! - (k-1)!$ alt-orders: for each of the $k-1$ candidates who

---

[4] If the CVRs are linked to the corresponding ballot cards, RAIRE and AWAIRE can use *ballot-level comparison* auditing, increasing efficiency. See, e.g., Blom et al. [2]. ONEAudit [9] can also be used with RAIRE and AWAIRE to take advantage batch subtotals or linked CVRs.

[5] In some countries, a ballot may comprise more than one piece of paper (card).

were not reported to have won, there are $(k-1)!$ elimination orders for the the other $k-1$ candidates that would make that candidate the winner.

Example 1. Consider a four-candidate election, with candidates W, X, Y, Z, where W is the reported winner. The outcome is confirmed if we can rule out every elimination order in which any candidate other than W is last (every *alt-order*):

$$[W, X, Y, Z], [W, X, Z, Y], [W, Y, X, Z], [W, Y, Z, X], [W, Z, X, Y], [W, Z, Y, X],$$
$$[X, W, Y, Z], [X, W, Z, Y], [X, Y, W, Z], [X, Z, W, Y], [Y, W, X, Z], [Y, W, Z, X],$$
$$[Y, X, W, Z], [Y, Z, W, X], [Z, W, X, Y], [Z, W, Y, X], [Z, X, W, Y], [Z, Y, W, X].$$

The other 6 elimination orders lead to W winning: they are not alt-orders. □

Each alt-order is characterized by a set of *requirements*, all of which must be true for that alt-order to be the actual elimination order. If any requirement for an alt-order fails, that rules out the alt-order—and every other alt-order that shares that requirement. AWAIRE used a single form of requirement:

Directly Beats. $\mathbf{DB}(i, j, \mathcal{S})$ holds if candidate i has more votes than candidate j when the only candidates remaining are $\mathcal{S} \supseteq \{i, j\}$: i cannot be the next candidate eliminated when exactly the candidates $\mathcal{S}$ remain.

If $\mathbf{DB}(i, j, \mathcal{S})$ is false, j has more votes than i when only $\mathcal{S}$ remain standing. In that case, j cannot be the next eliminated: i would be eliminated before it.

Each requirement is associated with a *test supermartingale* (TSM) called a *base TSM*. (A TSM is a stochastic process starting at 1 that, if the requirement is true, is a nonnegative supermartingale. A nonnegative supermartingale is like the fortune of a bettor in a series of games that are fair or biased against the bettor, when the bettor is not allowed to go into debt. Ek et al. [6] explains how TSMs are used in AWAIRE.)

In turn, each alt-order is associated with a TSM called an *intersection TSM*, a weighted average of the base TSMs for the requirements that characterize that alt-order. If every requirement for that alt-order is true, the intersection TSM for the alt-order is a nonnegative supermartingale starting at 1. The weights in the average are chosen adaptively to try to minimize the sample size required to confirm the reported outcome (i.e., to reject every alt-order) when the reported outcome is indeed correct.

Constructing the statistical tests of alt-orders from TSMs provides *sequential validity*: the evidence that the outcome is correct can be evaluated after each sampled ballot card is examined, with no statistical penalty for looking at the data repeatedly. For any requirement that is true, the chance that its base TSM ever reaches or exceeds $1/\alpha$ is at most α, by Ville's inequality. If any alt-order is true, the chance that its intersection TSM ever reaches the value $1/\alpha$ is at most α. Thus, if the audit stops without a full hand count only if every intersection TSM hits or exceeds $1/\alpha$, the audit has risk limit α.

Requirements are expressed in terms of the means of lists of numbers, one number per ballot card (for each requirement). An *assorter* (see Stark [7]) assigns a number to each card, depending on the vote preferences on the card and on the requirement. The assorter assigns the numbers in such a way that if its requirement is true, the mean of the list of numbers is no larger than $1/2$.

Example 2. Consider the requirement $\mathbf{DB}(\mathtt{X}, \mathtt{Y}, \mathcal{C})$ that candidate $\mathtt{X}$ beats candidate $\mathtt{Y}$ on first preferences. The corresponding assorter assigns a card the value 1 if it shows a first preference for candidate $\mathtt{Y}$, the value 0 if it shows a first preference for $\mathtt{X}$, and the value $1/2$ otherwise. If the mean of the resulting list of all B numbers is less than $1/2$, then the requirement $\mathbf{DB}(\mathtt{X}, \mathtt{Y}, \mathcal{C})$ holds.   □

Each requirement can be tested by testing the statistical hypothesis that the mean of its assorter values is at most $1/2$ from a random sample of values of its assorter. That is done by drawing ballot cards at random and computing the value of the assorter corresponding to the requirement from the preferences on each sampled card. The same sample can be used to test all requirements by computing the value of every assorter for each sampled card.

As in the previous implementation of AWAIRE, we use the ALPHA TSM with the truncated shrinkage estimator to test requirements and intersections of requirements from the sample of assorter values. See Stark [8] for more about ALPHA and Ek et al. [6] for details on how ALPHA is used in AWAIRE. Given the cards sampled in draws $t = 1, \dots, \ell$, let $(X_t)_{t=1}^{\ell}$ denote the values assigned by the assorter of a particular requirement. Let M_ℓ be the TSM for the requirement, evaluated after the ℓth card is drawn. It can be written as a product: $M_\ell := \prod_{t=0}^{\ell} m_t$. Here, $m_0 = 1$ is the initial value of the TSM and m_t reflects the evidence X_t provides about the requirement: if $m_t > 1$, X_t is evidence against the requirement. The TSMs for individual requirements are called *base TSMs*.

To test an alt-order statistically, we could test each of its requirements separately and reject the alt-order if we reject at least one of its requirements. However, doing this naively would increase the risk limit; this is an instance of the well-known problem of *multiple testing* in statistics. AWAIRE addresses multiple testing by forming a weighted average of the base TSMs called an *intersection TSM*, which is a nonnegative supermartingale starting at 1 if every requirement for that alt-order is true.

The weights are chosen *predictably*: the weights at time t depend on the data collected up to time $t-1$, but not on anything that has not been observed before the tth card is drawn. The intersection TSM is a product of weighted means of the terms of the base TSMs. When all the requirements hold, the intersection TSM is a nonnegative supermartingale starting at 1.

Multiple weighting schemes were investigated in [5]. One of the best and the simplest for AWAIRE was 'Largest,' which puts all weight on the base TSM that is largest at time $t-1$ (in the case of ties, it gives equal weight to the largest). We use 'Largest' below because of its simplicity and good empirical performance.

If every intersection TSM hits or exceeds $1/\alpha$, we can reject every alt-order: the audit stops without a full hand count and the reported outcome is certified. Otherwise, AWAIRE continues until the sample contains every ballot card: a full hand count. The chance the audit stops without a full hand count if any alt-order is correct is at most α, the risk limit.

RAIRE avoids multiple testing by pre-commiting, before sampling commences, to a sufficient set of requirements[6] that covers all alt-orders. RAIRE uses the CVRs to select a set of requirements that minimizes the expected number of ballot cards required to be sampled to certify the contest, on the assumption that the CVRs are accurate.

3 Improving AWAIRE

The original implementation of AWAIRE tracked all $k! - (k - 1)!$ alt-orders separately. The requirements characterizing each alt-order were all **DB**. Because there are so many alt-orders, the implementation became computationally impractical for more than 6 candidates.

The present contribution makes AWAIRE tractable for contests with far more candidates, using three tools: *incremental expansion*, *use of new requirements*, and *requirement abandonment*. The first of these helps the most, but for clarity we begin by describing the second. The new implementation of AWAIRE and the code and output for the figures and tables in this paper are at https://github.com/aekh/awaire.

3.1 Another Type of Requirement

We introduce a new requirement to AWAIRE, related to a RAIRE assertion. Candidate i *dominates* candidate j if i has more first-preference votes than there are ballots that rank j ahead of i (including ballots that mention j but not i). In other words, i has more votes before any candidate is eliminated than j could ever possibly get, no matter who else is eliminated. The new type of requirement is the complement of this condition:[7]

Does Not Dominate. DND(i, j) holds if candidate i does not dominate candidate j: there might be an elimination sequence that results in j having more votes than i.

If the requirement is false, i dominates j: j cannot possibly have more votes than i. The original implementation of AWAIRE used only **DB** requirements. Including **DND** requirements can reduce sample sizes and runtimes because the requirement **DND**(i, j) is shared by all alt-orders in which candidate i is eliminated before candidate j. Although **DND** requirements may need larger samples to reject than **DB** requirements, they still reduce runtime and there are only $k(k - 1)$ of them.

Like **DB**, the assorter for the requirement **DND**$(\mathtt{X}, \mathtt{Y})$ assigns a ballot card the value 0 if it shows a first preference for candidate $\mathtt{X}$ (so that card will be

---

[6] RAIRE uses the terminology 'assertions' in place of 'requirements'.

[7] Blom et al. [3] originally defined 'WO' assertions, later renamed to 'NEB' [2]. **DND** is the negation of these.

counted for candidate X), the value 1 if it shows a preference for candidate Y before candidate X or shows a preference for candidate Y and does not mention candidate X (so the card may eventually contribute a vote to in Y before X is eliminated), and the value 1/2 otherwise.

3.2   Suffix Representation and Incremental Expansion

Instead of tracking all alt-orders, we track *suffixes* of alt-orders. Each suffix of a set of alt-orders can be represented by a set of requirements that are shared by all alt-orders with that suffix. As the audit progresses, either it finds enough

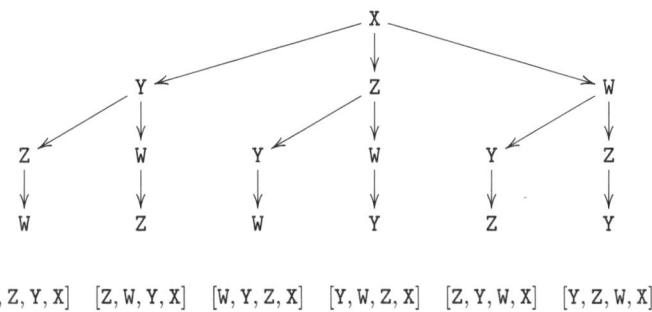

$$[W, Z, Y, X] \quad [Z, W, Y, X] \quad [W, Y, Z, X] \quad [Y, W, Z, X] \quad [Z, Y, W, X] \quad [Y, Z, W, X]$$

Fig. 1. The suffix tree for alt-orders with alternate winner X

evidence to reject a suffix (along with all alt-orders that include it), or it extends that suffix by one in all possible ways and tests those extended suffixes.

Example 3. Consider the alt-orders in Example 1 where X wins. Figure 1 illustrates how these alt-orders can be represented by a suffix tree. On the first level of the tree, the suffix $[\ldots, X]$ encompasses all alt-orders where X wins (listed at the bottom of the tree). One step below are three suffixes, $[\ldots, Y, X]$, $[\ldots, Z, X]$, $[\ldots, W, X]$, denoting the winner X but also the possible runner-ups (Y, Z, and W, respectively). The first of these represents the two complete alt-orders $[W, Z, Y, X]$ and $[Z, W, Y, X]$. □

Each suffix has an associated intersection TSM, a weighted combination of the base TSMs for requirements shared by all alt-orders with that suffix. If that intersection TSM hits or exceeds $1/\alpha$, we reject every alt-order with that suffix.

The base TSM for each active requirement is only computed once and stored in a dictionary (i.e., hash table). The test for each suffix can access a set of base TSM values and can determine weights to combine them into an intersection TSM for that suffix. The code can also remove from the database every requirement that is no longer useful, further reducing memory and CPU usage. Figure 2 shows the structure of the algorithm. The figure caption summarizes the steps, many of which are described below in more detail.

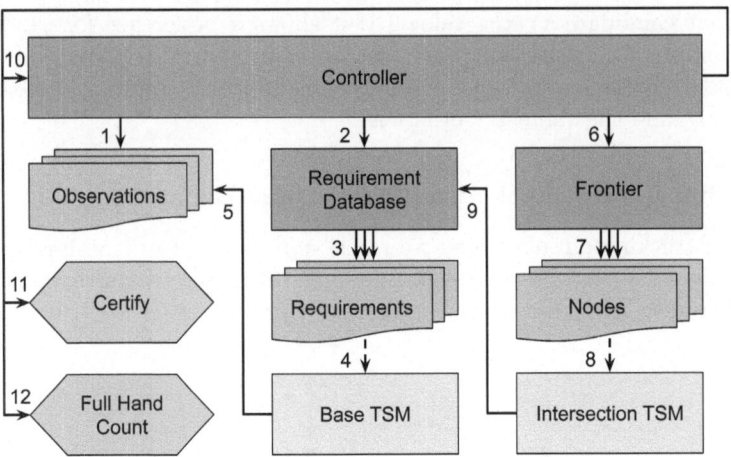

Fig. 2. An overview of the new implementation of AWAIRE. The process begins by (1) sampling some ballots at random. Then, the controller (2) prompts the requirement database, which (3) processes each requirement in the database. Each requirement has (4) a base TSM, the value of which is (5) calculated from the ballots seen so far. Once all requirements have been processed, the controller (6) prompts the frontier, which (7) processes and keeps track of all the nodes. Each node represents a suffix and has (8) an intersection TSM associated with it. To calculate the current value of the intersection TSM, it (9) requests the previous values of the node's associated base TSMs (used as weights) and how their values changed to reach the current values (used as returns). If a node's intersection TSM is above the risk threshold, we remove it; further, if a node's intersection TSM and/or base TSM(s) are not increasing enough or at all, the frontier may expand this node, introducing several children of longer suffixes. Once all nodes have been processed, AWAIRE either (10) continues sampling if nodes and unseen ballots remain, (11) certifies the election if no nodes remain, or (12) terminates as a full hand count if no unseen ballots remain but nodes remain. At any point in this process, auditors may decide to perform a full hand count instead of continuing to sample ballots at random; this cannot increase the risk

Suffix Trees. The alt-orders of a given k-candidate election can be represented by a forest of $k-1$ suffix trees, each rooted at the supposed winning candidate according to that alt-order. Each alt-order corresponds to the unique path from a leaf node to a root node. Recall the alt-orders defined in Example 1. The forest consists of 3 suffix trees rooted by the candidates other than the reported winner: X, Y and Z. The one for X is shown in Fig. 1; the other two are analogous. Each node in the forest corresponds to a suffix of alt-orders. For example, the node pictured under the root corresponds to suffix $[\ldots, Z, X]$ and subsumes (is the suffix of) the two alt-orders $[W, Y, Z, X]$ and $[Y, W, Z, X]$.

Node Frontier. We keep track of a dynamic *frontier* of nodes in this forest of suffixes, the nodes for which we calculate intersection TSMs to test alt-orders.

Every alt-order has a suffix in the frontier. If we can rule out each node in a frontier, we have ruled out every alternative winner of the election.[8]

Before sampling commences, the frontier is initialized with $|\mathcal{C}| - 1$ suffixes of the form $[\ldots, c]$, for each candidate c other than the reported winner, i.e., the roots of the forest of alt-orders. The requirements for the root node labelled c are $\{\mathbf{DND}(c', c) : c' \in \mathcal{C} - \{c\}\}$, since, for c to have won, no other candidate could have dominated c.

Example 4. Continuing with Example 1, the requirements for the suffix $[\ldots, \mathtt{X}]$ are $\{\mathbf{DND}(\mathtt{Y}, \mathtt{X}), \mathbf{DND}(\mathtt{Z}, \mathtt{X}), \mathbf{DND}(\mathtt{W}, \mathtt{X})\}$. The requirements for the other suffixes $[\ldots, \mathtt{Y}]$ and $[\ldots, \mathtt{Z}]$ are similar. □

Each node m has a watchlist of requirements that are necessarily true if its suffix is true. These are the requirements that are shared among the alt-orders represented by m. The weighting scheme for m is in essence no different than for the original implementation of AWAIRE except it uses only the base TSMs from the watchlist of requirements. Thus, some requirements and their base TSM values are ignored. If the intersection TSM for node m ever reaches $1/\alpha$, we can reject all elimination orders with that suffix. We remove node m from the frontier, its subtree is *pruned*.

Expanding Nodes. If none of a node's requirements appears to be false (e.g., all the base TSMs have decreased for a long time or are less than 1), we split that node. Given a node representing suffix $[\ldots, S]$ we split it to create the child nodes $\{[\ldots, c] \oplus S : c \in \mathcal{C} \setminus S\}$, where $\oplus$ represents sequence concatenation. Thus, we create a child node for each candidate not appearing in the suffix S of the expanded parent node.

Consider a suffix $[\ldots, c_\ell, c_{\ell-1}, \ldots, c_1]$ with the unmentioned candidates, implicitly eliminated before this suffix, represented by the set $\mathcal{U}$. The requirements of this suffix are given by: $\{\mathbf{DND}(c_j, c_i) : \ell \geqslant j > i \geqslant 1\}$, i.e., each candidate c_j eliminated before c_i *does not dominate* c_i; together with $\{\mathbf{DND}(c, c_i) : \ell \geqslant i \geqslant 1,\ c \in \mathcal{U}\}$, i.e., every unmentioned candidate c *does not dominate* any candidate c_i in the suffix; and $\{\mathbf{DB}(c_i, c_j, \{c_\ell, \ldots, c_1\}) : \ell \geqslant j > i \geqslant 1\}$, i.e., just before c_j is eliminated, every other remaining candidate c_i *directly beats* c_j.

Each node inherits all the requirements of its parent node, and adds more specific requirements relating to the newly added candidate $c_{\ell+1}$. We only need to add the requirements $\{\mathbf{DND}(c, c_{\ell+1}) : c \in \mathcal{U} \setminus \{c_{\ell+1}\}\}$ and $\{\mathbf{DB}(c_i, c_{\ell+1}, \{c_{\ell+1}, \ldots, c_1\}) : \ell \geqslant i \geqslant 1\}$ to the parent nodes requirements.

Example 5. Continuing our running example of Example 1, assume we decide to expand the node $[\ldots, \mathtt{X}]$. We add three child nodes: $[\ldots, \mathtt{Y}, \mathtt{X}], [\ldots, \mathtt{Z}, \mathtt{X}], [\ldots, \mathtt{W}, \mathtt{X}]$. The requirements for $[\ldots, \mathtt{Y}, \mathtt{X}]$ adds $\{\mathbf{DND}(\mathtt{Z}, \mathtt{Y}), \mathbf{DND}(\mathtt{W}, \mathtt{Y}), \mathbf{DB}(\mathtt{X}, \mathtt{Y}, \{\mathtt{X}, \mathtt{Y}\})\}$ to those inherited from its parent $[\ldots, \mathtt{X}]$. □

---

[8] RAIRE also uses suffix trees, but it computes a *static* frontier of the alt-order forest using the CVRs (before observing any sampled ballot cards).

When a node is expanded, its intersection TSM (up to the latest sample) is copied to all its children. This step ensures that its continued use will remain risk-limiting.

A critical ingredient for the improved AWAIRE is when and which nodes to expand. To decide *which node* to expand we score nodes by the value of its best performing base TSM. The higher the score the more likely we will be able to reject this suffix. So when we choose to expand a node we always choose one with the lowest score.

To decide *when* to expand a node we consider a few policies:

Every(i). We expand a node after every non-zero multiple of i ballots sampled.

Below(x). After every ballot, we expand every node that has a score below x.

These policies are quite myopic, only looking at the current node's score. We can also impose a look-ahead rule to avoid unnecessary expansions. If we choose a node m for potential expansion, we examine the child suffixes of node m and determine what their scores would be (by computing the base TSM for any newly introduced requirements). We only allow the expansion if:

Loose. Some child node has a better score than m.

Tight(y). Some child has a better score than m, and is also higher than y.

3.3   Requirement Database and Requirement Abandonment

The requirement database is a critical data structure of the algorithm as the number of requirements is $k(k-1)2^{k-2}$.[9] Thus, we have to aggressively restrict the number of requirements we track.

The requirement database is initially empty but nodes can *request* requirements needed for their intersection TSM, adding them to their watch-list and the database (if not already added). This happens when the frontier is created or a node is expanded. Adding a requirement to the database involves calculating its base TSM from ballot card 1 to the latest observed.

We can leverage some logical implications between requirements to decrease computation time, by deciding to *abandon* (i.e., set weight to 0 for the remaining samples) particular requirements when there is sufficiently strong evidence that they are true. Note that this will not compromise the risk limit, but it may increase the sample size required to terminate the audit (if a requirement that is actually false is erroneously abandoned). The two relationships we use are:

$$\neg \mathbf{DB}(i,j,S) \longleftrightarrow \mathbf{DB}(j,i,S) \qquad \text{and} \qquad \neg \mathbf{DB}(i,j,S) \longrightarrow \mathbf{DND}(i,j).$$

---

[9] This is fewer than the number of alt-orders due to the *order* of elimination being irrelevant for requirements; only the *set* of eliminations is relevant.

Considering the requirement on the left-hand side of these rules, if its base TSM exceeds $1/\alpha$ (our threshold of 'enough evidence' that the requirement is false[10]), we abandon the requirements on the right-hand side, since the evidence now suggests that they ought to be true.

Another way a requirement can be abandoned is when it has been mathematically proven to be true (i.e., we can show that the requirement must be true given the number of remaining samples).

Finally, if, due to node pruning, a requirement is no longer part of any node's watch-list, we need not process its base TSM. In that case we *park* the requirement to save computation time. If at another point this parked requirement is requested, we simply *unpark* it and calculate its base TSM values from the time it was parked to the latest observed ballot.

Table 1. Size of the final frontier for AWAIRE v2, showing the mean and 99th percentile frontier size across all experiments on contests with a given number of candidates. The second column shows the number of contests summarized in each row, and the third column shows the total number of alt-orders (max. possible frontier size). The three subcolumns refer to different ways to specify η_0 in ALPHA: either to 0.51, to the last-round margin (LRM), or to the reported assorter margins (AM)

Candidates	Contests	Alt-orders	Mean			99th percentile		
			0.51	LRM	AM	0.51	LRM	AM
4	5	18	5	7	7	11	11	11
5	50	96	7	9	10	36	37	40
6	25	600	10	15	16	34	60	55
7	17	4,320	31	38	44	379	372	455
8	7	35,280	13	35	35	57	218	259
11	2	4×10^7	5,005	5,471	6,194	21,171	24,190	25,762
18	1	6×10^{15}	17	937	81	17	22,711	694
19	2	1×10^{17}	794	6,879	1,299	3,068	82,947	10,889
36	1	4×10^{41}	170	3,463	740	1,318	51,669	5,075

4   Analyses and Results

We used the data from the 93 New South Wales Legislative Assembly Contests and 14 contests in the USA used by [3].[11] We also used datasets for three contests for Minneapolis Mayor (in 2013, 2017, and 2021),[12] for a total of 110 contests.

---

[10] Due to multiple testing, this does not necessarily allow us to reject the alt-orders it is part of. To do that we need to use intersection TSMs.

[11] https://github.com/michelleblom/margin-irv/ (visited 16 May 2024).

[12] https://vote.minneapolismn.gov/results-data/election-results/ (16 May 2024).

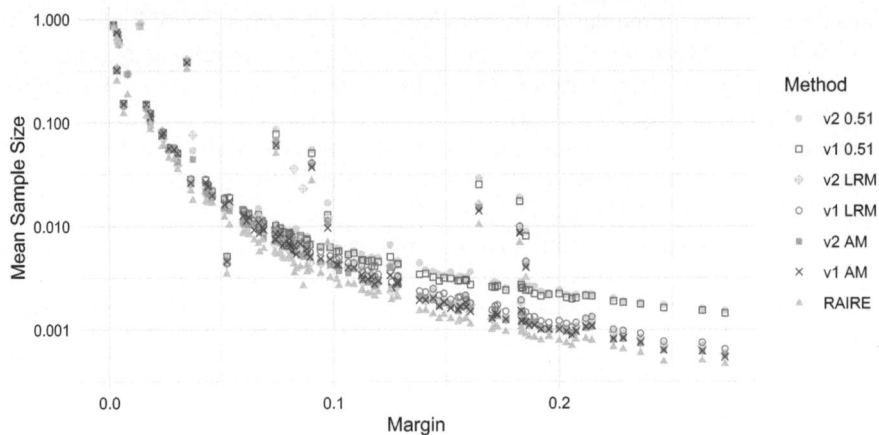

Fig. 3. Mean sample size (as a fraction of the total number of ballots) comparing AWAIRE v2, AWAIRE v1, and RAIRE at risk limit 0.05. All used the ALPHA test supermartingale with $d = 200$ in the truncated shrinkage estimator and $\eta_0 = 0.51$, the last-round margin (LRM), or the reported assorter margins (AM). We omitted the San Francisco Mayor 2007 contest (the margin was much larger than for the other contests), but see Table 2

The *reported margin* (in cards) of an election is the minimum number of cards that must have been mistabulated if the reported winner really lost. We use *margin* to mean *reported diluted margin*, the reported margin in cards divided by the number of cards from which the sample is drawn. We used `margin-irv` [4] to find margins for 109 of the contests; it did not find the margin for 2021 Minneapolis Mayor (19 candidates) in a week.

When the reported outcome is correct, audit sample sizes can generally be reduced by exploiting information about the tabulation available before auditing, for instance, the *reported last-round margin*. Often, the reported last-round margin is close to or equal to the actual reported margin in cards.[13]

We simulated 500 ballot-polling audits for every contest, with each audit corresponding to a randomly sampled (without replacement) order of the ballots. The same 500 sampled orders for each contest were used across all methods. The ballots were selected one at a time. After each ballot, the method under experiment was used to determine whether to terminate and certify the contest (with risk limit $\alpha = 0.05$), or continue sampling.

We compared the old and new implementations of AWAIRE (v1 and v2, respectively) and RAIRE. Each simulation had access to 32GB of RAM. For the

---

[13] Of the 109 contests for which we calculated the margin, 8 had last-round margins greater than their actual margin. The difference ranged from 11 to 2,539 ballots, equating up to a few percentage points in margin relative to the total number of ballots.

tuning parameters in the truncated shrinkage estimator for ALPHA, we used $d = 200$ and three choices of η_0:

- *0.51*: setting $\eta_0 = 0.51$, as recommended by [5]
- *LRM*: setting η_0 for all requirements using the last-round margin
- *AM*: setting η_0 to the reported assorter margin (for each requirement separately), which requires CVRs.

All experiments with RAIRE used AM.

In earlier extensive comparisons of expansion schemes in AWAIRE v2, **Below**(1)–**Tight**($e^{0.5}$) consistently performed the best. We used this scheme for all AWAIRE v2 experiments reported here. Additional experiments with and without requirement abandonment and **DND**s showed some performance improvements (without affecting sample sizes) when using the above expansion scheme. We have omitted the details due to space constraints.

4.1   Computational Performance

Incremental expansion lets the audit 'group reject' many alt-orders by rejecting nodes they share, rather than having to reject all $k! - (k-1)!$ alt-orders separately. One measure of the computation saved is the final frontier size (the number of nodes that were not expanded but instead pruned) compared to $k! - (k-1)!$, the total number of alt-orders and thus the maximum possible frontier size; see Table 1. Incremental expansion saves an exponential amount of memory.[14]

AWAIRE v2 was substantially faster, scaling exponentially better in k. For elections with 4–8 candidates it saved seconds for the smaller elections and up to 20 min on the larger elections. AWAIRE v1 could not complete the audit of any contest with more than 8 candidates (6 of the contests) regardless of the margin of victory, for lack of memory. AWAIRE v2 could complete all but 36 simulated audits (two using $\eta = 0.51$, 33 using LRM, and one using AM; all for the Minneapolis contests) out of 165,000, for lack of memory or time (48 h). This could be resolved by further experimentation with expansion schemes. We treated those 36 audits as full hand counts.

To stress-test the implementation, we added 'fake' candidates to a handful of contests. These candidates never get any votes, but the audit cannot foresee that, so it must include them in the search tree. The new implementation could easily handle 55 candidates in those simulations, and possibly more. The runtime was always within a minute *per ballot* on average, and only reached an hour *per audit* on average in the toughest cases. The largest real IRV election to the authors' knowledge had 36 candidates (Minneapolis Mayor 2013). CPU time per audit for RAIRE and our implementation of AWAIRE v2 were similar.

---

[14] The result for 18 candidates represents a single contest (San Francisco Mayor 2007) that was inexpensive to audit. There is little expansion with 0.51 and AM but quite a bit with LRM. Nonetheless, with LRM, the audit terminated after 24 ballots on average, compared to 60 for 0.51, since LRM expanded to nodes that were easy to reject. Using AM expanded to fewer nodes but on average terminated after 20 ballots.

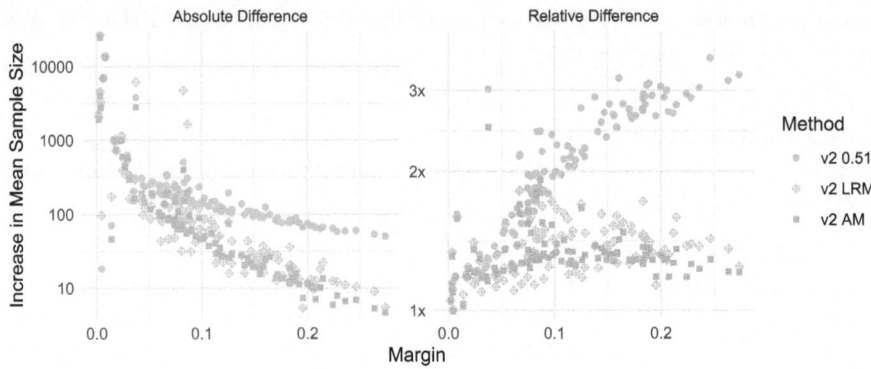

Fig. 4. Average number of cards sampled by AWAIRE v2 minus average number sampled by RAIRE, as a function of contest margin, to audit 109 contests at risk limit 0.05. Omitted: Lismore (left pane, AWAIRE v2 AM samples 91 fewer cards than RAIRE on average), Minneapolis Mayor 2013 using LRM (right pane, relative differences are beyond 4×), and San Francisco Mayor 2007 (both panes, margin too large)

Table 2. Contest sizes, no. candidates, margins, and audit sample sizes for 8 contests. Rows 5–11: mean sample size for AWAIRE with various settings and RAIRE. Bottom row: largest standard error of the mean sample sizes in each column

Contest:		Lismore	Aspen City Council	Monaro	Auburn	Macquarie Fields	Maroubra	Cessnock	San Francisco Mayor
Candidates:		6	11	5	6	7	5	5	18
Margin:		0.44%	1.38%	2.43%	5.15%	7.43%	10.1%	20.0%	34.0%
Ballots:		47,208	2,544	46,236	44,011	47,381	46,533	45,942	149,465
AWAIRE	v1 0.51	28,088	—	3,642	803	438	264	102	—
	v1 LRM	28,596	—	3,758	826	420	222	56	—
	v1 AM	27,851	—	3,660	709	357	196	46	—
	v2 0.51	27,204	2,200	3,446	794	440	286	110	60
	v2 LRM	27,282	2,303	3,245	626	317	191	47	24
	v2 AM	27,095	2,175	3,453	656	342	191	48	20
RAIRE		27,186	2,129	2,850	539	269	143	36	16
Std. err. (max.)		410.0	8.5	112.9	27.5	13.4	7.9	1.8	0.7

4.2 Statistical Performance

To quantify the statistical efficiency we used the sample size required to certify each contest, averaged across simulated audits.

The mean sample size as a proportion of the total number of ballots is shown in Fig. 3. Unsurprisingly, RAIRE is typically the most efficient since it uses CVRs, but AWAIRE v2 is close or on par (for Lismore). Having more information (LRM) is better than default (0.51) for both AWAIRE v1 and v2; v2 was slightly better than v1. The mean sample size for AWAIRE v2 was never more than v1 by more than 1.8% of the total number ballots or 55 ballots (despite having less information at the start), and was often slightly more efficient (likely due to the difference in initial bets).

For larger elections we can only compare RAIRE to AWAIRE v2. Figure 4 shows the absolute and relative increase in mean sample sizes for RAIRE (using error-free CVRs) and the new implementation. While the difference in the number of cards can be large for large elections with tiny margins, the relative difference is small; and while the relative difference is large for small elections, the difference in cards is small.

Table 2 shows detailed results for a few elections with various margins. The narrower the margin, the better RAIRE typically does (since it takes advantage of the accurate CVRs), but the relative difference is small. For the new implementation, using the LRM usually helps, but using individual assorter margins did not help more.

4.3   Robustness to CVR Errors

Ek et al. [6] illustrated the robustness of AWAIRE v1 compared to RAIRE when the CVRs have errors. We repeated that experiment using AWAIRE v2 for the Strathfield and Ballina contests; see Table 3. For each contest we re-labelled the candidates on the ballots and ran 200 simulated audits for each re-labeling and

Table 3. Average number of ballots required to certify the winner in the Strathfield (top, 46,644 cards cast) and Ballina (bottom, 47,865 cards cast) contests at risk limit 0.05 when the candidates are re-labeled, for RAIRE and the new implementation of AWAIRE (v2) with different ways of choosing η_0. 'F' means the audit led to a full hand count in every run. Notation for reported elimination orders: an integer means the candidate with that number is in that place in the order; a crossed-out integer means the given candidate is not in that place; and a dot ($\cdot$) means any unmentioned candidate can be in that place. The final row is the only order with a different winner. Ranges span the lowest and highest mean sample size of all permutations of a row

	Method:		AWAIRE v2		RAIRE
	Reported	0.51	LRM	AM	
Strathfield	12345	6,491	6,495	6,553	5,626
	$\cdot\cdot\cancel{3}45$	6,491	6,495	6,553	5,626
	$\cdot\cdot 4\cdot 5$	6,491	6,495	17,125–17,183	45,945
	$\cdot 4\cdot\cdot 5$	6,491	6,495	20,642–20,681	45,014
	$4\cdot\cdot\cdot 5$	6,491	6,495	20,848–20,879	45,014
	12354	F	F	F	F
Ballina	1234567	3,777	3,836	3,707	2,737
	$\cdot\cdot\cdot\cancel{4}567$	3,777	3,836	3,682–3,730	2,737
	$\cdot\cdot\cdot\cdot 6\cdot 7$	3,777	3,836	3,802–4,598	47,422–F
	$\cdot\cdot\cdot\cdot\cancel{5}67$	3,777	3,836	4,409–5,556	47,422–F
	$\cdot\cdot\cdot 6\cdot\cdot 7$	3,777	3,836	5,323–6,320	F
	$\cdot\cdot 6\cdot\cdot\cdot 7$	3,777	3,836	6,478–7,203	F
	$\cdot 6\cdot\cdot\cdot\cdot 7$	3,777	3,836	8,019–8,439	F
	$6\cdot\cdot\cdot\cdot\cdot 7$	3,777	3,836	7,876–8,307	F
	1234576	F	F	F	F

method. In all renumberings but the last, the winner is unchanged. The workload for approaches that do not use (erroneous) information to set assorter margins was unchanged by renumberings that do not change the winner. RAIRE become much worse as the CVRs increasingly became less accurate; AWAIRE v2 using AM was affected less. For Ballina, RAIRE often led to an unnecessary full hand count.

5   Discussion

The new implementation of AWAIRE (v2) has comparable statistical efficiency to the original (v1) but requires substantially lower computational resources, allowing audits of IRV elections with up to 55 candidates. Using an incremental expansion strategy for AWAIRE does not undermine its risk-limiting properties. It amounts to giving zero weight to the base TSMs for a subset of requirements for a group of alt-orders. Expanding the frontier is equivalent to changing the weights from zero to something positive, using past samples to inform the choice of weights. Because only past samples are used to select the weights, the stochastic process is still a TSM.

Future work includes understanding how to better leverage CVRs in AWAIRE when using incremental expansion, e.g., how to 'pre-expand' the frontier, perhaps guided by RAIRE-produced assertions; using AWAIRE for comparison audits including those based on assorter means for groups of CVRs [9]; experimenting with expansion strategies and other weighting schemes and ALPHA tuning parameters; and experimenting with more varieties of CVR errors.

References

1. Appel, A., Stark, P.: Evidence-based elections: create a meaningful paper trail, then audit. Georgetown Law Technology Review (2020). https://georgetownlawtechreview.org/wp-content/uploads/2020/07/4.2-p523-541-Appel-Stark.pdf
2. Blom, M., et al.: You can do RLAs for IRV: the process pilot of risk-limiting audits for the San Francisco District Attorney 2019 instant runoff vote. In: Proceedings of E-Vote-ID 2020, pp. 296–310 (2020)
3. Blom, M., Stuckey, P.J., Teague, V.J.: Ballot-polling risk limiting audits for IRV elections. In: Krimmer, R., Krimmer, R., et al. (eds.) E-Vote-ID 2018. LNCS, vol. 11143, pp. 17–34. Springer, Cham (2018). https://doi.org/10.1007/978-3-030-00419-4_2
4. Blom, M., Stuckey, P.J., Teague, V.J.: Computing the margin of victory in preferential parliamentary elections. In: Krimmer, R., et al. (eds.) E-Vote-ID 2018. LNCS, vol. 11143, pp. 1–16. Springer, Cham (2018). https://doi.org/10.1007/978-3-030-00419-4_1
5. Ek, A., Stark, P., Stuckey, P.J., Vukcevic, D.: Efficient weighting schemes for auditing instant-runoff voting elections. In: Proceedings of the 9th Workshop on Advances in Secure Electronic Voting (2024)

6. Ek, A., Stark, P.B., Stuckey, P.J., Vukcevic, D.: Adaptively weighted audits of instant-runoff voting elections: AWAIRE. In: Volkamer, M., et al. (eds.) Electronic Voting, pp. 35–51. Springer, Cham (2023). https://doi.org/10.1007/978-3-031-43756-4_3

7. Stark, P.B.: Sets of half-average nulls generate risk-limiting audits: SHANGRLA. In: Bernhard, M., et al. (eds.) FC 2020. LNCS, vol. 12063, pp. 319–336. Springer, Cham (2020). https://doi.org/10.1007/978-3-030-54455-3_23

8. Stark, P.B.: ALPHA: audit that learns from previously hand-audited ballots. Ann. Appl. Stat. **17**(1), 641–679 (2023). https://doi.org/10.1214/22-AOAS1646

9. Stark, P.B.: Overstatement-net-equivalent risk-limiting audit: ONEAudit. In: Essex, A., et al. (eds.) Financial Cryptography and Data Security, pp. 63–78. Springer, Cham (2024). https://doi.org/10.1007/978-3-031-48806-1_5

A Framework for Voters' Trust Repair in Internet Voting

Leo Fel[✉] [ⓘ]

University of Luxembourg, Esch-Sur-Alzette, Luxembourg
leo.fel@uni.lu

Abstract. Research on voters' trust in i-voting has been exclusively related to building trust in the process of i-voting adoption, with no work addressing the question of trust repair. This article introduces a framework for trust repair in i-voting by integrating insights from trust repair in other research areas, as well as concepts developed for and used in the e-voting literature. The article traces the process of trust repair from the different beliefs influencing voters' trust in both the human and technological dimensions of an i-voting system, through the influence of the internal and external stakeholders, to trust violations and the i-voting organisers' strategies for trust repair and the 'arsenal' of measures at their disposal. The article highlights the importance of detecting the emergence of events that may violate trust among voters, understanding the severity and dimensions of trust violation, and strategically navigating trust repair. It also outlines open questions and identifies avenues for future research.

Keywords: i-voting · voters · trust · trust repair · framework

1 Introduction

Trust goes hand in hand with the introduction of novel voting methods. This is particularly true when these new technologies involve the extensive use of information and communications technology (ICT), as is the case with internet voting (i-voting). Creating, building, and establishing trust is an important and challenging task, which should be undertaken before i-voting is even offered to voters, as it is commonly seen as a conditio sine qua non for its adoption. Such a view is unsurprising as elections lie at the heart of democracy and are a joint exercise of a mutually unknown multitude of voters, aimed at transferring power to elected representatives, which presents a basis for building trust in society in all other matters. Elections and voting are, therefore, trust exercises in themselves, and trust in the used voting method is imperative to fulfil its societal purpose.

In recent years, interest in studying trust in internet voting (i-voting) and the closely related, but distinct, electronic voting (e-voting) has increased, although the main body of research has been conducted from a technical perspective [15]. Surprisingly, research on trust repair and its related aspects in the context of i-voting (e.g., areas of potential trust violation, and trust repair strategies and mechanisms, and preventive tactics) has

D. Duenas-Cid et al. (Eds.): E-Vote-ID 2024, LNCS 15014, pp. 54–71, 2025.
https://doi.org/10.1007/978-3-031-72244-8_4

not garnered much interest in the literature. This has been the case not for the lack of i-voting situations that might be perceived as damaging to voters' trust and necessitating consequent action for trust repair, but those events and responses have not yet been studied through the lens of trust repair.

This article seeks to address that research gap and to open a new direction in the research on trust in i-voting. First, it provides definitions of terms relevant to trust in i-voting and presents a review of existing research on trust repair in areas such as marketing, management, organisation, and civil society research. Second, the article incorporates these insights into existing concepts used for i-voting research. This results in a conceptual framework for voters' trust repair, with each element explained in turn. Third, the article presents findings relevant to trust repair in i-voting and provides few notable real-world examples from cases of trust violation and trust repair in i-voting. Practical implications and applicability for i-voting practitioners and researchers are discussed, highlighting the importance of timely detection and addressing of trust violations, and offering suggestions on how strategies for trust repair can be crafted. Finally, the article provides avenues for future research on trust repair in i-voting, with open questions to be answered.

2   Theoretical Background and Literature Review

2.1   Trust in I-voting

Since i-voting became an object of scientific interest, trust has been one of the most used and mentioned terms, although definitions and understandings vary among scientific fields. Moreover, trust has not usually been addressed as a principal element but instead as an ancillary component in research. The lead in i-voting research has been taken by computer science, which shaped the approach to and definition of trust. Computer scientists and social scientists, at first glance, appear to have had opposite objectives when it comes to trust – while computer scientists have viewed the need for trust as something 'bad' and have focused on minimising parts of voting technologies which one had to trust, social scientists (or more precisely psychologists) have tended to focus on maximising trust, viewing it as a desirable 'good' in and of itself [32]. This has resulted in two differing views on trust: bad trust, i.e., "something that people establish because they have to, not because the system is inherently trustworthy", and good trust, i.e., "something that people establish because they want to, owing to the system's trustworthiness" [32]. Without delving into this differentiation any further, which may not even be fruitful, our understanding of trust in this article is in line with the social science understanding of trust as a desirable characteristic, "a mechanism that helps us to reduce social complexity" [32], thus serving as "the bond of society or a lubricant for social relations" [34].

Although trust might be characterised as "an immaterial bond, including subjective evaluations and social projections" [13], which is somewhat vague and amenable to an emotivist or sentimental reading, its deliverables are "hard and measurable results" [2]. The desirability of trust and subsequent palpable effects of trust initiate a debate about what constitutes trust in i-voting and how the trustor and trustee should be defined. Trust in i-voting research is relied on and borrows from adjacent scientific fields, particularly trust in technology research in which two sets of beliefs are inconsistently utilised in trust constructs, with a tension between the human-like and system-like attributes of technology [25]. Lankton, McKnight, and Trip demonstrate that the two sets of trusting beliefs are compatible by pairing human-like beliefs (integrity, ability/competence, benevolence) with corresponding system-like trusting beliefs (reliability, functionality, and helpfulness) [25]. In the first pairing, "integrity", the belief that a trustee adheres to principles acceptable to the trustor, corresponds to "reliability", the belief in the consistent proper operation of the technology. The second pairing involves two human-like beliefs on one part, which are "ability", i.e., the trustee's skills, competencies, and characteristics that influence a specific domain, and "competence", i.e., the belief that the trustee has the ability to do what the trustor needs done, which corresponds with "functionality", the technology's capability, functions, or features to meet the trustor's needs, on the other part. The third and final pairing is between "benevolence", the belief that the trustee will act in the trustor's interest beyond selfish motives, and "helpfulness", the belief that the technology provides adequate and responsive support to users. It is argued that the distinctive feature in choosing trusting belief constructs to apply to a specific technology is the level of humanness, i.e., "aspects of technologies and users' interactions with technologies that can make them seem more or less human-like and, thereby, exhibit different levels of 'humanness'" [25]. The authors conclude that the technology's humanness has to be addressed when considering technology trust constructs and that the type of trusting beliefs has an influence on outcomes – human-like trust beliefs have stronger influence when technology is perceived as high in humanness by users, and vice versa, that system-like trust beliefs have stronger influence if technology is perceived as low in humanness. In the context of i-voting, Erb, Duenas-Cid, and Volkamer argue that "the trustee is no longer a moral agent but a technological artifact created by humans that has limited capabilities" while also noting that "the role played by those stakeholders having the capacity to provide trust or distrust of the system even if not directly related to its functioning" should be acknowledged [15]. The authors choose to mainly focus on system-like trusting beliefs when assessing trust in i-voting, simultaneously asserting that the nature of trust in this context is considerably more complex and intertwined and cannot be simply reduced to trust in the technological dimension of i-voting.

I-voting is commonly introduced as supplementary to traditional voting methods, primarily paper voting. As such, it is subject to high expectations and even more rigorous evaluations, backmarked against the standards of these traditional methods. Its distinct characteristics, such as its technological basis and remoteness, create and pose unique complexities and challenges not present in traditional settings. Trust in i-voting is substantially conditioned by its underlying mechanics or operations, which are not as intuitive to a lay voter as traditional paper voting.[1] Due to its technological complexity and sophistication, voters' beliefs are, to a certain extent, shaped by external stakeholders' views on a specific i-voting ecosystem, which is combined with its human and technological dimensions. In the literature, this notion is recognised by Pieters [32], who borrows Luhmann's argument that one has to reduce complexity to "properly function in a complex social environment", and Ehin and Solvak [14] who utilise 'the cue-taking

---

[1] Pieters [32] argues that comprehending all aspects of paper voting is also beyond the capacity of a lay voter - it appears superficially more evident and understandable, but the possible challenges are merely „black-boxed" in our experience of democracy.

approach' grounded in theories of bounded rationality, explaining how people are more prone to rely on cues from other trusted social actors under conditions of information scarcity, complexity, high uncertainty, limited time, and low information processing ability. Similarly, Crane [9] uses 'trustworthiness cues', while Ferin, Dirks, and Shah introduce the concept of 'trust transferability', according to which a third party contributes to providing trust-related information [17]. For the reasons mentioned, trust in i-voting can certainly be considered, at least in part, as intermediated trust.

2.2 Trust Repair

Research on trust can be grouped into six areas: 1) antecedents/preconditions for trust, 2) the process of trust-building, 3) contextual determinants of trust-building, 4) decision-making processes in trust, 5) implications and uses of trust, and 6) lack of trust, distrust, mistrust, and trust repair [28]. This last category is actually an 'all-other-kinds' category where different aspects of trust and trust repair, even those that are not closely related, are included. In i-voting research, trust repair has been out of researchers' sight, which might be explained by the fact that i-voting has not been broadly adopted, and, therefore, the dominant body of research focuses on trust building as a prerequisite for the adoption of i-voting. Although initial trust-building is more prevalent in real-world practice than trust repair, it does not imply trust repair does not occur where i-voting is introduced or experimented with. It is already intuitively understood that establishing trust in i-voting is just the first step and that voters' perceptions should be governed after the initial rollout of an i-voting system as part of "continuous supervision of actors' perceptions regarding the Internet voting system" [36]. As trust repair has not been extensively studied in the i-voting domain, we are directed to look at 'usual suspects' from relatable research areas, primarily marketing, management, organisation, and civil society research. In those areas, various topics related to trust repair have captured scholarly attention, from the causes and consequences of trust violations and their multilevel character to the severity, intentionality, and timing of trust violations and the affected trustworthiness dimensions, to strategies and mechanisms for trust repair, as well as comparisons of the pre- and post-repair levels of trust [26]. Two approaches are used to study trust repair: the variance approach (the "what") and the process approach (the "how"), with time as central to explaining how trust repair happens [3].

Trust repair "entails improvement in a trustor's trust after it was damaged by a trust violation" [3]. More elaborately, it is a process directed at restoring cooperation between the trustor and trustee and making the trustor willing to be vulnerable again by re-establishing their positive expectations [21]. Trust repair is a response to reductions in the perception of one or more dimensions of trustworthiness (cognition, affect, behaviour, and intended behaviour) [2], which decrease the existing level of trust. Since there is no unifying or umbrella term, different terms are used to describe a decrease in the existing level of trust, such as trust violation [10], transgression [6], erosion [2], breach [30], or damage [22]. We will go with 'trust violation' as the used term in this article.

A shared assumption is that trust violations should be "repaired" or "fixed" if they emerge, if not avoided. This assumption reflects the social sciences' understanding of trust as desirable, with benefits for both the trustor and trustee. Building trust is a lengthy and time-consuming process, while trust violations can occur unexpectedly and, within a short period, undo all previous efforts, overshadowing the established trust. In other words, "trust can take years to build but be lost in a day" [23]. When there are existing elements of distrust or reduced perceptions of trust, repairing trust may necessitate even more effort and time than initially building it [19]. The subjective perceptions of trust violations, which differ among stakeholders, coupled with the complexities of power relations and interests, make trust repair even more challenging [1].

What is more, trust violations are not confined to the particular transgressing organisation but often transcend the boundaries and spill over to other organisations in a sector, so even blameless organisations are affected and (have to) engage in trust repair and differentiation from organisations involved in trust violation [4]. An interesting area of trust repair research is preventive tactics at individual, organisational, and sectoral levels, which have a twofold purpose - to prevent the occurrence of trust violations by influencing potential causes or, if the violation still occurs, to mitigate the impact of the violation by making consequences less severe [6]. For instance, those tactics include training of staff, job-level checks and balances, and staff evaluations at the individual level, then audits, governance practices, and internal controls at the organisational level, and finally, sector-level regulation and oversight at the sectoral level [6].

It might be argued that the dominant narrative in extant research, even when it is not clearly and explicitly stated, is that trust repair is somewhat mechanical in its nature [4], as if it is a broken part of machinery that can be perfectly repaired so that no one notices any difference or it is an elastic band that is stretched and then returned to its initial position. This mechanistic view of trust repair is an oversimplification, if not a complete fabrication, for at least two reasons. First, there is a point of no return regarding trust violations, i.e. trust cannot always be repaired. And second, repaired trust is different (not necessarily of lesser quality) than unbroken trust. In other words, trust repair is much more like medical healing than mechanical repair [26]. The term 'trust repair' is widely spread in research with some exceptions (e.g. trust restoration), so we will stick with that term, bearing in mind that it is not mechanic repair one may think of when seeing this term.

Three related but distinct stage models help us explain how the process of trust repair itself is constructed in a series of steps or phases which follow each other in a consciously led trust repair process, and those models are utilised in organisational trust repair [21]. For trust repair in i-voting, the model formulated by Gillespie and Dietz [20] is particularly pertinent and effective. This approach strategically addresses trust violations, starting with an immediate response (step 1) and progressing to a diagnostic phase (step 2) that informs the development of reforming interventions (step 3), which are then evaluated for their effectiveness (step 4). In contrast, the two other stage models place more emphasis on the trustee's acknowledgement of the trust violation and willingness to accept responsibility, accompanied by subsequent penance. In instances of trust violations, an immediate response is considered beneficial, at least to communicate acknowledgement of reduced trust perceptions and outline the steps necessary to identify the cause. However, this is not always the case, as responding to a trust violation does not necessarily require positive action from the trustee. Some research suggests that defensive strategies may benefit the trustee more in the short term than genuine communication [18]. A transgressing organisation might deny the occurrence of the trust violation, downplay the problem to minimise its significance [4], and continue with a business-as-usual approach [6]. The next stage in trust repair involves diagnosing the incident, determining the severity of trust damage, and identifying the affected trustworthiness dimensions to orchestrate effective trust repair, as "the context-specific nature of trust affects the choice of trust repair mechanism(s)" [2]. What works in one context or country may not work in another, as "an appropriate social ritual to restore a relationship is culturally and contextually bound" [1]. Interventions or mechanisms for trust repair are systematised into a framework for organisational and institutional trust repair consisting of six mechanisms by Bachmann et al. [1]. This framework is probably the most comprehensive of its kind and is widely cited in trust repair research, particularly in empirical studies. The trust repair mechanisms are as it follows: 1. Sense-making, 2. Relational, 3. Regulation and controls, 4. Ethical culture, 5. Transparency, and 6. Transference. Each trust repair mechanism has a common assumption, foci, and underlying mechanism, accompanied by practical examples of measures from real-world cases. The table below provides detailed descriptions of each trust repair mechanism Fig. 1.

| | Trust repair mechanism | | | | | |
	Sense-making	Relational	Regulation and controls	Ethnical culture	Transparency	Transference
Assumption	A shared understanding or accepted account of the trust violation is required for effective trust repair.	Trust repair requires social rituals and symbolic acts to resolve negative emotions caused by the violation and re-establish the social order in the relationship.	Trust repair requires formal rules and controls to constrain untrustworthy behaviour and hence prevent a future trust violation .	Trust repair requires informal cultural controls to constrain untrustworthy behaviour and promote trustworthy behaviour, and hence prevent a future trust violation.	Transparently sharing relevant information about organizational decision processes and functioning with stakeholders helps restore trust.	Trust repair can be facilitated by transferring trust from a credible party to the discredited party.
Foci	Cognition and social influence	Emotions and social rituals	Formal organization and institutional environment	Informal organization and broader cultural context	Reporting and monitoring	Third party involvement
Underlying mechanism	Collective learning	Remorse and redemption	Formal control	Informal control	Information sharing and accountability	Reputation spillover
Tradition	Organization theory	Psychology and sociology	Sociology, management, and organization science	Philosophy, organization science, and management	Public management and corporate governance	Social networks and sociology
Practical examples	Investigations, public inquiries, explanations and accounts.	Explanations, apologies, punishment, penance, compensation, redistribution of power and resetting expectations.	Regulation, laws, organizational rules, policies, controls, contracts, codes of conduct, sanctions and incentives.	Cultural reforms, induction and socialization, professional training, leadership and role modelling.	Corporate reporting, external audits, public inquiries and whistleblower protection.	Certifications, memberships, affiliations, awards and endorsements.

Fig. 1. A framework of six trust repair mechanisms for repairing organizational and institutional trust, adapted from Bachmann et al. [1]

Trust repair measures do not function in isolation. Quite the contrary, they are interdependent and often rely on each other [1]. Therefore, before implementing trust repair measures, it is important to understand their interactions. Some measures can enhance the effects of others, while in some cases, they may have negative consequences. Hence, trust repair is a serious undertaking, and its management requires a systematic approach.

2.3 E-voting Frameworks

The proposed trust repair framework borrows its building blocks from established frameworks in i-voting research. We utilise Krimmer's "The E-voting Mirabilis" [24] and its adapted version, "The Mirabilis of Internet Voting System Failure" by Spycher-Krivonosova [36], who integrates Toots' information system failure framework [37] with Krimmer's model. Elements from these concepts help us identify relevant stakeholders, their mutual relationships, and their roles in trust-building and trust-repair processes. "The E-voting Mirabilis" is a conceptual framework for the analysis of ICT in elections, comprising four dimensions affecting e-voting adoption (1. Technology; 2. Law; 3. Politics; 4. Society), and five stakeholder group that are of help in e-voting adoption (1. Citizens, Voters; 2. Politicians, Candidates; 3. Election Management; 4. Inventors, Vendors; 5. Media, Observers) [24]. Krimmer lists stakeholders as leaves of the e-voting mirabilis without any special division or relations among them. Spycher-Krivonosova adapts Toots' information system failure framework with elements of Krimmer's Mirabilis and divides stakeholders into two groups named "Stakeholders" (citizens, voters; politicians, candidates; media; observers) and "Project Organization" (election management and vendors) [36]. This distinction is made between those in charge of i-voting, i.e., stakeholders responsible for delivering elections, and other stakeholders outside this internal process.

3 Framework for Voters' Trust Repair in Internet Voting

This framework integrates insights from trust repair research across multiple scholarly fields with established e-voting frameworks. By leveraging current knowledge on trust repair, we gain an understanding of how voters' trust in i-voting is formed, the influence of external stakeholders on voters' trust, the nature and impact of trust violations, and the basic propositions of trust repair. Furthermore, the integration of trust repair research findings allows us to delineate the step-by-step processes involved in trust repair, the mechanisms available for trust repair, and the comparative quality of repaired versus pre-violation trust. The established e-voting frameworks help identify stakeholders and their relations and clarify the roles of the trustor and trustee, as well as other stakeholders within the i-voting context Fig. 2.

The constitutive elements of the framework will be thoroughly explained in the subsequent subsections, but it is useful to provide a brief overview and outline the basic assumptions and relationships. Voters have two types of trusting beliefs toward i-voting: human-like beliefs and system-like beliefs. These beliefs are influenced by numerous stakeholders, given that many voters cannot fully understand the technological aspects of i-voting. Voters' beliefs refer to both the human (i-voting organisation) and technological dimensions (i-voting system), forming the basis for their overall perceptions of i-voting. I-voting organisers have a dual role within this framework, acting as both trustees and trust repairers. This group includes decision-makers, electoral management bodies, and vendors. When these perceptions erode, a trust violation occurs, necessitating trust repair. Trust repair takes place when i-voting organisers respond to trust violations. To ensure successful trust repair, it is essential to assess the affected beliefs/dimensions, the available trust repair measures, how these measures interact, their suitability for

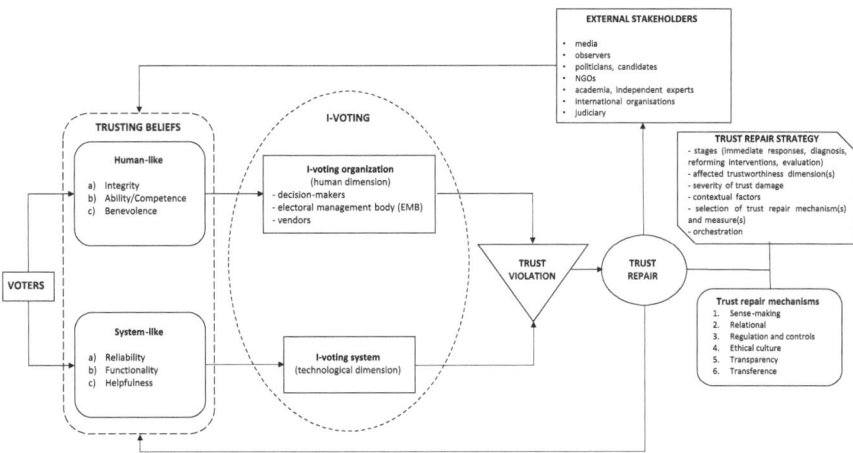

Fig. 2. A Framework for Voters' Trust Repair in I-voting, integrating concepts from [1, 20, 24–26, 36]

specific trust violation areas, the appropriate mix of measures for each case, and any contextual specifics before beginning the trust repair process. Trust repair is overseen by i-voting organisers, who direct it toward both voters and external stakeholders, as trust in i-voting is intermediated trust.

The framework presented in this article is developed for politically binding elections. While it is tailored for this specific context, it may also be adapted appropriately for other forms of i-voting (e.g., interparty elections).

3.1 Voters

We adopt a macro perspective with voters as a collective of individuals eligible to vote in an election with their "collectively held trust perceptions" [5], which are conceptualised as generalised or aggregated trust. Trustors are voters as an enmassed group of people, with acknowledgement of their individual characteristics playing a role in trust building and trust repair, but going beyond individual determinants of trust (which are usually applied to trust in i-voting research, like TAM and UTAUT models [13]), with generalised trust in mind and trust repair as a systematic endeavour to improve the violated trust of a larger collective.

3.2 Trusting Beliefs

Trust in i-voting is conceptualised as a multifaceted, multilevel, and multi-relational construct involving human-like trust beliefs (integrity, benevolence, and competence) and system-like trust beliefs (reliability, functionality, and helpfulness) directed toward the respective human and technological dimensions of i-voting. Both sets of beliefs shape voters' trust, as i-voting features a human component in its organisers and a technological component in its ICT infrastructure. This distinction in trusting beliefs can be applied to various aspects of i-voting systems, revealing potential areas for trust violations and underscoring the importance of considering both human and technological factors in trust repair management. Understanding the dual nature of trusting beliefs is crucial for identifying which beliefs are affected by trust violations so that an appropriate trust repair strategy can be tailored for each case.

Whether human-like or system-like beliefs weigh more and what is their proportion in building trust in i-voting is an open question. However, as mentioned, some researchers underline a degree of perceived technology's humanness [25], which might suggest higher relevance of system-like beliefs because i-voting is, from the perspective of voters, a tool for expressing their preferences. Other researchers equally rightly argue that i-voting is a rather sophisticated technology and trust in i-voting rests on 'the cue-taking approach' used by voters, especially partisan voters [14], pushing trust in i-voting in the direction of human-like beliefs on the imaginary continuum of trust in i-voting with two opposite sets of beliefs on both ends. Nonetheless, human-like and system-like trust beliefs undoubtedly influence voters' trust, and violations in either dimension necessitate trust repair.

3.3 I-voting

I-voting as a whole is divided into two subgroups: i-voting organisation (human dimension) and i-voting system (technological dimension), each corresponding to two distinct types of trusting beliefs.

I-voting Organisation Three stakeholder groups fall into the i-voting organization category: decision-makers, electoral management bodies (EMBs), and vendors. These stakeholders represent the human dimension of i-voting, and voters' human-like trusting beliefs are directed at them when assessing the trustworthiness of i-voting. All of these groups are involved in creating institutional and legal frameworks and managing i-elections, making them accountable for the performance of i-voting. They are not only the subjects of voters' assessments, through which trust in i-voting can be built or violated, but they also stand on the front lines when trust violations occur and must manage trust repair.

Decision-makers possess the final authority to adopt, reject, or discontinue i-voting. In instances of trust repair, they are significantly engaged in sense-making by commissioning investigations into the causes of trust violations, usually with the assistance of a broad circle of stakeholders. These stakeholders may be internal, from within the i-voting organization, or external, potentially from other countries, which is relatively common. This investigation has twofold goals: to understand what went wrong and to give recommendations for improvements, resulting in amending existing or introducing new regulations and practices on i-voting. For instance, Switzerland was not successful in introducing i-voting as a general voting method in 2019, and before continuing or starting again with their i-voting project, a report followed by a broad consulation was published with a set of measures to be implemented in a redesigned i-voting project [16].

EMBs are engaged in day-to-day operations and have the best overview of the current state of an i-voting system. They employ staff from various backgrounds, including legal and computer experts. While their role in trust building is already recognised, they also play a crucial role in trust repair as first-line responders during times of uncertainty and trust violations. Their position as trustees necessitates a strategic approach to both preventing and addressing trust violations.

In developing i-voting solutions, EMBs often collaborate with companies that specialise in the technical aspects of i-voting. Given that the i-voting market is relatively small and resembles an oligopoly, these companies typically engage in other business activities or offer their services internationally. Such an international presence can result in trust violations in other markets where these private vendors operate, raising questions about the i-voting systems they support, even in countries where no trust violation has yet occurred. Potential trust violations attributed to a particular vendor can impact the specific i-voting system involved and cause a spillover effect on other i-voting projects the vendor manages in different countries. Such spillovers can influence the entire i-voting market, compelling stakeholders in other countries who are not at fault to differentiate themselves from the offending entity and undertake trust repair with their stakeholders [4].

I-voting System An i-voting system is the technological basis of i-voting, encompassing all hardware and software elements required to run and support i-voting, as well as auxiliary applications and services. These supplementary components, although not necessary for the technological execution of i-voting, are incorporated to serve various purposes, including improving transparency and building voter trust, such as verifiability tools.

3.4 External Stakeholders

External stakeholders, as defined in this concept, are stakeholders external to an i-voting system in terms of the accountability of its development and functioning. In other words, these stakeholders are not responsible for election delivery but have the power to influence voters' trust in i-voting by claiming that some internal stakeholders (i-voting organisation) or the i-voting system itself cannot be trusted, or if they question some aspect of trust in the human or technological dimension of i-voting. The trust of those stakeholders in i-voting is transferred to voters' beliefs about i-voting and influences their trust in either a positive or negative way. External stakeholders can facilitate or hinder trust. In other words, they can either produce or induce trust damage or partner in trust repair.

In this framework, there are three additional modifications: voters as a central stakeholder group in the model, additional stakeholder groups added, and a regrouping of two stakeholder groups to "I-voting organisation" or "Internal stakeholders" and "External stakeholders". A vast majority of the listed stakeholders come from Krimmer's "Mirabilis of the E-voting model" [24] and its adapted version, "The Mirabilis of Internet Voting System Failure" by Spycher-Krivonosova [36]. The latter includes: 1. Media, 2. Observers, 3. Politicians, candidates, 4. NGOs, 5. Academia, independent experts, 6. International organisations, 7. Judiciary. The first three groups of stakeholders are the same as from Krimmer's and Spycher-Krivonosova's model, further complemented by four groups of stakeholders who play a notable role in I-voting but, for some reasons, have not yet been included in existing models. These stakeholder groups have influenced voters' trust in e-voting and I-voting.

Political parties have significant influence on shaping voters' trust in i-voting, vividly demonstrated in the Estonian example [14] - voters who vote for a party that supports i-voting are more likely to trust i-voting in comparison to those who vote for parties with a negative attitude towards i-voting, and this "partisan gap in trust" cannot be reduced to differences in the socio-demographic profiles of voters, with potential to lead to the polarization of trust and usage of i-voting along party lines. Moreover, i-voting has also been utilized in inter-party elections, where potential trust violations could impact voters' confidence in politically binding elections [38].

The discontinuation of Dutch e-voting resulted primarily from a campaign by an NGO called "We Don't Trust Voting Computers". How academia and independent experts can play a role in voters' trust was demonstrated in Estonia in 2014 when a group consisting of university researchers, e-voting observers, independent researchers, and advisors, led by Professor J. Alex Halderman, published a security analysis [35] of the Estonian i-voting system in which they identified significant vulnerabilities, demonstrating potential client-side and server-side attacks that could alter election outcomes or compromise voter secrecy. Their analysis highlighted the lack of end-to-end verifiability and inadequate procedural controls, leading to their recommendation to discontinue its use for the time being. On the other hand, these groups can positively influence trust with their engagement in monitoring i-voting.

International organisations are also important stakeholders, yet not recognised by current models. The Council of Europe has served as a forum for discussions and the exchange of experiences among countries engaged in the adoption of e-voting and i-voting from the early days. Moreover, the CoE's role in setting international standards in e-voting (recommendations from 2004 [7] and 2017 [8]) can also impact voters' trust - it is possible to test one's own country's i-voting against set international criteria and to signal that some of those standards are not (fully) respected, thus undermining trust among the electorate. The OSCE/ODIHR observes elections and publishes after-election reports that describe the overall electoral process, including the voting method, and provide their opinions and recommendations based on findings gathered during their observer mission. For instance, the report on the Estonian 2023 parliamentary elections contains recommendations aimed at election authorities for addressing election stakeholders' concerns, implementing technical and organisational measures, and establishing transparency practices [31]. These publicly available reports create expectations among stakeholders as a to-do list for i-voting organisers, who are expected to tick off the given recommendations. This may create a perception of the recommendations as tasks rather than suggestions. Potential non-adherence to these recommendations can initiate a loop of trust erosion, starting within the expert community, which can subsequently be transferred to ordinary voters.

The last newly added group is the judiciary, a separate branch of power with a supervisory role in elections. Case law in e-voting is rich, and certain landmark judgments have influenced trust in e-voting [12].

3.5 Trust Violation

Trust violations can occur as a single event or as a series of events, both leading to a reduction in voters' perceptions of i-voting. For example, the abandonment of the general i-voting roll-out in Switzerland, although mainly perceived as triggered by the detection of critical vulnerabilities in the source code, "has fuelled the already heated debate over the future development of internet voting in Switzerland" [11]. Trust violations in i-voting can be further divided by causes, type, severity, timing, intentionality, and consequences [26]. Types of trust violations correlate to three basic categories of human-like and corresponding system-like trusting beliefs (integrity vs. reliability, ability/competence vs. functionality, benevolence vs. helpfulness). Not all trust violations have the same impact on voters' trust, and more severe trust violations must be addressed with greater urgency before the violation reaches a point where damage becomes irreparable, and the whole i-voting system is abandoned.

When it comes to the timing of trust violations, the magnitude of the violations and their consequences differ if they occur in the early phases of development of i-voting or early enough before elections. In 2014, Halderman's report [35] was published just a couple of days before the European elections, which necessitated an immediate response from the Estonian electoral administration that completely denied their findings and tried to assure voters that everything was alright. Trust violations may also happen during the voting period, as occurred in Estonia in 2023, where minor issues such as a delay due to manual data upload and a mismatch in district data arose. These issues, attributed to human error and delayed updates, were promptly addressed by officials, ensuring that the integrity of the voting process was not compromised [27].

Accurate detection of the nature of trust violation(s) helps create a trust repair strategy based on „careful planning, coordination and combined implementation of trust repair mechanisms that best repair affected or important trustworthiness dimensions" [2].

3.6   Trust Repair in I-Voting

Trust repair in i-voting and other studied entities, most of which are service industry brands operating in the market, have to be distinguished. In i-voting, the competition is not with other providers of the same voting method but with other voting methods altogether. The question is not which alternative provider of i-voting voters will turn to in cases of trust violations, but rather which other voting method they will choose, and whether i-voting will survive at all. The high standards set for i-voting mean that maintaining trust is crucial, and violations of this trust can lead to significant, sometimes irreversible, consequences. When trust issues become too great or frequent, the simpler and more practical response is often to abandon i-voting altogether. This approach is favoured over the arduous and uncertain process of trust repair, reflecting the lower resilience of alternative voting methods to sustain trust violations. In simpler terms, new voting methods are seen as alternative, optional and have to be trustworthy, and demands for them are stricter than those for established voting methods, which are seen as default, as well as the mere fact that there is an alternative you can choose between, it introduces risk analysis and the situation of trust [32].

Trust repair is a thoughtful and directed process, not just a point in time, especially in the context of i-voting. It begins by opening communication channels and immediately responding to trust violations. This initial response should acknowledge the occurrence of the violation and assure stakeholders that necessary steps will be taken to identify the causes and repair trust. It is often not immediately clear what exactly went wrong, and it may take some time to determine what happened. Even so, the immediate effects of a trust violation can severely negatively influence voters' trust. Following the initial response, the next step is diagnosing or sense-making of trust violations by understanding all their aspects. It is essential to ensure that everyone is aligned on what constitutes the trust violation(s), whether it is recognised as a violation by all, and the severity of the violation. Stakeholders might have dissimilar understandings of what happened, the event's nature, its significance, whether there is a need for trust repair, and if so, how it should be done. Understanding stakeholders' views is essential for designing effective trust-restoring measures and avoiding exacerbating the situation. Apart from perceptual distinctions or biases, power asymmetries, in this case, stem from disproportions in the specialist knowledge of the technological base of i-voting – understanding and thus having justified trust is reduced to "an elite intelligent few" [29]. Therefore, trust in i-voting is not only shaped by voters' immediate interactions with the system but also by external stakeholders, primarily because of the complexity of i-voting.

The notion that relational trust repair measures are culturally and contextually bound has two repercussions for trust repair. First, in crafting a (relational) trust repair response, i-voting organisers should be aware of the cultural environment in which trust repair takes place. What works in Estonia may not work in Switzerland or France, and vice versa. For instance, the notion of voting privacy and remoteness differs in Switzerland, which has a positive experience with postal voting, and in Estonia, which uses the revote option with the last cast ballot counted. In contrast, in France, even if revoting could be introduced from a technological standpoint, it is not feasible due to cultural and legal constraints, as voting is framed as a one-off activity, and revoting would infringe on the solemnity of the voting act. The second repercussion is that trust violations might be framed differently by voters in different countries, to the extent that what constitutes a trust violation in one country might not even be perceived as such in another. Since trust violations are essentially perceptions, they reflect cultural specificities. Additionally, because i-voting trust violations can spill over to other countries, it is feasible to plan and design different social rituals suited to each specific country rather than adopting a one-size-fits-all mindset for trust repair.

Engaging renowned experts or other trusted entities in trust repair operations - appointing them to working bodies, giving them access to documentation, and involving them in sense-making, monitoring, and evaluating the success of trust repair - can endorse the trust repair process. This creates a dual source of verification: both i-voting organizers and independent experts. Moreover, trust repair is not the sole task of the transgressing organization but involves blameless organizations within a certain organizational field [4]. Trust violations can have spillover effects from one country to another, even if the affected i-voting system is not involved. In i-voting, spillover effects of trust violations can lead to decreased trust perceptions among voters in other countries where the violation did not occur. This is partly because technical weaknesses that triggered trust violations in one context may also be present in other i-voting systems. Additionally, new demands for implementing measures in one context can influence other contexts. For instance, verifiability has steadily become an indispensable part of i-voting practices, and even when it is not legally required, pressure from other countries can lead the public to demand its introduction. The rejection or poor implementation of such measures can undermine voters' trust. Blameless organizers should monitor events in other contexts to learn from them, undertake preventive measures, engage in trust repair processes to address stakeholder concerns, and differentiate themselves from transgressing organizers. In such cases, an i-voting organiser should engage in trust repair to manage voters' perceptions, and this should consist of shared trust repair strategies between the transgressing organisation and the blameless organisation and also should have a distinct differentiation strategy to distance themselves from the transgressing organisation [4].

As the mechanistic view of trust repair has been previously discarded, it is recognized that initial trust and repaired trust are not necessarily of the same quality – repaired trust can be at a lower level, the same, or even at a higher level. Time is an important variable, as repaired trust differs shortly after the repair intervention and in a longer-term perspective [26]. Evaluating the efficiency of trust repair, particularly by comparing pre- and post-levels of voters' trust and assessing the trust repair strategy, is crucial for guiding successful trust repair.

Prevention of trust violations can be achieved through 'recalibration practices' [19] which help maintain the optimal level of trust through early interventions. These practices detect 'cracks' in trust before they become more serious and eventually convert to distrust, potentially reaching a point of no return. Transparency measures are indispensable for building trust in i-voting and preventing trust violations or mitigating their severity. The 2019 Swiss i-voting project was discontinued after significant security vulnerabilities were disclosed during a bug bounty program, allowing anyone to inspect the Swiss i-voting system's source code [16]. Interestingly, a measure to build trust in i-voting, code disclosure, enabled the detection of security vulnerabilities and thus led to trust violation. Although it was a rather big blow for Swiss aspirations to generalize i-voting later that year, the author argues that the procedure through which vulnerabilities were found – the strategic disclosure of information through an organized bug bounty program – enabled the relaunch of the Swiss i-voting project soon after. Utilising transparency measures can mitigate the severity of potential trust violations by reframing the nature of trust violations from integrity-based or benevolence-based to competence-based, so such violations are perceived as the result of technical incompetence rather than a breach of integrity. If a trust violation affects competence, it is local and technical and can be resolved by improved practices, additional technical measures, enhanced skills, etc. On the other hand, integrity and benevolence-based violations might be much more detrimental and cast doubts on the overall intentions of the i-voting organization, thus leading to the point of no return with irreparably damaged trust of voters and other stakeholders. Therefore, the Swiss example demonstrates how transparency measures, i.e. strategic disclosure of source code, serve for continuous improvement and as a shield from more deleterious implications of integrity and benevolence-based trust violations.

4   Avenues for Future Research

Trust repair in i-voting is a nascent research area without any prior systematic account, which opens a range of potentially interesting and useful (sub)topics for future research. Each avenue would enhance the proposed framework, deepen our knowledge of trust repair in i-voting, and provide sound advice for i-voting practitioners.

The framework can facilitate case study research by providing theoretical lenses for detecting real-world trust breaches and following trust repair interventions in countries that offer i-voting to some extent to their voters. In the European context, that might be Estonia and France, but also Switzerland, with its long and rich history marked with ups and downs and the attempt to generalise i-voting in 2019. Those practices and experiences may help detect different causes, consequences, and nature of breaches, the response strategies applied to restore trust, and the level of trust before and after the breach. Trust repair strategies are not static, and it is important to understand how they are recalibrated and adjusted when Plan A does not go as planned.

Cross-cultural aspects of trust repair in i-voting can be studied by comparing trust repair management across those countries, with the potential to identify and separate generalities that hold for all cases from particularities related to a specific case. Trust violations can have transnational effects, where a trust violation in one country influences voters' perceptions and trust levels in another. Research should explore the differentiation strategies employed by blameless stakeholders to repair trust in their country and distance themselves from violations elsewhere.

Although the presented framework emphasises voters as trustors, trust restoration can be applied to different stakeholder groups, and future research can focus on a particular stakeholder group as trustors whose trust is negatively affected and necessitates repair. Preventive measures are part of good trust repair management, and understanding how they are designed and how effective they are in preventing or mitigating trust breaches in the context of i-voting is another promising avenue.

Time is another aspect of trust repair that is getting more attention from researchers. The process approach is dynamic and sees time as central to explaining trust repair, whereas the dominant variance approach is static in nature [33]. Answering "how" and not only "why" can deepen our understanding of trust repair in i-voting. In the end, measuring the effectiveness of trust repair efforts is important to comprehend their impact on voters and other stakeholders, providing insights that can lead to more nuanced and effective trust repair strategies in the future.

5 Conclusion

While trust in i-voting is not a novel research topic, trust repair has yet to capture scholarly attention despite trust violations and subsequent trust repair in practice. This article introduces trust repair in the context of i-voting, presenting a systematic account through developing a conceptual framework for voters' trust repair in politically binding elections. By integrating insights from various research domains within the i-voting context, this article advances the understanding of how trust can be repaired after violations occur. The framework maps out the interplay between human and technological dimensions of trust and the roles of internal and external stakeholders, offering a nuanced perspective on trust violations and trust repair in i-voting.

In the academic context, the article contributes to the literature by shifting the focus from trust building to trust repair. It systematically identifies the elements influencing trust repair, from detecting trust violations to the required trust repair responses. By grounding these insights in theoretical and practical considerations, the framework sets the stage for scholarly inquiry into trust repair in i-voting as a new subtopic of a broader and already established trust in i-voting research. Moreover, the article lists a range of possible research avenues in the realm of trust repair, which could enrich the understanding of trust repair in i-voting.

The framework provides i-voting organisers with the available 'arsenal' of trust repair measures. It explains how those measures correspond to and are appropriate for specific areas of trust damage, thus assisting i-voting organisers in developing trust repair management plans that include response strategies for trust violations and preventive measures to mitigate or avoid such violations. Understanding and embracing trust (repair) management as a proactive, rather than merely a reactive activity when trust violations occur, is of utmost importance for maintaining voters' trust in i-voting, preventing potential trust violations, and successfully addressing those that occur.

Disclosure of Interests.   The author has no competing interests to declare that are relevant to the content of this article.

References

1. Bachmann, R., Gillespie, N., Priem, R.: Repairing trust in organizations and institutions: toward a conceptual framework. Organ. Stud. **36**(9), 1123–1142 (2015). https://doi.org/10. 1177/0170840615599334
2. Bolat, E., et al.: Service brand rehab: Diagnosing trust repair mechanisms. Qual. Market Res. **23**(4), 797–819 (2020). https://doi.org/10.1108/QMR-12-2017-0187
3. Bozic, B.: Consumer trust repair: a critical literature review. Eur. Manag. J. **35**(4), 538–547 (2017). https://doi.org/10.1016/j.emj.2017.02.007
4. Bozic, B., Siebert, S., Martin, G.: A strategic action fields perspective on organizational trust repair. Eur. Manag. J. **37**(1), 58–66 (2019). https://doi.org/10.1016/j.emj.2018.04.005
5. Brattström, A., Faems, D., Mähring, M.: From trust convergence to trust divergence: trust development in conflictual interorganizational relationships. Organ. Stud. **40**(11), 1685–1711 (2019). https://doi.org/10.1177/0170840618789195
6. Chapman, C.M., Hornsey, M.J., Gillespie, N., Lockey, S.: Nonprofit scandals: a systematic review and conceptual framework. Nonprofit Voluntary Sect. Q. **52**(1_suppl), 278S–312S (2023). https://doi.org/10.1177/08997640221129541
7. Council of Europe: Recommendation Rec(2004)11 of the Committee of Ministers to member states on legal, operational and technical standards for e-voting. Council of Europe, Strasbourg (2004)
8. Council of Europe: Recommendation CM/Rec(2017)5 of the Committee of Ministers to member States on standards for e-voting. Council of Europe, Strasbourg (2017)
9. Crane, B.: Revisiting who, when, and why stakeholders matter: trust and stakeholder connectedness. Bus. Soc. **59**(2), 263–286 (2020). https://doi.org/10.1177/0007650318756983
10. de Visser, E.J., Pak, R., Shaw, T.H.: From 'automation' to 'autonomy': the importance of trust repair in human–machine interaction. Ergonomics **61**(10), 1409–1427 (2018). https:// doi.org/10.1080/00140139.2018.1457725
11. Driza Maurer, A.: The swiss Post/Scytl transparency exercise and its possible impact on internet voting regulation. In: Krimmer, R., et al. (eds.) Electronic Voting. E-Vote-ID 2019. LNCS, vol. 11759, pp. 83–99. Springer, Cham (2019). https://doi.org/10.1007/978-3-030-30625-0_6

12. Driza Maurer, A., Barrat, J. (eds.): E-Voting Case Law: A Comparative Analysis. Ashgate Publishing, Farnham (2015). https://doi.org/10.4324/9781315581385
13. Duenas-Cid, D.: A theoretical framework for understanding trust and distrust in internet voting. In: Seventh International Joint Conference on Electronic Voting - E-Vote-ID 2022 Proceedings, pp. 57–62. University of Tartu Press, Tartu (2022). https://doi.org/10.15157/dis s/020
14. Ehin, P., Solvak, M.: Party cues and trust in remote internet voting: Data from Estonia 2005–2019. In: Krimmer, R., et al. (eds.) Electronic Voting. E-Vote-ID 2021. LNCS, vol. 12900, pp. 83–97. Springer, Cham (2021). https://doi.org/10.1007/978-3-030-86942-7_6
15. Erb, Y., Duenas-Cid, D., Volkamer, M.: Identifying factors studied for voter trust in E-voting – Review of literature. In: E-Vote-ID 2023, 8th International Joint Conference on Electronic Voting Proceedings. Gesellschaft für Informatik, Bonn (2023)
16. Federal Chancellery Ch: Redesign and relaunch of trials Final report of the Steering Committee Vote électronique (SC VE). Federal Chancellery, Bern (2020)
17. Ferrin, D.L., Dirks, K.T., Shah, P.P.: Many routes toward trust: a social network analysis of the determinants of interpersonal trust. Acad. Manag. Proc. **2003**(1), C1–C6 (2003). https://doi.org/10.1037/0021-9010.91.4.870
18. Fuoli, M., van de Weijer, J., Paradis, C.: Denial outperforms apology in repairing organizational trust despite strong evidence of guilt. Publ. Relat. Rev. **43**(4), 645–660 (2017). https://doi.org/10.1016/j.pubrev.2017.07.007
19. Gillespie, N.: Trust dynamics and repair: an interview with Roy Lewicki. J. Trust Res. **7**(2), 204–219 (2017). https://doi.org/10.1080/21515581.2017.1373022
20. Gillespie, N., Dietz, G.: Trust repair after an organization-level failure. Acad. Manag. Rev. **34**(1), 127–145 (2009). https://doi.org/10.5465/amr.2009.35713319
21. Gillespie, N., Siebert, S.: Organizational trust repair. In: Searle, R., Nienaber, A.-M., Sitkin, S.B. (eds.) The Routledge Companion to Trust, pp. 284–301. Routledge, London (2018). https://doi.org/10.4324/9781315745572-20
22. Hou, J., Zhang, C., Guo, H.: How nonprofits can recover from crisis events? the trust recovery from the perspective of causal attributions. Voluntas **31**, 71–93 (2020). https://doi.org/10.1007/s11266-019-00176-7
23. International IDEA: Introducing Electronic Voting: Essential Considerations. International IDEA, Stockholm (2011)
24. Krimmer, R.: The evolution of E-voting: Why voting technology is used and how it affects democracy. Doctoral thesis, Tallinn University of Technology (2012)
25. Lankton, N.K., McKnight, D.H., Tripp, J.: Technology, humanness, and trust: rethinking trust in technology. J. Assoc. Inf. Syst. **16**(10), 880–918 (2015). https://doi.org/10.17705/1jais.00411
26. Lewicki, R.J., Brinsfield, C.: Trust Repair. Annu. Rev. Organ. Psych. Organ. Behav. **4**, 287–313 (2017). https://doi.org/10.1146/annurev-orgpsych-032516-113147
27. Liive, R.: E-hääletamine algas paari väheolulise viperusega. Digigeenius (2023), https://digi.geenius.ee/rubriik/uudis/e-haaletamine-algas-paari-vaheolulise-viperusega/. Accessed 14 May 2024
28. Lyon, F., Möllering, G., Saunders, M.N.K.: Introduction: The variety of methods for the multi-faceted phenomenon of trust. In: Lyon, F., Möllering, G., Saunders, M.N.K. (eds.) Handbook of research methods on trust, pp. 1–15. Edward Elgar Publishing, Cheltenham (2012). https://doi.org/10.4337/9780857932013.00008
29. Mercuri, R.T., Neumann, P.G.: The risks of election believability (or lack thereof). Commun. ACM **64**(6), 24–30 (2021). https://doi.org/10.1145/3461464
30. Nelson, C.A., Cui, A.P., Walsh, M.F.: Breach of trust and repair: the impact of salespersons words and actions on buyer trust. Qual. Market Res. **24**(3), 375–395 (2021). https://doi.org/10.1108/QMR-08-2019-0101

31. OSCE/ODIHR: Estonia parliamentary elections 5 March 2023, ODIHR election expert team: Final report. OSCE/ODIHR, Warsaw (2023)
32. Pieters, W.: Acceptance of voting technology: between confidence and trust. In: Stølen, K., et al. (eds.) Trust Management. iTrust 2006. LNCS, vol. 3986, pp. 283–297. Springer, Berlin (2006). https://doi.org/10.1007/11755593_21
33. Siebert, S., Martin, G., Bozic, B.: Organizational recidivism and trust repair: a story of failed detectives. J. Organ. Effectiveness People Perform. **5**(4), 328–345 (2018). https://doi.org/10.1108/JOEPP-07-2018-0054
34. Six, F., Verhoest, K.: Trust in Regulatory Regimes: Scoping the Field. In: Six, F., Verhoest, K. (eds.) Trust in Regulatory Regimes, pp. 1–36. Edward Elgar, Cheltenham (2017). https://doi.org/10.1080/21515581.2017.1364028
35. Springall, D., et al.: Security analysis of the Estonian internet voting system. In: Proceedings of the 2014 ACM SIGSAC Conference on Computer and Communications Security, pp. 703–715. ACM, New York (2014). https://doi.org/10.1145/2660267.2660315
36. Spycher-Krivonosova, I.: The Impact of Internet Voting on Election Administration: Directing Implementation Towards a Blessing or a Curse. TalTech Press, Tallinn (2022). https://doi.org/10.23658/taltech.16/2022
37. Toots, M.: Why E-participation systems fail: the case of Estonia's Osale.ee. Gov. Inf. Q. **36**(3), 546–559 (2019). https://doi.org/10.1016/j.giq.2019.02.002
38. von Nostitz, F., Sandri, G., Esteve, J. B..: Regulating i-Voting within countries and parties. In: Barberà, O., Sandri, G., Correa, P., Rodríguez-Teruel, J. (eds.) Digital Parties. Studies in Digital Politics and Governance, pp. 57–76. Springer, Cham (2021). https://doi.org/10.1007/978-3-030-78668-7_3

Efficient Cleansing in Coercion-Resistant Voting

Rosario Giustolisi[1] and Maryam Sheikhi Garjan[2(✉)]

[1] IT University of Copenhagen, Copenhagen, Denmark
rosg@itu.dk
[2] Brandenburg University of Technology, Cottbus, Germany
sheikhig@b-tu.de

Abstract. Coercion resistance is a strong security property of electronic voting that prevents adversaries from forcing voters to vote in a specific way by using threats or rewards. There exist clever techniques aimed at preventing voter coercion based on fake credentials, but they are either inefficient or cannot support features such as revoting without leaking more information than necessary to coercers. One of the reasons is that invalid ballots cast due to revoting or coercion need to be removed before the tallying. In this paper, we propose a coercion-resistant Internet voting scheme that does not require the removal of invalid ballots, hence avoids the leakage of information, but still supports revoting. The scheme is very efficient and achieves linear tallying.

1 Introduction

The utilization of ICT solutions is becoming more prevalent, particularly within electoral processes. The EU Commission has recently acknowledged [12] that Internet voting facilitates elections and encourages the digitalization of many sectors and activities in society. However, Internet voting is risky. A shift towards Internet voting would introduce unprecedented challenges to election correctness. The most obvious one is voter coercion, in which a coercer forces a voter to cast a ballot in a particular way.

Most cryptographic schemes achieve coercion resistance by either deniable revoting or fake credentials. In deniable revoting, voters update or nullify previously cast votes while being under coercion. Schemes based on deniable revoting normally assume over-the-shoulder coercion and that the voter has always a chance to revote after being coerced. These assumptions are not needed in fake credentials as coercers cast ballots using fake credentials. Such ballots are removed from the tally during the so-called cleansing phase. Cleansing is a critical process that traditionally follows voting and precedes tallying, in which the talliers verifiably remove the ballots that should not be counted due to revoting or coercion. Efficient coercion-resistant voting schemes based on fake credentials have been proposed in the literature, but they publicly leak more information than necessary to coercers during cleansing. For example, information about ballots with the same credentials and those with invalid credentials is leaked out in

D. Duenas-Cid et al. (Eds.): E-Vote-ID 2024, LNCS 15014, pp. 72–88, 2025.
https://doi.org/10.1007/978-3-031-72244-8_5

JCJ [18]. A recent attempt [8] aimed at preventing information leakage during cleansing achieves quasi-linear tallying, yet it is inefficient. Inefficiency originates from the fact that the the scheme rely on the multiparty computation (MPC) technique called CGate [27] and on mixnets [2] to prevent information leakage. CGate introduces heavy costs due to computations on bit-wise encryptions in the cleansing phase.

In this paper, we propose an Internet voting scheme that offers a new trade-off between coercion-resistance and efficiency. Assuming that the tally servers are trusted for coercion-resistance, we can avoid the leaking of any information during cleansing very efficiently and achieve linear tallying. Our scheme is based on noise ballots that obfuscate the ballots cast by voters, and on a cleansing procedure that excludes invalid and noise ballots without the need to remove ballots, therefore without leaking any information during cleansing publicly. The scheme guarantees a version of coercion-resistance that accounts for revoting and noise ballots. Our definition is based on a recent one by Cortier et al. [8]. The scheme is also very efficient as it provides linear tallying, and does not require MPC or mixnets. It relies on exponential ElGamal [11] and (disjunctive) non-interactive zero-knowledge proofs (NIZKP) of knowledge [10].

Contributions. The main contribution of this paper is a new Internet voting scheme that provides coercion-resistance without leaking any information during cleansing efficiently. We prove that our scheme satisfies coercion resistance under the DDH assumption in the random oracle model. Cleansing in our scheme is particularly efficient, and the complexity of tallying is linear. We provide a prototype implementation of our scheme in Python to demonstrate that the scheme provides fast cleansing and tallying.

2   Related Work

The concept of the fake credential paradigm, introduced in JCJ [19], has been widely acknowledged as an effective method to achieve coercion resistance. In JCJ, tallying has a quadratic complexity in the number of votes. This is due to the cleansing steps required to eliminate invalid and revote ballots. Efforts have been made to enhance the efficiency of JCJ. Civitas [7] groups voters into blocks to reduce the tallying time. Weber et al. [31] use hash tables instead of plaintext equivalence tests (PET). Other approaches [16,28–30] use a mix of hash tables and PET to remove ballots due to revoting and invalid credentials in linear time. Rønne et al. [26] advance a version of JCJ with linear-time tallying based on fully homomorphic encryption. Araújo et al. [3] use different cryptographic primitives than JCJ to achive tallying in linear time. However, all the schemes outlined above have the same cleansing leakage as JCJ [8].

To avoid information leakage at cleansing, Cortier et al. [8] propose CHide, a *cleansing-hiding* scheme that uses MPC and mixnets. Tallying is quasi-linear but MPC introduces several exponentiations and computations with bit-wise encryptions inducing a heavy cost for CHide. Differently from CHide, our work requires

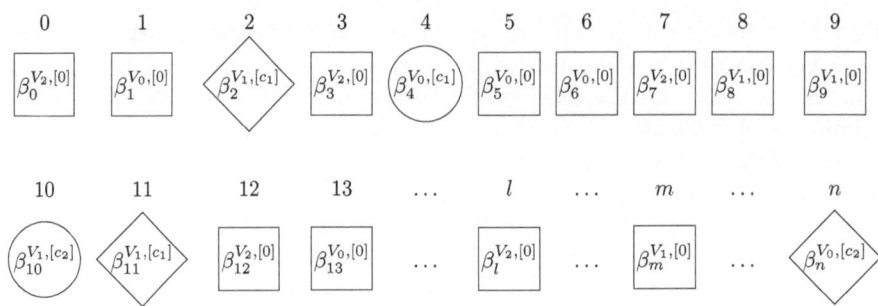

Fig. 1. In the voting phase, the bulletin board is filled with ballots. Ballots cast by a voter under coercion are in diamond, while coercion-free cast ballots are in circle. Noise ballots are in square. Inside each square bracket is the chosen candidate. In this example, the last ballot on the bulletin board is a coerced one and is for candidate $[c_2]$.

noise ballots and that the tally servers are trusted for coercion-resistance. However, even considering a large number of noise ballots, our scheme is faster than CHide since it has no MPC or mixnets and it is fully parallelizable while guaranteeing *publicly* cleansing-hiding.

Schemes based on deniable vote updating [1,4,6,13,17,20–22,24,25] add noise ballots to mitigate information leakage to coercers. They require either that the voter can cast a ballot after being coerced or inalienable authentication at voting (i.e. over-the-shoulder coercion). Our scheme is based on fake credentials and does not have such assumptions.

The first formal definition of coercion-resistance [19] sets the coercer's advantage to distinguish between a real and an ideal game that simulates the voting scheme. Later, various definitions based on a real-ideal games have been proposed [18]. A general approach that defines quantitative coercion-resistance has been proposed in [21] as δ-coercion resistance. In this approach, the coerced voter has a specific strategy to evade coercion. Coercion resistance is ensured if the adversary cannot distinguish whether the coerced voter evades coercion with an advantage greater than δ. Grewal et al. [15] introduced a relaxed version of coercion-resistance in which voters can signal coercion attempts. We aim to a non-relaxed versions of coercion-resistance instead. More recently, Cortier et al. [8] proposed a definition of coercion resistance based on the one introduced in JCJ that captures revoting and the addition of noise ballots. We use this definition to prove that our scheme is coercion-resistant.

3   Overview

In the voting phase, the bulletin board receives ballots from voters and coercers, as well as, noise ballots from voting authorities. It is important that the distributions used to sample the number of noise ballots and to determine the time to cast each of them are unpredictable [21] otherwise a coercer can learn the

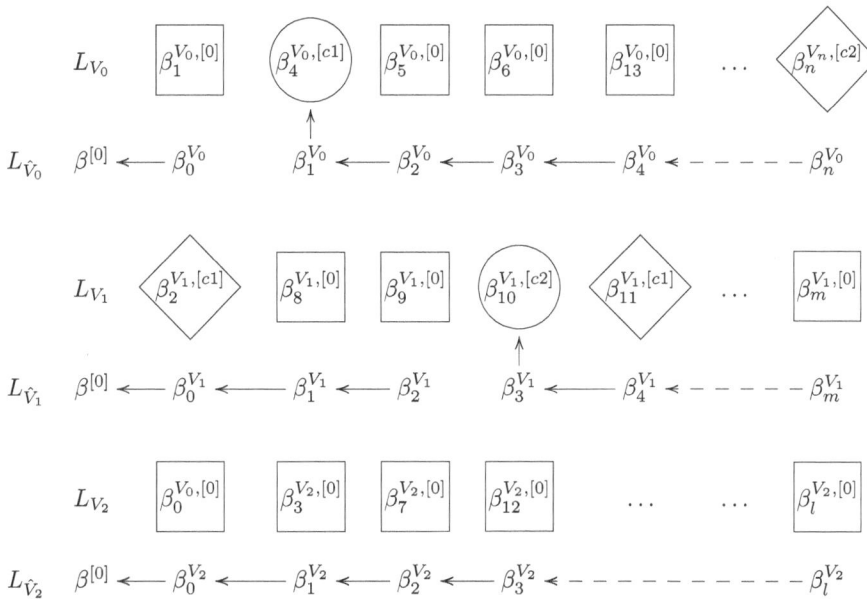

Fig. 2. Our cleansing technique in practice. Each voter list contains the ballots with the public identity of voter V_i. Arrows indicate which ballots are re-randomized to generate the cleansing lists. V_2 captures a voter who abstains from voting. The last ballots in the cleansing lists are those considered for tallying.

voting cast behaviour of voters and significantly distinguish the amout of noise ballots from the real ones. Voters can also generate and cast noise ballots to mitigate forced-abstention attacks and the extent to which the effectiveness of coercion resistance is dependent on authorities controlling noise ballot generation. In each ballot, it is indicated in clear to which voter the ballot should be assigned. Figure 1 shows an example of a bulletin board filled with some ballots.

In the cleansing phase, the tally servers associate each ballot to the assigned voter according to their cast time, generating public *voter lists* of ballots. For example, in Fig. 2, the voter list for voter V_0 is L_{V_0}. The goal is that at the end of cleansing, the last ballot of each voter list encrypts the last vote cast with the valid credential, if any, or an encryption of zero. To do so, for each voter, the tally servers generates a *cleansed list* that will contain the same number of ballots of the voter list. In Fig. 2 the cleansed list for voter V_0 is $L_{\hat{V}_0}$. The tally servers populate the cleansed list by checking, in order, the credential encrypted in each ballot from the corresponding voter list. If the ballot has the correct credential, the tally servers add to the cleansed list a new ballot that is the re-randomization of the ballot with the correct credential. Otherwise, the new ballot is the re-randomization of the previous ballot in the cleansed list. The tally servers re-randomize tha ballots using ElGamal re-encryption and prove in zero-knowledge (i.e. using disjunctive NIZKP) the correctness of the re-randomization. The last ballots in the cleansing lists can homomorphically added to obtain the final tally.

3.1 Threat Model

The list of participants is the same as JCJ. We consider voters, a registration authority, a bulletin board, and tally servers. Differently from JCJ, we require an authority (e.g. the tally servers) generating noise ballots. Voters may be dishonest and collude with the attacker. The attacker may attempt to coerce honest voters. The registration authority provides credentials to voters therefore is assumed to be honest. The bulletin board is assumed to present the same content to all readers therefore is an honest, append-only list of data that is publicly accessible. Therefore, it is susceptible to denial of service attacks as it receives anonymous ballots. The tally servers are responsible for tallying and publishing the final election results on the bulletin board. These servers form an honest majority t-out-of-n threshold encryption system and are trusted for coercion resistance. The communication channels between the voters and the registrar are untappable, and the voters send their ballots to the bulletin board via anonymous channels. Civitas [7] is an example of techniques that implement distributed participants with the related trust assumptions outlined above. Finally, we consider a computationally bounded adversary whose aim is to break ballot privacy, verifiability, deniable revoting, and coercion resistance.

3.2 Cryptographic Primitives

The only two cryptographic primitives required in our scheme are ElGamal encryption and NIZKP.

Let λ and κ be the security parameters. Let $\mathbb{G}$ be a cyclic group of prime order p and generators $g, g_1, g_2 \in \mathbb{G}$. We denote the integers modulo p with $\mathbb{Z}_p$ and write $r \xleftarrow{\$} \mathbb{Z}_p$ for r being chosen uniformly from $\mathbb{Z}_p$. The encryption scheme is the modified ElGamal encryption scheme [19] for group $\mathbb{G}$, with generators g_1, g_2 of order p and message space $\mathbb{M} = g_1{}^b$, where $b = \{0, 1\}$ consisting of the following algorithms:

- $\mathsf{TKeyGen}(1^\lambda)$, which, on input of security parameter 1^λ, outputs a pair of ElGamal decryption and encryption keys (sk, pk) where $sk = (x_1, x_2), x_1, x_2 \xleftarrow{\$} \mathbb{Z}_p$, and $pk = g_1^{x_1} g_2^{x_2}$.
- $\mathsf{Enc}(pk, m; r)$, which, given a public key pk, a message $m \in \mathbb{M}$, and some randomness $r \xleftarrow{\$} \mathbb{Z}_p$, outputs a ciphertext $(c_1, c_2, c_3) = (g_1^r, g_2^r, m \cdot pk^r)$.
- $\mathsf{Dec}(sk, ct = (c_1, c_2, c_3))$, which outputs $m = (c_1)^{-x_1} \cdot (c_2)^{-x_2} \cdot c_3$.
- $\mathsf{ReEnc}(pk, ct = (c_1, c_2, c_3); r)$, which, using randomness $r \xleftarrow{\$} \mathbb{Z}_p$, outputs the reencryption of ct namely $(c_1 \cdot g_1^r, c_2 \cdot g_2^r, c_3 \cdot pk^r)$.
- $\mathsf{CKeyGen}(1^\kappa)$ which, on input security parameter 1^κ, outputs the credential σ, where $\sigma \xleftarrow{\$} \mathbb{G}$.

For verifiability, we use NIZKP of knowledge based on the Fiat-Shamir transforma to prove relations. We define the following relations to verify the proper construction of a voter's ballot and the computation of the tally.

The *proof of well-formed encryption* assures the verifier that ct is an accurate encryption of a message m and randomness r known to the prover, using the public encryption key pk. The corresponding relation is defined as $R_{enc} = \{((ct, pk), (r, m)) \in R_{enc} \text{ iff } ct = \mathsf{Enc}(pk, m; r)\}$ to compute NIZKP of knowledge π_{enc}. We also prove that $m \in \mathbb{M}$, where $\mathbb{M}$ denotes the range of the messages.

The *proof of correct decryption* assures the verifier that ct is decrypted to m by applying the knowledge of secret encryption key sk on ciphertext ct. The decryption relation is defined as $R_{dec} = \{((pk, m, ct), sk) \in R_{dec} \text{ iff } m = \mathsf{Dec}(sk, ct) \wedge pk = g^{sk}\}$ to compute the NIZKP of knowledge π_{dec}.

The *proof of correct re-encryption* assures the verifier that ct' is a valid re-encryption of ciphertext ct using randomness r with respect to a public encryption key pk. The corresponding relation $R_{r_{enc}}$ is defined as $R_{r_{enc}} = \{((pk, ct, ct'), r) \in R_{r_{enc}} \text{ iff } ct' = \mathsf{ReEnc}(pk, ct; r)\}$ to compute a NIZKP of knowledge $\pi_{r_{enc}}$.

We use disjunctive NIZKP of knowledge as introduced by Cramer et al. [9] for verifiable cleansing in the tally phase. Let $R_d = R_1 \vee R_2$ and $x = (x_1, x_2)$, a disjunctive NIZKP relation R is defined as follows:

$$\{((x_1, x_2), \omega) \in R_d \text{ iff } (x_1, \omega) \in R_1 \vee (x_2, \omega) \in R_2\}$$

To generate a proof for a defined relation, we use the function $\mathsf{Proof}(x, \omega)$, which takes a public statement x and a secret witness ω of the defined relation, and outputs the corresponding proof. We assume that the function Proof takes the corresponding relation as implicit input. For disjunctive NIZKP of knowledge, we use the function $\mathsf{DisjProof}(x, \omega)$ to compute the related proof.

4 Formal Description

The algorithms defining the schemes are as follow.

- $\mathsf{Setup}(1^\lambda, (t, n), \mathbb{I}, \mathbb{C}) \rightarrow ((pk_T, sk_T), (pk_R, sk_R))$: on input of the security parameter 1^λ, threshold parameter (t, n) electoral roll $\mathbb{I}$, and candidate list $\mathbb{C}$ computes $(pk_T, sk_T) \xleftarrow{\$} \mathsf{TKeyGen}(1^\lambda)$ and $(pk_R, sk_R) \xleftarrow{\$} \mathsf{SKeyGen}(1^\lambda)$.
- $\mathsf{Register}(1^\kappa, \mathbb{I}, (sk_R, pk_R), pk_T) \rightarrow (\mathbb{L}, \{(id, \sigma, \hat{ct})\}_{id \in \mathbb{I}}$: on input of the security parameter 1^κ, sk_R, pk_R, pk_T, and $\mathbb{I}$ do the following.
    - Compute $\sigma \xleftarrow{\$} \mathsf{CKeyGen}(1^\kappa)$ to create a voting credential for voter id.
    - Compute $\hat{ct} \xleftarrow{\$} \mathsf{Enc}(pk_T, \sigma; r_{id})$
    - Add the tuple $(id, \hat{ct})$ to the registered voter roll $\mathbb{L}$.
    - Append the signed voter roll $\mathbb{L}$, to the public bulletin board, $\mathcal{BB}$.
    - Return $(id, \sigma, \hat{ct})$ to the voter id.
- $\mathsf{Vote}(\hat{ct}, \sigma, c) \rightarrow \beta$: on implicit input the tallier public key pk_T, secret credential σ, candidate option $c \in \mathbb{C}$, do the following.

- Compute $ct_\sigma \xleftarrow{\$} \mathsf{Enc}(pk_T, \sigma; r)$ and $ct_c \xleftarrow{\$} \mathsf{Enc}(pk_T, c; r_c)$.
- Run $\pi \xleftarrow{\$} \mathsf{Proof}(x, \omega)$, where $x = (pk_T, \hat{ct}, ct_\sigma, ct_c)$ and $\omega = (r_c, c, r, \sigma)$:

$$(x, \omega) \in R_\beta \text{ iff } ct_c = \mathsf{Enc}(pk_T, c; r_c) \wedge ct_\sigma = \mathsf{Enc}(pk_T, \sigma; r).$$

- Return the ballot $\beta = (ct_c, ct_\sigma, \hat{ct}, \pi)$ on $\mathcal{BB}$.

- $\mathsf{Validate}(\mathcal{BB}, \beta) \rightarrow \top/\bot$: on input a ballot $\beta = (ct_v, ct_\sigma, \hat{ct}, \pi)$ and implicit input (pk_T, L) checks that i) $\hat{ct} \in L$, ii) β does not already appear in $\mathcal{BB}$, and iii) $\top \leftarrow \mathsf{Verify}(x, \pi)$. If any of the checks fail, it returns $\bot$ otherwise $\top$.

- $\mathsf{Append}(\mathcal{BB}, \beta) \rightarrow \mathcal{BB}$: on input a ballot $\beta = (ct_c, ct_\sigma, \hat{ct}, \pi)$ updates $\mathcal{BB}$ by appending the ballot β.

- $\mathsf{VerifyVote}(\mathcal{BB}, \hat{ct}, \sigma, c, \beta) \rightarrow \bot/\top$: on input a ballot $\beta = (ct_c, ct_\sigma, \hat{ct}, \pi)$, secret credential σ, public credential $\hat{ct}$, and vote option c checks that β is on $\mathcal{BB}$ and that $\mathsf{Validate}(\mathcal{BB}, \beta) = \top$. If any of the checks fail return $\bot$ otherwise $\top$.

- $\mathsf{Tally}(\mathcal{BB}, sk_T) \rightarrow (R, \Pi)$: on input $\mathcal{BB}$ and the decryption key sk_T apply cleansing and compute the election result as follows: Let $N = |\mathbb{L}|$, where $\mathbb{L}$ is the set of public credentials of registered voters on $\mathcal{BB}$. Let $L_{\hat{ct}}$ be a voter list of ordered ballots based on the submission time such that $\hat{ct} \in \mathbb{L}$, where $\beta_i = (ct_{c_i}, ct_{\sigma_i}, \hat{ct}, \pi_i)$ and $\beta_i \in L_{\hat{ct}}$. Filter the ballots as follows:
  - Arrange the ballots with public credential $\hat{ct}$ in the order they appear on $\mathcal{BB}$ and store them in $L_{\hat{ct}}$.
  - Initialise the cleansed list $L_{\hat{ct}_T} = [\hat{ct}, ct_0]$ for each $\hat{ct} \in \mathbb{L}$, where $ct_0 = \mathsf{Enc}(pk_T, 0; 0)$ denotes a null vote ballot.
  - Run $\mathsf{Append}(\mathcal{BB}, L_{\hat{ct}}) \rightarrow \mathcal{BB}$ and $\mathsf{Append}(\mathcal{BB}, L_{\hat{ct}_T}) \rightarrow \mathcal{BB}$.
  - If $\mathsf{Dec}(sk_T, \frac{ct_{\sigma_i}}{\hat{ct}}) = 1$, given $ct_{\sigma_i} \in \beta_i$ and $\hat{ct} \in L_{\hat{ct}_T}$, then compute $ct_{T_i} \xleftarrow{\$} \mathsf{ReEnc}(pk_T, ct_{c_i}; r_{T_i})$ and run $\pi_i \xleftarrow{\$} \mathsf{DisjProof}(x, \omega)$, where $x = (L_{\hat{ct}}, L_{\hat{ct}_T}, pk_T, ct_{T_i})$ and $\omega = (sk_T, r_{T_i})$

$$(x, \omega) \in R_{eq} \text{ iff } ct_{T_i} = \mathsf{ReEnc}(pk_T, ct_{c_i}; r_{T_i}) \wedge \mathsf{Dec}(sk_T, \frac{ct_{\sigma_i}}{\hat{ct}}) = 1$$

  - Else compute $ct_{T_i} \xleftarrow{\$} \mathsf{ReEnc}(pk_T, ct_{T_{i-1}}; r_{T_i})$ and run $\pi \xleftarrow{\$} \mathsf{DisjProof}(x, \omega)$, where $x = (L_{\hat{ct}}, L_{\hat{ct}_T}, pk_T, ct_{T_i})$ and $\omega = (sk_T, r_{T_i})$

$$(x, \omega) \in R^{Uneq} \text{ iff } ct_{T_i} = \mathsf{ReEnc}(pk, ct_{T_{i-1}}; r_{T_i}) \wedge \mathsf{Dec}(sk_T, \frac{ct_{\sigma_i}}{\hat{ct}}) \neq 1$$

  where $R_T = R^{eq} \vee R^{Uneq}$ and $i \geq 1$.
  - Set (ct_{T_i}, π_i) as a last vote ballot in $L_{\hat{ct}_T}$ and run $\mathsf{Append}(\mathcal{BB}, L_{\hat{ct}_T}) \rightarrow \mathcal{BB}$.

  Compute $T_i = \prod_{k=1}^{N} ct_k^i$, where $ct_k \in L_{\hat{ct}_T}$ denotes the last vote ciphertext. The tally t_i for candidate c_i is produced by decrypting T_i with the key sk_T. Compute the result $R = (t_1, \ldots, t_{|C|})$ and Π, i.e. all Fiat-Shamir proofs including the proof for correct decryption of the result. Output (R, Π).

- $\mathsf{VerifyTally}(\mathcal{BB}, (R, \Pi)) \rightarrow \bot/\top$: on input $\mathcal{BB}$, result (R, Π), verifies the correctness of (R, Π) on $\mathcal{BB}$. If any of the checks fail return $\bot$ otherwise $\top$.

The scheme is organized in the following four phases.

Setup phase: The algorithm $\mathsf{Setup}(1^\lambda, (t,n), \mathbb{I}, \mathbb{C}) \rightarrow ((pk_T, sk_T), (pk_R, sk_R))$ allows, respectively, tallying servers and registrars to generate the key pairs $(pk_T, sk_T)^1$ and (pk_R, sk_R). The bulletin board $\mathcal{BB}$ is initialized with the lists of candidates $\mathbb{C}$, eligible voters identities $\mathbb{I}$, pk_R, and pk_T.

Registration phase: The registration authority registers the voter with $id \in \mathbb{I}$ to the election by running $\mathsf{Register}(1^\kappa, \mathbb{I}, sk_R, pk_R, pk_T) \rightarrow (\mathbb{L}, \{(\sigma_{id}, \hat{ct}_{\sigma_{id}})\}_{id \in \mathbb{I}}))$, which returns to each voter id, a secret credential $\sigma_{id} \in \mathbb{G}$, and a public credential $\hat{ct}_{\sigma_{id}}$. Then it sets a voting roll $\mathbb{L}$ of the voters' public credential (e.g. $(id, \hat{ct}_{\sigma_{id}})$). Finally, it executes $\mathsf{Append}(\mathcal{BB}, \mathbb{L}))$, which appends the signed $\mathbb{L}$ on $\mathcal{BB}$.

Voting phase: A voter makes a choice of a candidate from $\mathbb{C}$, selects a public credential $\hat{ct}_{\sigma_{id}}$ from $\mathbb{L}$ on $\mathcal{BB}$, encrypts and generates the proof for their ballots. The voter then submits their ballot to $\mathcal{BB}$ through an anonymous channel. The voters use NIZKP to prove the relation R_β. The voter proves in zero-knowledge that they know the vote and their choice is well-formed. The voter runs $\mathsf{VerifyVote}(\mathcal{BB}, \hat{ct}, \sigma, c, \beta) \rightarrow \bot/\top$ to verify their ballot and check that it is included in the bulletin board.

Trustees generate noise ballots identical to the voters' ballots to provide re-voting deniability and participation privacy. To generate a noise ballot, the trustee computes $\mathsf{Vote}(pk_T, \sigma', \hat{ct}, c') \rightarrow \beta'$ using a fake credential σ' generated by the trustees and a random candidate $c' \in \mathbb{C}$. Both voters and trustees can generate these noise ballots.

Tallying phase: The tallying servers execute $\mathsf{Tally}(\mathcal{BB}, sk_T) \rightarrow (R, \Pi)$. Anyone can verify the process of tallying and result R of tallying by executing $\mathsf{VerifyTally}(\mathcal{BB}, R, \Pi)$, which checks Π w.r.t. $\mathcal{BB}$ and R. The tally servers use disjunctive NIZKP of knowledge π to prove that $(x, \omega) \in R_T$, where $R_T = R^{eq} \vee R^{Uneq}$. The tally phase proceeds as follows.

- The tallying servers eliminate ballots that contain invalid proofs or unregistered public credentials.
- The tallying servers arrange the ballots based on their public credentials. The ballots with credential $\hat{ct}$ are stored in the list $L_{\hat{ct}}$.
- The tallying servers initiate a list called $L_{\hat{ct}_T} = [ct_0, \hat{ct}]$ corresponds to the original list $L_{\hat{ct}}$.
- The tallying servers generate a new vote ballot ct_T corresponding with $\beta_{\hat{ct}} = (ct_v, ct_\sigma, \pi) \in L_{\hat{ct}}$. If $\mathsf{Dec}(sk_T, \frac{ct_{\sigma_i}}{\hat{ct}}) = 1$, then ct_T is a re-randomiztion of $ct_c \in \beta$. The tally servers prove $(x, \omega) \in R^{eq}$ and simulate the relation R^{Uneq}. Otherwise, they re-randomize the last vote ciphertext in $L_{\hat{ct}_T}$. In this case, the they prove $(x, \omega) \in R^{Uneq}$ and simulate the R^{eq}.
- In homomorphic tallying, the final ballots of each tally list $L_{\hat{ct}_T}$ are multiplied, and the resulting ciphertext is decrypted. The tally servers provide proof of correct decryption. Furthermore, the steps of tallying with corresponding proofs are added to $\mathcal{BB}$ to ensure universal verifiability.

---

[1] The secret key is generated in a distributed way, thus no single server learns the key.

Algorithm 1. RealCR

Require: $\mathcal{A}, 1^\lambda, 1^\kappa, n_A, \mathbb{I}, \mathbb{C}, \mathcal{B}$

1: $\mathcal{BB} \leftarrow \emptyset$
2: $((pk_T, sk_T), (pk_R, sk_R)) \leftarrow \mathsf{Setup}(1^\lambda, 1^\kappa, \mathbb{I}, \mathbb{C})$
3: $\{\sigma_i; i \in \mathbb{I}\}, \mathbb{L} \leftarrow \mathsf{Register}(1^\kappa, \mathbb{I}, (sk_R, pk_R), pk_T)$
4: $A \leftarrow \mathcal{A}(\mathbb{L})$ ▷ corrupt voters
5: $(j, c_\alpha) \leftarrow \mathcal{A}(\{\sigma_i; i \in A\})$ ▷ coerce a voter j who has vote intention c_α
6: **if** $|A| \neq n_A \vee j \notin \mathbb{I}\backslash A \vee c_\alpha \notin \mathbb{C} \cup \{\phi\}$ **then** Return 0
7: **end if**
8: $B \leftarrow \mathcal{B}(\mathbb{I}\backslash A, \mathbb{C})$
9:        ▷ samples a sequence of pairs (i, c_i) with $i \in \mathbb{I}\backslash A) \cup \{-i \in \mathbb{Z}|i > 0\}$ and $c_i \in \mathbb{C}$
10: **for** $(-i, *) \in B, i \in \mathbb{I}$ **do** $\sigma_i^f \leftarrow \mathsf{Fakecred}()$ ▷ ballots sent for the voter i with invalid creds
11: **end for**
12: $b \xleftarrow{\$} \{0, 1\}$
13: $\sigma_j^f \leftarrow \sigma_j$
14: **if** $b == 1$ **then**
15:        Remove all $(j, *) \in B$
16: **else**
17:        Remove all $(j, *) \in B$ but the last, which is replaced by (j, c_α) if $c_\alpha \neq \phi$ and removed otherwise
18:        $\sigma_j^f \leftarrow \mathsf{Fakecred}(\sigma_j)$
19: **end if**
20: $\mathcal{A}(\sigma_j^f)$ ▷ A learns σ_j^f
21: **for** $(i, c_i) \in B$ (in this order) **do**
22:        $M \leftarrow \mathcal{A}(\mathcal{BB})$ ▷ cast ballots
23:        $\mathcal{BB} \leftarrow \mathcal{BB} \cup \{m \in M | \mathsf{Validate}(m, BB) = 1\}$
24:        $\mathcal{BB} \leftarrow \mathcal{BB} \cup \{\mathsf{Vote}(i, \sigma_i, c_i)\} \cup \{\mathsf{Vote}(i, \sigma_i^f, c_i)\}$
25: **end for**
26: $M \leftarrow \mathcal{A}(\mathcal{BB}, \text{"last honest ballot sent"})$
27: $\mathcal{BB} \leftarrow BB \cup \{m \in M | \mathsf{Validate}(m, BB) = 1\}$
28: $(R, \Pi) \leftarrow \mathsf{Tally}(BB, sk_T)$
29: $b' \leftarrow \mathcal{A}()$

---

5   Security

We prove that our scheme ensures coercion resistance under the DDH assumption in the random oracle model. We informally argue that our scheme provides ballot privacy and universal verifiability. Our scheme satisfies ballot privacy if the underlying ballot encryption scheme is non-malleable under chosen plaintext attack (NM-CPA) secure under the DDH assumption in the random oracle model [5]. Universal verifiability means that anyone can refer to the public bulletin board to verify the correctness of the tally result produced by tally servers.

Algorithm 2. IdealCR

Require: $\mathcal{A}, 1^\lambda, 1^\kappa, n_A, \mathbb{I}, \mathbb{C}, \mathcal{B}$

1: $A \leftarrow \mathcal{A}(1^\lambda, 1^\kappa)$ ▷ corrupt voters
2: $(j, c_\alpha) \leftarrow \mathcal{A}()$ ▷ coerce a voter j who has vote intention c_α
3: **if** $|A| \neq n_A \vee j \notin \mathbb{I} \backslash A \vee c_\alpha \notin \mathbb{C} \cup \{\phi\}$ **then** Return 0
4: **end if**
5: $B \leftarrow \mathcal{B}(\mathbb{I} \backslash A, \mathbb{C})$ ▷ sample a sequence of pairs (i, c_i) with $i \in \mathbb{I} \backslash A) \cup \{i \in \mathbb{Z} | i < 0\}$
     and $c_i \in \mathbb{C}$
6: $b \xleftarrow{\$} \{0, 1\}$
7: **if** $b == 1$ **then**
8:      Remove all $(j, *) \in B$
9: **else**
10:      Remove all $(j, *) \in B$ but the last, which is replaced by (j, c_α) if $c_\alpha \neq \phi$ and
     removed otherwise
11: **end if**
12: $(c_i)_{i \in A}, c_\beta \leftarrow \mathcal{A}(|B_i|)_{i \in \mathbb{I}})$ ▷ $|B_i|$ is a number of pairs $(i, c_i) \in B$ and $(-i, c_i) \in B$
     for voter i.
13: **if** $(b == 1) \wedge (c_\beta \in \mathbb{C})$ **then**   ▷ c_β is the coercer vote for the voter j
14:      $B \leftarrow B \cup \{(j, c_\beta)\}$
15:      $B \leftarrow B \cup \{(i, c_i) | i \in A, c_i \in \mathbb{C}\}$
16: **end if**
17: $X \leftarrow result(cleanse(B))$
18: $b' \leftarrow \mathcal{A}(X)$
19: Return 1 if $b' == b$ else 0

5.1 Coercion Resistance

Our scheme ensures coercion resistance, meaning that a coercer should not be able to determine the validity of a voter's credential based on the election result. Additionally, the data published on the bulletin board during the voting and tally phases should not reveal whether a registered voter abstained from voting or revoted. It is assumed that the bulletin board is honest and that the communication channels between the voters and the public board are anonymous. The registration is untappable and the registration authority and the tally servers are trusted for coercion resistance. We adapt the definition of coercion-resistance by Cortier et al. [8] that takes into account revoting and the addition of noise ballots by tally servers. The main modification is in the ideal experiment in which, instead of giving the total number of ballots, we give to the adversary $\mathcal{A}^I$ in the ideal experiment each voter's number of ballots (including noise ballots). In doing so, the adversary $\mathcal{A}^R$ in the real experiment and $\mathcal{A}^I$ have the same knowledge about the number of ballots regarding a public credential, and not about the number of ballots cast by a voter. For simplification, we consider a single honest tallier. For a quantitative analysis of the effectiveness of coercion resistance depending on noise generation we refer to the one done in [25].

Theorem 1. *Our scheme provides coercion resistance under the DDH assumption in the random oracle model.*

Proof. We construct a probabilistic polynomial time algorithm S which is given a DDH test instance to simulate the election protocol process for $\mathcal{A}^R$ (Algorithm 1). Our goal is to prove that the advantage of $\mathcal{A}^R$ in the real experiment is only negligibly higher than that of $\mathcal{A}^I$ (Algorithm 2). This is important because if there is a non-negligible advantage $\mathcal{A}^R$ over $\mathcal{A}^I$, then the simulator S can solve the DDH problem with a non-negligible probability.

The group of voters who have been corrupted is denoted by A, while the voters who have valid credentials are denoted by $S = \mathcal{I} \setminus A$. $\mathcal{B}$ denotes a distribution of pairs (i, c) where $c \in \mathbb{C}$ and i represents a voter with valid credentials. A voter with fake credentials or noise ballots, is represented by $(-i, c)$. The distribution $\mathcal{B}$ models a voter's abstention with $(i, *)$, revoting with i appears in several pairs, and $(-i, c)$ as a ballot with a fake credential for the voter i. The ballots with fake credentials can be added either by any participant. Note that both the real and ideal experiments assume that there are noise ballots in $\mathcal{B}$ regardless of how many ballots a voter casts.

The challenger of DDH problem constructs the test quadruple (g_1, g_2, h_1, h_2) based on the coin d. If $d = 1$, the simulator S receives a DDH instance; otherwise, a random instance is given. The simulator S, which is given (g_1, g_2, h_1, h_2) and a distribution $B \in \mathcal{B}$, simulates the election process for $\mathcal{A}^R$. If the test instance is DDH instance, $\mathcal{A}^R$'s view will be the same as their view in the real coercion-resistance experiment. Otherwise, $\mathcal{A}^R$'s view will be the same as $\mathcal{A}^I$'s in the ideal coercion-resistance experiment. The election process is simulated as follows:

1. **Setup.** Given the test quadruple (g_1, g_2, h_1, h_2), the simulator S who controls the tally servers and registrar simulates the setup phase for $\mathcal{A}^R$. The simulator S, who knows the secret key of the tally server $sk_T = (x_1, x_2)$ and the secret key of the registrar sk_R outputs the electoral roll $\mathbb{I}$, the candidate list $\mathbb{C}$, the register keys (pk_R, sk_R), and tally server keys (pk_T, sk_T), where $pk_T = (g_1^{x_1} g_2^{x_2}, (g_1, g_2))$.
2. **Registration.** The simulator S generates credentials $\{\sigma_i \in \mathbb{G}\}_{i \in \mathcal{I}}$, encrypts them using pk_T, stores them in $\mathbb{L}$, and publishes the registration list $\mathbb{L}$.
3. **Adversarial corruption.** $\mathcal{A}^R$ selects a set A of n_A voters to corrupt.
4. **Adversarial coercion.** $\mathcal{A}^R$ selects the voter that they want to coerce and also chooses the vote c_α as the coerced voter's vote.
5. **Validity check** The simulation terminates if any of the following happens: $|A| \neq n_A$, $j \notin \mathcal{I} \setminus A$, or $c_\alpha \notin \mathbb{C} \cup \{\varnothing\}$ where $\varnothing$ denotes the choice to abstain.
6. **Bit flip.** Given a distribution B, S flips a random bit $b \in \{0, 1\}$. If $b = 0$ and $c_\alpha \neq \varnothing$, S eliminates all valid pairs of voter j except the last one, replaces the last pair $(j, c) \in B$ with (j, c_α), and gives a fake credential σ^f to $\mathcal{A}^R$. On the other hand, if $b = 1$, S removes all valid pairs $(j, c) \in B$ and gives the coerced voter's credential σ to $\mathcal{A}^R$.
7. **Adversarial ballot casting.** $\mathcal{A}^R$ casts some of the ballots with credentials of the corrupted voters, as well as that of the coerced voter j.
8. **Honest voter simulation.** S generates a ballot for all pairs in B, namely the honest voters and their noise ballots as follows:
   - S selects the public credential $\hat{ct}$ from the registered voting roll $\mathbb{L}$ corresponding with voter i.

- $\mathcal{S}$ computes $\mathsf{Dec}(sk_T, \hat{ct}) = \sigma_i$. For a noise ballot, it generates a random fake credential σ_i^f. Note that $\mathcal{S}$ knows the encryption secret key sk_T.
- Given test quadruple (g_1, g_2, h_1, h_2) and the encryption secret key $sk_T = (x_1, x_2)$, $\mathcal{S}$ computes new public key $\bar{pk}_T = (h_1^{x_1} h_2^{x_2})$ where (h_1, h_2) denotes corresponding the new generators.
- Given the vote ciphertext $\bar{ct}_{c_i} = (h_1^{r_{c_i}}, h_2^{r_{c_i}}, c_i(\bar{pk}_T)^{r_{c_i}})$ and credential ciphertext $\bar{ct} = (h_1^{r_i}, h_2^{r_i}, \sigma_i(\bar{pk}_T)^{r_i})$, $\mathcal{S}$ simulates the zero-knowledge proof π_i using programmable random oracle, and returns $\bar{\beta}_i = (\bar{ct}_{c_i}, \bar{ct}_{\sigma_i}, \hat{ct}, \pi_i)$.

  Note that the simulated honest voter ballot, denoted by $\bar{\beta}_i$, is different from the actual ballot β_i, which is generated by an honest voter i using a public key $pk_T = (g_1^{x_1} g_2^{x_2}, (g_1, g_2))$. We will demonstrate the advantage of $\mathcal{A}^R$ to distinguish this difference is equivalent to determining whether (g_1, g_2, h_1, h_2) is a Decisional Diffie-Hellman (DDH) instance (i.e., $d = 1$) or not.

9. **Adversarial last ballot casting** Adversary $\mathcal{A}^R$ casts the final set of ballots corresponding with the corrupted voters and the coerced voter j.
10. **Tallying** $\mathcal{S}$ simulates an honest tallier using the secret key sk_T. The correctness of each step in this phase can be verified publicly.
    a. **Proof checking** $\mathcal{S}$ verifies the proof of the ballot cast by $\mathcal{A}^R$. It then initialises the lists $(L_{\hat{ct}}, L_{\hat{ct}_T})$ for each $\hat{ct} \in L$ and for the all cast ballots.
    b. **Checking credentials and generating tally ballots** $\mathcal{S}$ generates cleansed ballots for $L_{\hat{ct}_T}$. It uses sk_T to decrypt the comparison result of credentials. Then $\mathcal{S}$ generates a voting ciphertext corresponding with each ballot $\beta \in L_{\hat{ct}}$ and the relation R_T. It then simulates a NIZKP of knowledge for the relation R_T. Note that $\mathcal{S}$ re-randomizes the adversary ballots using public key pk_T and honest voters using public key $\bar{pk}_T$.
    c. **Decryption** $\mathcal{S}$ homomorphically adds the last ballots from $\{L_{\hat{ct}_T}\}_{\hat{ct} \in \mathcal{I} \setminus A}$ and decrypts the result using secret key sk_T. Similarly, the last ballots of $\{L_{\hat{ct}_T}\}_{\hat{ct} \in A}$ are added and decrypted. $\mathcal{S}$ computes the final result R and simulates the decrypting proof Π.
12. **Adversarial output.** Adversary $\mathcal{A}^R$ outputs a bit b'. $\mathcal{S}$ returns $d' = b'$ for the test instance of DDH problem.

If $d = d' = 1$, namely, $(g_1, g_2, h_1, h_2) = (g, g^a, g^b, g^{ab})$, the view of $\mathcal{A}^R$ from the simulation of the election process is indistinguishable from the real coercion resistance experiment $\mathbf{Exp}^{cr-real}$. Additionally, if $d = d' = 0$, the view of $\mathcal{A}^R$ from the simulation of the election is equal to the $\mathcal{A}^I$ in the ideal coercion resistance experiment $\mathbf{Exp}^{cr-ideal}$. The adversary $\mathcal{A}^I$ in experiment $\mathbf{Exp}^{cr-ideal}$ is given a list of numbers corresponding to the number of ballots per voter i and the final result. This means that the advantage of $\mathcal{S}$ in distinguishing the test (g_1, g_2, h_1, h_2) in DDH problem can be reduced to the advantage of $\mathcal{A}^R$ in $\mathbf{Exp}^{cr-real}$ over $\mathcal{A}^I$ in $\mathbf{Exp}^{cr-ideal}$. Formally,

$$Adv_{\mathcal{S}}^{DDH} = Adv_{\mathcal{A}^R}(\mathbf{Exp}^{cr-real}) - Adv_{\mathcal{A}^I}(\mathbf{Exp}^{cr-ideal}).$$

We now show that if $d = 1$ i.e. $(g_1, g_2, h_1, h_2) = (g, g^a, g^b, g^{ab})$. The view of $\mathcal{A}^R$ in the simulation process of $\mathbf{Exp}^{cr-real}$ is indistinguishable from the view of $\mathcal{A}^R$ in $\mathbf{Exp}^{cr-real}$. Let $\bar{pk}_T = (h_1^{x_1} h_2^{x_2}, (h_1, h_2))$ be the encryption public key used by $\mathcal{S}$, $\bar{ct}_c = \mathsf{Enc}(\bar{pk}_T, c; r)$, $c \in \mathbb{C}$. Since $d = 1$ we have $h_1 = g_1^b$, $h_2 = g_2^b$,

$$\mathsf{Enc}(\bar{pk}_T, c; r) = (h_1^r, h_2^r, c(\bar{pk}_T)^r) = (g_1^{br}, g_2^{br}, c(g_1^{x_1} g_2^{x_2})^{br}) = \mathsf{Enc}(pk_T, c; br)$$

The equation above shows that $\mathsf{Enc}(\bar{pk}_T, c; r)$ and $\mathsf{Enc}(pk_T, c; br)$ are different in the randomness. $\mathsf{Enc}(pk_T, c; br)$ and $\mathsf{Enc}(pk_T, c; t)$ have the same distribution of randomness for $t \overset{\$}{\leftarrow} \mathbb{Z}_p$, hence $Pr[\mathcal{S} = 1 | d = 1] = Adv_{\mathcal{A}^R}(\mathbf{Exp}^{cr-real})$, where $Adv_{\mathcal{A}^R}$ is defined as $|Pr[\mathbf{Exp}_{ES,\mathcal{A}^R}^{cr-real}(1^\lambda, 1^\kappa, \mathbb{I}, \mathbb{C}, n_c) = 1] - \frac{1}{2}|$.

We also prove that if $d = 0$ then $(g_1, g_2, h_1, h_2) = (g, g^a, g^b, g^z)$ where $z \overset{\$}{\leftarrow} \mathbb{Z}_p$. The view of $\mathcal{A}^R$ in the simulation process of $\mathbf{Exp}^{cr-real}$ can be presented by the view of $\mathcal{A}^I$ in $\mathbf{Exp}^{cr-ideal}$. Let $az' = z$ and $b + b' = z'$,

$$
\begin{aligned}
\mathsf{Enc}(\bar{pk}_T, c; r) &= (h_1^r, h_2^r, c(\bar{pk}_T)^r) \\
&= (g_1^{br}, g_2^{zr}, c(g_1^{bx_1} g_2^{zx_2})^r) \\
&= (g_1^{br}, g_2^{zr+br-br}, c(g_1^{bx_1} g_2^{rzx_2 - rbx_2 + rbx_2})) \\
&= (g_1^t, g_2^t g_2^{zr-br}, c(pk_T)^t g_2^{rzx_2 - rbx_2}) \\
&= (g_1^t, g_2^t g_2^{t'}, c(pk_T)^t g_2^{t'}))
\end{aligned}
$$

The random group element $g_3^{t'}$ completely hides vote c, and the adversary $\mathcal{A}^R$ does not learn anything from $\mathsf{Enc}(\bar{pk}_T, c; r)$. In this case, the view of $\mathcal{A}^R$ in the simulation process of $\mathbf{Exp}^{cr-real}$ can be compared to the view of $\mathcal{A}^I$ in $\mathbf{Exp}^{cr-ideal}$ where in the latter $\mathcal{A}^I$ is given a list containing the total number of ballots of each voter as $Pr[\mathcal{S} = 1 | d = 0] = Adv_{\mathcal{A}^I}(\mathbf{Exp}^{cr-ideal})$. $\square$

5.2 Ballot Privacy

A voting scheme ensures ballot privacy if the information published during the election does not reveal how a voter voted. We informally show that our scheme achieves ballot privacy based on the following assumptions:

- the ballot encryption scheme with the NIZKP of knowledge is NM-CPA secure
- the registrar and the public bulletin board are honest
- up to t talliers and a subset of voters can be corrupted

A voting system can be vulnerable to replay attacks if an attacker can copy a voter's ballot from the bulletin board and then submit it as their own legitimate ballot, violating ballot privacy. Our ballot encryption scheme includes NIZKPoK, which prevents malleability during the voting phase. Since the registrar and the majority of talliers are honest, no legitimate ballot can be generated with honest voter credentials. In the tally phase, the manipulation of the voting ballot beyond re-randomization and nullifying defined in the relation R_T is prevented, as the talliers generate NIZKPoK for each ballot during the tally phase.

6 Verifiability

For verifiability, we consider the voting device being trusted and an adversary that can corrupt a subset of voters. First, we show that the final result is accurate and computed on the last ballots on the bulletin board. Assume that the adversary outputs a set of final ballots, the result R, and the corresponding proof Π at the tally phase. The *last* ballots from the tally processed lists namely $\{L_{\hat{ct}_T}\}_{\hat{ct} \in \mathbb{L}}$ form a set i.e., $T = \{ct_{T_1}, ct_{T_2}, \ldots, ct_{T_n}\}$. The set T, the result R, and the proof of valid decryption are published on the $\mathcal{BB}$. The homomorphic property of ElGamal and the soundness of proof of valid decryption verifies that the result R is obtained from the decryption of $\Pi_{i=1}^n ct_{T_i}$. We can conclude that $\mathsf{VerifyTally}(R, \Pi)$ only returns $\top$, when R is the correct result of $T = \{ct_{T_1}, ct_{T_2}, \ldots, ct_{T_n}\}$ on $\mathcal{BB}$.

We show that each ballot $\beta = (ct_c, ct_\sigma, \hat{ct}, \pi)$ on $\mathcal{BB}$ corresponds to one of the following sets: i) the ballots of the honest voters who have checked their ballots; ii) the ballots with fake credential σ^f; iii) the ballots of the corrupted voters.

The knowledge soundness of the proof π on the ballot β ensures that β is well-formed and valid. Thus, one can verify that the ballot β on $\mathcal{BB}$ is either a well-formed ballot with real or fake credential. Given that i) the registration authority is honest, ii) up to the threshold of tallier are dishonest, iii) DDH problem assumption holds, and iv) the knowledge-soundness of NIZKP proves that if $\beta \in \mathcal{BB}$ has a valid credential, it is cast by either honest voters or corrupted voter. In addition, the adversary cannot generate a new ballot with a legitimate credential except by using the corrupted voter's credential. The cleansing process on the tuples $(ct_c, ct_\sigma) \in L_{\hat{ct}}$ result in either a vote $c \in \mathbb{C}$ or $c = 0$. The tally servers generate a new pair (ct_T, π_T) corresponding to $(ct_c, ct_\sigma) \in L_{\hat{ct}}$ based on the relation $R_T = R^{eq} \vee R^{Uneq}$. The knowledge soundness of the proof π_T ensures that ct_T is either a re-randomized version of ct_c or the null vote with deterministic randomness ct_0. According to relation R_T, ct_T is a re-randomization of ct_c if the decryption of ct_σ and $\hat{ct}$ are equal, or ct_0 otherwise.

Table 1. Tallying times (including cleansing) in our scheme.

nr. of ballots	1000			10000			100000			1000000		
nr. of candidates	2	4	10	2	4	10	2	4	10	2	4	10
tallying time	2 s	3 s	5 s	18 s	30 s	50 s	3 m	5 m	8 m	30 m	50 m	1.3 h

7 Performance and Conclusion

Our prototype is written in Python [14]. We use the zksk library [23] for the implementation of the disjunctive zero-knowledge proofs. We run our experiments in a M2 MacBook Pro laptop with 16GB of RAM. Table 1 shows the average times to tally the results according to different numbers of ballots and candidates. The prototype implementation confirms that the tallying time is linear to the number of the ballots, which also includes the noise ballots. Since each voter list can be cleansed independently from the others, cleansing is fully parallelizable in our scheme. This means that our scheme can accommodate a very large number of noise ballots and still provide fast tallying. Better performance can be achieved by implementing the scheme in a more efficient language.

In conclusion, we presented a scheme that provides an efficient cleansing procedure for coercion-resistant voting. Since any participant can cast a ballot for any candidate, the scheme is subject to ballot flooding attacks. This is mitigated by fast cleansing and can be further mitigated by using slot times for casting ballots. With this work, we introduce a new trade-off between coercion-resistance and efficiency, and aim at stimulating the voting community to further investigate the implications of publicly cleansing-hiding in coercion-resistant voting.

References

1. Achenbach, D., Kempka, C., Löwe, B., Müller-Quade, J.: Improved coercion-resistant electronic elections through deniable re-voting. {USENIX} J. Election Technol. Syst. ({JETS}) **3**, 26–45 (2015)
2. Aranha, D.F., Battagliola, M., Roy, L.: Faster coercion-resistant e-voting by encrypted sorting. Cryptol. ePrint Arch. (2023)
3. Araújo, R., Foulle, S., Traoré, J.: A practical and secure coercion-resistant scheme for remote elections. In: Dagstuhl Seminar Proceedings (2008)
4. Bernhard, D., Kulyk, O., Volkamer, M.: Security proofs for participation privacy and stronger verifiability for helios. Tech. rep, TU Darmstadt (2016)
5. Bernhard, D., Pereira, O., Warinschi, B.: How not to prove yourself: pitfalls of the fiat-shamir heuristic and applications to helios. In: ASIACRYPT 2012, pp. 626–643. Springer (2012). https://doi.org/10.1007/978-3-642-34961-4_38
6. Clark, J., Hengartner, U.: Selections: internet voting with over-the-shoulder coercion-resistance. In: Danezis, G. (ed.) Financial Cryptography and Data Security, pp. 47–61. Springer, Berlin Heidelberg, Berlin, Heidelberg (2012)
7. Clarkson, M.R., Chong, S., Myers, A.C.: Civitas: toward a secure voting system. In: 2008 IEEE Symposium on Security and Privacy (2008), pp. 354–368 (2008)
8. Cortier, V., Gaudry, P., Yang, Q.: Is the JCJ voting system really coercion-resistant? Cryptol. ePrint Arch. (2022)
9. Cramer, R., Damgård, I., Schoenmakers, B.: Proofs of partial knowledge and simplified design of witness hiding protocols. In: CRYPTO '94 (1994)
10. Cramer, R., Gennaro, R., Schoenmakers, B.: A secure and optimally efficient multi-authority election scheme. Eur. Trans. Telecommun. **8**(5), 481–490 (1997)
11. Elgamal, T.: A public key cryptosystem and a signature scheme based on discrete logarithms. Inf. Theor. IEEE Trans. **31**(4), 469–472 (1985)
12. EU Commission: Compendium of e-voting and other ICT practices. https://commission.europa.eu/publications/compendium-e-voting-and-other-ict-practices_en. 06 Dec 2023
13. Giustolisi, R., Garjan, M.S., Schuermann, C.: Thwarting last-minute voter coercion. In: 2024 IEEE Symposium on Security and Privacy (SP) (2024)

14. Giustolisi, R., Sheikhi, M.: Scheme prototype (2024). https://github.com/fgiustol/Evoteid24
15. Grewal, G.S., Ryan, M.D., Bursuc, S., Ryan, P.Y.: Caveat coercitor: coercion-evidence in electronic voting. In: IEEE Symposium on Security and Privacy (2013)
16. Haghighat, A.T., Dousti, M.S., Jalili, R.: An efficient and provably-secure coercion-resistant e-voting protocol. In: Privacy, Security and Trust (2013)
17. Haines, T., Mueller, J., Querejeta-Azurmendi, I.: Scalable coercion-resistant e-voting under weaker trust assumptions. In: ACM SAC'23 (2023)
18. Haines, T., Smyth, B.: Surveying definitions of coercion resistance. IACR Cryptol. ePrint Arch. 822 (2019)
19. Juels, A., Catalano, D., Jakobsson, M.: Coercion-resistant electronic elections. In: ACM Workshop on Privacy in the Electronic Society (2005)
20. Kulyk, O., Teague, V., Volkamer, M.: Extending helios towards private eligibility verifiability. In: E-Voting and Identity - VoteID 2015 (2015)
21. Kusters, R., Truderung, T., Vogt, A.: A game-based definition of coercion-resistance and its applications. In: IEEE Computer Security Foundations (2010)
22. Locher, P., Haenni, R., Koenig, R.E.: Coercion-resistant internet voting with ever-lasting privacy. In: Financial Cryptography and Data Security: FC 2016 International Workshops, pp. 161–175. Springer (2016). https://doi.org/10.1007/978-3-662-53357-4_11
23. Lueks, W., Kulynych, B., Fasquelle, J., Le Bail-Collet, S., Troncoso, C.: Zksk: a library for composable zero-knowledge proofs. In: WPES (2019)
24. Lueks, W., Querejeta-Azurmendi, I., Troncoso, C.: VoteAgain: a scalable coercion-resistant voting system. In: USENIX Security (2020)
25. Müller, J., Pejó, B., Pryvalov, I.: Devos: deniable yet verifiable vote updating. Proc. Priv. Enhancing Technol. (2024)
26. Rønne, P.B., Atashpendar, A., Gjøsteen, K., Ryan, P.Y.A.: Coercion-resistant voting in linear time via fully homomorphic encryption: towards a quantum-safe scheme. CoRR **abs/1901.02560** (2019)
27. Schoenmakers, B., Tuyls, P.: Practical two-party computation based on the conditional gate. In: International Conference on the Theory And Application of Cryptology and Information Security, pp. 119–136. Springer (2004). https://doi.org/10.1007/978-3-540-30539-2_10
28. Smyth, B.: Athena: a verifiable, coercion-resistant voting system with linear complexity. Cryptology ePrint Arch.(2019)
29. Spycher, O., Koenig, R., Haenni, R., Schläpfer, M.: Achieving meaningful efficiency in coercion-resistant, verifiable internet voting. Gesellschaft für Informatik eV (2012)
30. Spycher, O., Koenig, R., Haenni, R., Schläpfer, M.: A new approach towards coercion-resistant remote e-voting in linear time. In: Financial Cryptography and Data Security, pp. 182–189. Springer (2012). https://doi.org/10.1007/978-3-642-27576-0_15
31. Weber, S.G., Araujo, R., Buchmann, J.: On coercion-resistant electronic elections with linear work. In: ARES, pp. 908–916. IEEE (2007)

Absentee Online Voters in the Northwest Territories: Attitudes and Impacts on Participation

Nicole Goodman[1]([✉]) [ID], Helen A. Hayes[2] [ID], and Stephen Dunbar[3]

[1] Brock University, St. Catharines, ON, Canada
nicole.goodman@brocku.ca
[2] McGill University, Montreal, QC, Canada
helen.hayes@mcgill.ca
[3] Elections Northwest Territories, NWT, Yellowknife, NT, Canada
stephen_dunbar@electionsnwt.ca

Abstract. Despite being deployed in Canadian municipal elections since 2003, online ballots were not used in binding elections at higher levels of government until the Northwest Territories' adoption of online voting for absentee voters in its territorial elections in 2019 and 2023. Municipal and Indigenous use of online voting in Canada are well studied, but implementation at higher orders of government have not yet been examined. Drawing on an original data set of online voters in the 2023 Northwest Territories territorial election, we examine who votes online in higher order elections, attitudes towards the voting mode, and its impact on engagement. Throughout our analysis, we simultaneously compare these data to original data from online voter exit surveys conducted during the 2022 Ontario municipal elections. We find that uncommitted voters outside of Yellowknife would not have voted without the online option. Similarly, for municipal voters, we find that age and past voting record correlate with whether the online option influenced electors to cast a ballot.

Keywords: Online voting · Canada · Subnational elections · Absentee Voters · Participation · Northwest Territories · Ontario

1 Introduction

For more than two decades, Canada has been a hotspot for online voting use. But, until recently, online voting activity, and research studying it, has solely focused on community elections in Canada: municipally and among Indigenous communities. In the past several years, however, higher orders of government, including some territorial and provincial election agencies, have either adopted online voting for special groups of voters (e.g., absentee voters) or undertaken plans to do so (e.g., for military service) [1]. In 2022, for example, the Yukon introduced online voting in its school board elections, while in 2019 and 2023, the Northwest Territories (NWT) offered online ballots to absentee voters in its territorial elections. Using online voting in higher order elections

D. Duenas-Cid et al. (Eds.): E-Vote-ID 2024, LNCS 15014, pp. 89–106, 2025.
https://doi.org/10.1007/978-3-031-72244-8_6

prompt questions about its efficacy and uptake beyond the municipal arena, including whether voters report similar attitudes towards voting online. The unique geography and infrastructure of the NWT also raise questions about the potential of online voting to engage electors who might not otherwise have had the capacity or willingness to vote. While studies of online voting in Canada have examined the attitudes of voters, candidates, and administrators towards the local online voting experience [1 − 4], there has yet to be an examination of online voter attitudes in a higher-level government election or a comparison of provincial/territorial voter attitudes to municipal voters. Additionally, while research has probed whether online voting engages less committed voters [5] it has not done so in the context of such a geographically dispersed territory.

Unlike other Canadian provinces and territories, the NWT is an interesting case given the rural and remote character of some parts of the territory, which can be characterized by weaker broadband and physical infrastructure [6]. The territory can often encounter challenges delivering election materials, including paper ballots, to communities. Several communities can only be accessed by airplanes, and some are inaccessible when river crossings are not solidly frozen in the fall months. In addition, the northern location of the territory means it can experience unpredictable weather, including heavy fog and blizzards, which can complicate ballot and election delivery. Relying on mail voting as an alternative can also prove unreliable given delays in mail delivery due to inclement weather and lack of road infrastructure. In fact, the territories are the only locale in Canada where the national postal service does not guarantee delivery times. This unique rurality presents a challenge to delivering both paper-based and online elections.

To understand voter perceptions of online voting in the context of a higher-level (territorial) election and its potential impact on engagement, this article draws upon a unique data set of persons who registered to vote online as part of the absentee voter program in the 2023 NWT territorial election. This is the first time such data has been collected in Canada, thereby contributing significantly to the study of online voting implementation in the country. We consider who is applying to vote online, including age, geographic location, and digital profile. We also look at respondent rationales for casting an online ballot and attitudes towards the voting mode. Finally, we consider online voting's potential to engage electors. As a point of comparison, we draw upon original data collected from online voters during the 2022 Ontario municipal elections where voting by internet is open to the general population in select municipalities. Online voter attitudes in municipal elections are well studied [1, 5, 7] and this comparison allows us to establish whether there are differences in voter perceptions territorially and municipally.

Drawing upon this data, the article answers three important questions: (1) who is voting online in the NWT, (2) how do online voter attitudes compare in municipal and territorial elections, and (3) what factors predict non-voting without an online option? Answering these questions is imperative to understanding the effects that order of government may have on who votes online, voters' attitudes towards the franchise when it presents novel opportunities to access the ballot box, and whether it can encourage voting in rural and/or northern contexts.

2   Literature Review

2.1   Online Voter Characteristics and Reasons for Use

The introduction of online voting in Canada was followed by a push to understand the characteristics of its users. Little has been written on the demographic characteristics of "an online voter" in Canada [8], with notable exception of Goodman et al.'s (2024) recent study of Ontario municipal elections, which finds that online voters tend to be older homeowners with higher incomes who often sit left-of-center on the political spectrum. Interestingly, these findings mirror the characteristics associated with other convenience voting methods [9], including mail-in and telephone voting.

In studies of online voting in Canada, including in municipal [8] and Indigenous voting contexts [10, 11], convenience is often cited as the primary reason for voting online. This implies that ease of voting holds considerable importance for uptake because the online option can reduce the perceived costs of casting a ballot [12, 13]. This is particularly relevant in NWT, because the territory's rurality can present serious obstacles to accessing ballots. As a consequence, NWT voters may place a heightened importance on ballot accessibility or convenience when deciding to vote.

In terms of attitudes, studies have found that online voting in Canada has, generally, had a positive effect on satisfaction with local democracy [1], and that it correlates with strong support for use at all three levels of government. In fact, studies have shown that *municipal* online voters report being likely to recommend the voting mode to others and have few concerns with its security [3, 15]. Voters' satisfaction is relevant because governments typically hesitate to enact changes without public backing, as they are expected to consider voter preferences and have, historically, been responsive to them [14]. For online voting to be adopted more broadly [15], it is reasonable to believe that electors must look favourably upon the franchise.

2.2   Engagement

There are mixed results regarding the effect of internet voting on turnout in the literature. Some studies find little to no effect [16 − 18] while others paint a more optimistic picture of the voting mode as a possible solution to counter declining turnout [13, 19]. This optimism stems from its ability to be conducted remotely, reducing the need for physical presence at polling stations [13], and its support of equality in the voting process by enabling older individuals or individuals with disabilities to vote independently [20].

Within this vein, there is a second strand of research on internet voting and engagement focused on who decides to vote by internet. On the one hand, there are studies which argue that voting online is a tool to make voting easier for the already engaged [21]. Conversely, however, studies across multiple jurisdictions over time point to the ability of online voting to bring less committed voters into the voting process [5, 7, 22, 23]. Studies of Switzerland [22, 24], Estonia [23, 25], and Canada [5, 7] all document the ability of internet ballots to encourage voting among abstainers, occasional voters, or both. The theoretical reasoning behind both strands of research is similar: making voting easier and reducing the costs or barriers to accessing ballots can encourage certain voters to turnout [9, 19].

Since the perceived costs of voting are not the same for everyone, there are certain situations where we might expect internet voting to reduce voting costs more significantly. The time needed to travel to a polling location may be longer in rural areas where there are fewer polling locations. Likewise, in the case of the NWT, receiving and returning a ballot from a remote community with poor mail service may make online voting additionally appealing. Remote or convenience voting modes have been regarded in the literature as having the potential to make voting easier for groups of voters that face additional barriers to accessing the ballot box [27].

Looking to absentee voters - a group that often depends on remote voting - results have also been mixed. Work by Berinsky et al. (2001) [9], for example, suggests that alternative voting options for absentee voters, including vote-by-mail, do not improve voter turnout, but rather make voting more convenient for those already likely to vote. However, there is optimism regarding the potential of online voting to reduce barriers and positively affect participation for *other* special groups of voters. Germann (2021) [19], for example, finds that the extension of online voting increases expatriate turnout among Swiss voters. Likewise, in their assessment of internet voting deployment for citizens abroad in French consular elections, Dandoy and Kernalegenn (2021) [38] find that voting mode choice affects participation. These results are encouraging for deployments like in the NWT. Other Canadian research has shown that internet voting can be a tool to engage voters with less habitual voting histories [5, 7]. There is reasonable expectation to assume that a similar result could extend to the NWT where voting costs may be greater [12, 26] due to its remoteness and poor mail service.

Variables of Interest. Based on the literature, several variables stand out as potential predictors of electors' uptake of online voting. First, as noted above, voting history is a key variable of interest [5, 7]. Having a disability could also increase voting costs and therefore encourage voting by internet [20]. This supposition is supported by studies which document that internet voting can make the voting process more equal by canceling out mobility challenges or the need for assisted voting [28]. Third, rurality, and the perception of unreliable mail-service service, is another factor that may drive some voters to cast a ballot remotely online. Studies have shown that distance to the polls can have a marked impact on participation [29] and that convenience voting can be most helpful for voters on the margins [30].

Fourth, experience using the internet could affect an individual's ability to cast an online ballot [11]. Finally, age is a key variable in studies of voting by internet that could predict whether voters would have cast a ballot with or without the voting mode [1, 7].

After looking at who is voting online and their attitudes towards the voting mode, we consider the effect of these variables on engagement, measured by self-reports that respondents would not have voted otherwise in the 2023 NWT territorial election. Where possible, we compare these results to Ontario municipal voters.

3 Background and Context

3.1 Northwest Territories: Context

Spanning over 1.3 million square kilometres of northern Canada, the Northwest Territories is home to 45,000 residents in 33 communities, a third of which do not have permanent roads, and are dependent upon air travel, river transport, or winter ice roads. Most post-secondary students must travel out of territory for schooling and an increasing number of residents remain but spend their winters in the south.

Many areas of the territory experience challenges with internet access and quality. According to the NWT Bureau of Statistics' 2019 Community Survey, 16% of households reported not having home internet, either through a home internet service or a cellular data plan. More specifically, in the capital city of Yellowknife, where half of the territory's population resides, 7% of households do not have home internet access. This number exceeded 50% of households in most small communities [31]. This is relevant given the expected influence of internet access, usage, and comfortability on an individuals' likelihood of voting online [32].

The 2023 NWT territorial election was conducted in a unique context, following the wake of an exogenous shock wherein 70% of the territorial population was subject to a mandatory evacuation order due to widespread wildfires. With no legal authority to operate a polling station outside of the Northwest Territories, various alternatives, including an electronic absentee ballot were considered. Unclear whether communities would suffer further damage from the wildfires or the extent to which residents would be displaced, the Legislative Assembly passed *An Act to Postpone Polling Day for the 2023 General Election* on August 28, 2023 to delay the election past its planned date of October 3rd. The Chief Electoral Officer issued instructions on August 29, 2023 that the displacement or absence of a person from an electoral district as a result of the wildfire did not constitute a change to their place of ordinary residence, even if that residence no longer existed. Fortunately, all evacuation orders were lifted by mid-September. The postponed date of the election was set to November 14, 2023. Voters were informed of the available voting methods through both social and traditional media platforms. Post-secondary students received three emails over the course of the election notifying them of the option to vote online.

3.2 Legislative Context and History of Online Voting

Given Canada's multi-level governance structure, the authority, decision-making capabilities, and existence of municipalities are determined by provincial and territorial laws. This includes the regulation of municipal elections, with each province and territory having its own legislation governing the process. This means that the legislative authority to trial and use online voting or any electronic voting mode in sub-national elections rests with provincial and territorial governments.

In Canada, only Nova Scotia and the NWT have legislated the option to use online voting for their provincial and territorial elections.[1] Shortly after NWT's 2015 election,

---

[1] In NWT's *Local Authorities Elections Act*, online voting is not permitted for use in NWT's municipalities.

the then-Chief Electoral Officer recommended amending the *Elections and Plebiscites Act*, 2006 to permit electronic voting for special voting opportunities based on a belief that this is where voters wanted the future of elections to go [33]. The *Act* was amended in 2018 to allow the option of electronic voting for absentee voters.

3.3   Online Elections: Comparing NWT and Ontario

Online voting was first adopted for use by absentee voters in the 2019 NWT territorial general election. Elections Northwest Territories (Elections NWT) defines an absentee voter as a person who is registered to vote but is "unable to make it to an ordinary or advance poll" (*Elections and Plebiscites Act*, 2006). While absentee voters may apply to cast an online ballot because they are out of the territory entirely, they could also do so because they are outside of their district within the territory, or simply because they know in advance that they will be unable to attend a physical poll. Absentee ballots can be cast online or by mail. To cast an online ballot, voters were required to register with Elections NWT. Applications were approved if a voter was on the Register of Territorial Electors at the address that corresponded to their identification. In 2019, 489 votes were cast online, representing 3.7% of all ballots cast. This represents a sizable increase from when the absentee program offered the mail option only: 162 ballots were requested in 2011 and 244 in 2015. In 2023, online ballots accounted for 3.5% of all votes cast (375 total votes). There were 395 accepted applications, and 19 cancelled applications due to acclamations in those ridings.

In Ontario, by comparison, online voting is open to all voters in the select municipalities whose local councils adopt the voting mode. In the 2022 municipal elections, for example, online ballots were deployed in 222 of 414 municipalities that ran local elections. Decisions regarding the types of voting methods offered (for example, whether online ballots are offered alongside other voting modes or on their own) are at the discretion of local governments. As such, some cities decide to require online voter registration, while others do not. Because of this autonomy some cities have used online voting for over two decades, while for others it is a new addition. Thus, diffusion of online voting is more widespread across Ontario and uptake is greater given that it is offered to a much larger segment of the voting population. In terms of uptake, among municipalities that offered both online and paper voting in the 2018 Ontario local elections, approximately 57% of all votes were cast electronically [1] while in the case of NWT use represented 3.5% of all ballots cast.

While differences in online voting availability, diffusion and uptake make the samples distinct, the NWT represents the first point of comparison to understand more about online voter attitudes and engagement in higher order elections and how this matches up against municipal data.

4   Methods

The data informing this article come from a survey of persons registered to vote online in the 2023 NWT territorial election. A total of 395 electors registered to vote online (of 20,550 eligible electors) with 375 casting an online ballot. The survey invitation was sent to all persons who registered to vote online, regardless of how they voted.

The survey was programmed and distributed via the Qualtrics interface in English and French and was administered via email between April 9 and April 30, 2024.[2] An initial invitation was sent out in week one, with three reminder messages following in each of the subsequent weeks. A total of 392 valid email invitations were sent (three bounced back) and 171 persons completed the survey for a response rate of 44%. Respondents ranged in age from 18 to 78 years old, with a mean age of 48 years. There is a similar age distribution among the full population of online voters, which has a mean age of 44 years (see Fig. 1 below), albeit those aged 18 to 24 and 55 to 64 are slightly overrepresented in our sample. Respondents reported on average having "some university" education and an annual household income between $110,001 and $150,000. Geographically, there was representation from across the territory, with 67% respondents residing in the capital city, Yellowknife. About 25% of respondents reside in communities that are regional centres (Hay River, Inuvik, Fort Smith), and 9% in smaller, more rural communities. This geographic breakdown is closely aligned with the population of online voters in the territory (58.4% from Yellowknife, 27.7% in regional centres, and 13.9% from small communities).

We compare the responses of territorial voters with a dataset of municipal voters programmed and administered by Schlesinger Group Ltd during the 2022 Ontario municipal elections. Like the NWT survey, respondents self-selected to take part in the Ontario survey, but were recruited immediately following their online voting experience (rather than several months after voting, as was the case in NWT). Once voters had cast a ballot and exited the online voting system, they were prompted with a thank you screen that invited them to take part in a survey about their voting experience.[3] Surveys were available for completion during the voting period of each municipality, which, in total, lasted from September 26 to October 24, 2022 across the 24 municipalities that took part in the study. The survey was completed by 29,284 voters for a response rate of 16%. In terms of geography and size, participating municipalities were located across the province: 42% are considered small with fewer than 10,000 electors, 46% are medium sized, with electorates between 10,000 and 99,000, and 13% are large municipalities, with more than 100,000 electors.

Both the NWT and Ontario surveys were written and conducted in similar ways. Recruitment for both surveys was conducted online and Letters of Consent were compiled based on the same template. Both surveys were programmed using online platforms and had similar question sequencing with many identical questions. These included questions probing perceived satisfaction with voting online, reason for use, concerns, desirability to see the voting mode used in the future, trust, perceived risk, digital access and literacy, voting history, and standard socio-demographic items. The NWT survey

---

[2] While it would have been ideal to conduct the survey immediately following the 2023 territorial election, it was not possible as a lengthy ethics process is required for research conducted in the Northwest Territories wherein 33 Indigenous communities are able to weigh in on the research plan. Honouring this important process and responding to all comments meant that the research needed to be undertaken in April after the certificate was approved.

[3] There were a few exceptions to this recruitment approach in cases where one vendor refused for its clients to take part in the research. In these cases, voters were redirected to the municipal webpage which offered the option to take part in a voting experience survey.

also asked whether respondents had voted online in the 2023 territorial election since the survey invitation was extended to everyone who registered but may not have voted online. As such differences in data collection across the samples was minimal, although the memory of municipal voters may have been fresher.

Differences in response rates could be attributed to the fact that NWT respondents were sent an initial request and three reminders while Ontario municipal respondents only had one opportunity to complete a survey. The NWT response rate after the initial message was 19%, which is closed to the 16% in Ontario. Overall, we believe these differences are minimal and that the samples are appropriate for comparison.

In terms of limitations, all data is self-selected, and most respondents are voters (all Ontario municipal respondents and nearly all NWT respondents). While not necessarily representative of the total populations, there are similarities in the age and geographic location of NWT voters as described above. Comparable data is not available for Ontario, however, past comparisons suggest the age distributions of exit surveys and actual online voters are similar [3]. Additionally, it is possible that past turnout was over-reported based on social desirability [34]. This should be considered when interpreting the findings below.

5   Results

5.1   Who is Voting Online as an Absentee Voter in NWT?

First, we consider who votes online in a territorial election by looking at age and geography. We then turn to survey items on digital literacy - an important consideration given the rurality of the territory and the digital infrastructure challenges faced by some residents.[4] Note here that digital literacy refers to voters' capacity – or perceived capacity – to use online systems and/or digital technologies, including computers and other internet-enabled devices and platforms. Data on age and geographic location was collected by Elections NWT for all online voters. Figure 1 compares the percentages of all NWT voters (online and paper) in the 2023 election with online voters and NWT survey respondents by age group. Overall, we see that proportionately young people aged 18 to 34 were more likely to cast an online ballot than a paper one. Likewise, voters aged 45 + were proportionately less likely to opt for the online option compared to the traditional paper ballot. Interestingly, voter data from Ontario municipal elections overtime has shown, to the contrary, that older voters aged 50 + are the most likely users of online ballots [1, 3, 7]. In the case of absentee voters, however, it could be that younger people away at school or middle-aged voters traveling for work or busy with their families may make better use of online voting than when it is offered to the entire electorate. The limited post-secondary opportunities in the NWT support this line of reasoning. Overall, persons of all ages are voting online as absentee voters in the NWT: the youngest online voter in the 2023 election was 18, while the oldest was 95.

---

[4] Recall that availability of online voting differs in the NWT and Ontario. In the NWT, online voting is limited to absentee voters in territorial elections, while in Ontario, online voting is used solely in municipal elections and is open to entire electorates.

In terms of geography, there was a fairly even distribution of ballots cast across the territory: 36.4% of all votes were cast in Yellowknife districts, 30.4% in regional centres, and 33.2% in small communities. By comparison, 58.4% of *online* ballots were cast for Yellowknife districts, 27.7% for regional centre districts, and 13.9% for small community districts. This tells us that online ballots were used by voters across communities of varying urbanity and infrastructure, although, the voting mode was most heavily drawn upon by residents of the capital city. This is unsurprising given the improved digital infrastructure and access to travel in Yellowknife. Overall, persons of all ages and geographies in the territory voted online as absentee voters.

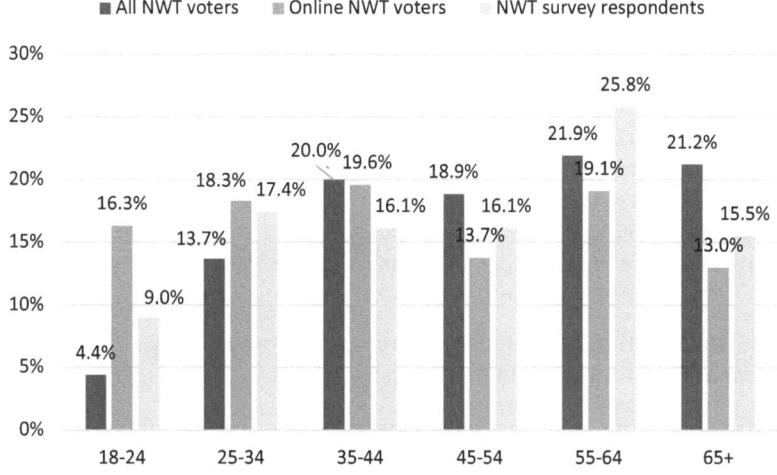

Fig. 1. Percentage of all NWT voters, online voters, and survey respondents by age group

To understand who is choosing to cast an online absentee vote in NWT, we also look at measures of digital literacy, including home internet access, frequency of use, and perceived ability to use the internet. This allows us to understand whether a respondent has direct access to the internet and the quality of that connection, their experience being online, and their confidence using it. We compare these results to responses to the same questions from the Ontario municipal survey.

Despite expecting these items to be lower for NWT voters given the rurality of the territory and challenges with digital infrastructure, we find the opposite is true. All NWT respondents report having an internet connection at home (compared to 1% of Ontario municipal respondents who do not). Furthermore, territorial respondents report having more stable cable connections (81.8% NWT compared to 58.3% in Ontario). With respect to access, 99.4% of NWT respondents in our sample reported using the internet daily compared to 94.8% of municipal respondents.[5] Conducting a cross-tabulation, Kendall's tau-b reveals that the difference between community size/urbanity and internet use is significant (tau-b $= 0.177$, sig. $= 0.036$). Finally, when asked about their ability to use the internet, a greater percentage of NWT respondents describe their ability as 'very

---

[5] Reported frequency of use is slightly higher among respondents from Yellowknife than other smaller communities.

good' (66.1%) or 'good' (28.5%) compared to Ontario municipal voters (61% and 27.5% respectively).

Taken together, NWT respondents report having better access, more frequent use, and greater confidence in their ability to use the internet than Ontario's municipal voters, even when considering responses from voters in Ontario's most urban and tech connected cities. These findings are contrary to the digital profile of the territory [6] and point to online voting attracting absentee voters who are more digitally connected. Online voters outside of Yellowknife do report being less digitally connected, but these differences are marginal at best (e.g., using the internet once a day instead of multiple times daily). It could be that while online voting is a much-needed measure of accessibility for territorial voters, it better reduces accessibility barriers for residents who are already comfortable using technology. While it is possible that less digitally skilled absentee voters could opt for a mail ballot option, data shows this is not the case. Only 48 mail-in ballots were requested by absentee voters, 35 of which were from incarcerated electors who did not have the online voting option. Applications for mail-in ballots have consistently dropped since the introduction of online voting [35], and the small number being applied for, and cast, suggest that less connected residents are not opting for this alternative. Future studies could examine this phenomenon further. It could be that some very rural voters - who have both poor mail delivery *and* connectivity - simply opt not to vote.

5.2   How Do Territorial Online Voters Feel About Online Ballots? How Does This Compare to Municipal Online Voters?

Respondents of both the NWT and Ontario surveys were asked to identify the main reason they chose to vote online. Note that some categories were collapsed or treated as missing data.[6] The striking difference between NWT and Ontario respondents is that Ontario municipal online voters were more likely to have said they voted online for convenience (80.2% municipal versus 28.3% NWT), whereas territorial voters were far more likely have cast an online ballot based on accessibility (6.3% municipal compared to 57.8% NWT) (see Fig. 2). This finding is distinct from all previous data obtained from municipalities and First Nations in Canada [8, 11, 36]. While online voters in municipalities and First Nations likewise experience challenges related to rurality and remoteness, it is possible that these issues are not as severe as they are in NWT. This difference could also be attributed to the fact that online voting in NWT was offered to absentee voters only, while deployments in municipalities and First Nations have been extended to the entire voting population. Twenty-one NWT residents (of 395) applied for absentee ballots outside of Canada.[7]

---

[6] For the NWT survey responses for 'accessibility' (53%), 'no polls near me' (4.2%), and 'concerns about mail delivery' (0.6%) were grouped together given that they all pertain to access of ballots. For the Ontario municipal dataset, response options 'Internet and telephone were my only choice' (2.17%), 'Internet was the only method offered in my municipality' (1.44%), 'suggestion from friends or family' (0.96%), suggestion from a candidate' (0.3%) and 'health and safety concerns' (5.66%) were treated as missing data.

[7] Application locations included Bosnia, Ecuador, Italy, Mexico, Netherlands, New Zealand, Pakistan and the United States.

Aside from differences between convenience and access, there are similarities across the other rationales cited for voting online. 'Positive past experience' with the voting mode is slightly higher for municipal voters. This is to be expected given the longstanding use of online voting in Ontario municipalities. Similar percentages of respondents chose 'found it interesting' and 'privacy' as their primary reason for use. 'Other' was modestly higher among territorial respondents, however all but one of these responses pertain to accessibility. These included being outside of the territory or having medical or mobility issues.

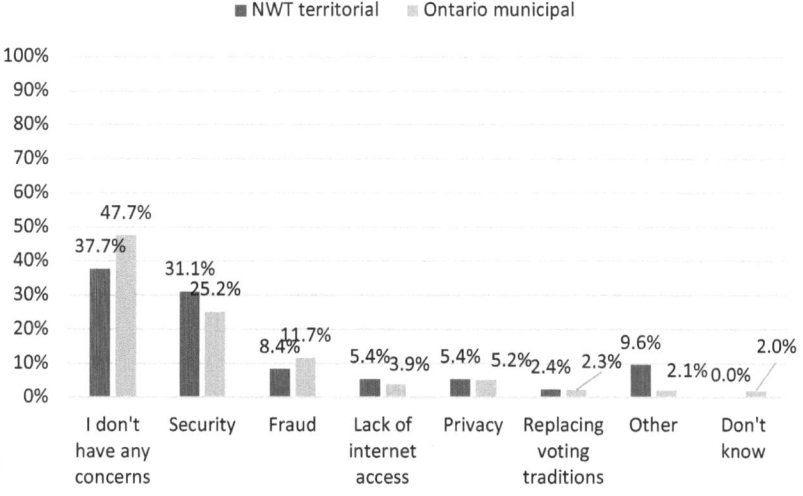

Fig. 2. Main reason for voting online.

Respondents were also asked to identify their top concern with voting online. This question gives us a sense of respondents' support for the voting mode. Presumably, a high percentage of certain concerns, like security and fraud, could contribute to weaker support for online ballots. The largest proportion of NWT respondents report having no concerns with voting online (37.7%), followed by security (31.1%), 'other' (9.6%)[8] and fraud (8.4%) (see Fig. 3). Lack of internet access only accounted for 5.4% of concerns. On the one hand, this is surprising given the digital infrastructure challenges faced by the territory. But, on the other hand, perhaps it is to be expected given that 67% of respondents reside in in the capital city of Yellowknife, which has high levels of home internet access. Looking at respondents' geography and their reported top concern, we see that lack of internet access is proportionately identified as a greater issue in regional centres and small communities, albeit only slightly. In fact, differences in concerns based on rurality were minimal overall, though respondents from regional centres and smaller communities were more likely to be unconcerned. Finally, items such as privacy (5.4%)

---

[8] These comments focus mostly on technical issues casting a vote online such as difficulty navigating the voting site and issues with connectivity and concerns about ballot verification. That is, being able to verify that your ballot was both recorded as intended and counted as cast.

and fear of online voting replacing voting traditions (2.4%) occupied an equally small share of responses.

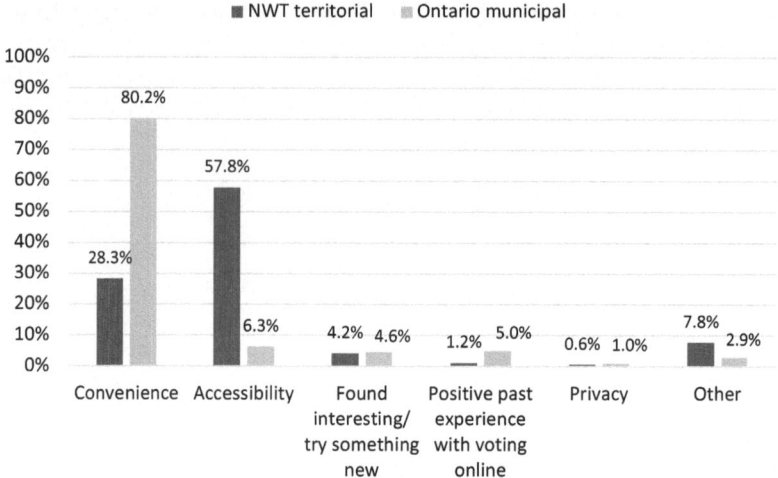

Fig. 3. Top concern with online voting.

Ontario municipal online voters, by comparison, had fewer concerns with online voting. Municipal respondents were more likely to say that they do not have concerns about casting a ballot online (47.7%), and fewer respondents identified security as their top concern (25.2%). Most other items were similar across the two samples, apart from fraud, which a greater percentage of municipal voters selected as their top concern (11.7% compared to 8.4% among NWT respondents). The fact that NWT respondents were more likely to report concerns could be related to the newness of online voting in territorial elections. Similar trends in responses are found among municipal respondents whose cities adopted online voting for the first or second time. Often, as the voting mode is made available overtime, concerns tend to lessen.

Considering satisfaction and willingness to recommend online voting to others, we find similarities across territorial and municipal samples (see Table 1). Respondents from both groups report satisfaction with the online voting process (96.4% grouping together 'very' and 'fairly' satisfied categories). A slightly greater percentage of municipal online voters say they are 'very satisfied' compared to territorial voters; however, it is not uncommon for online voters to report slightly lower satisfaction in the first couple of elections it is offered. Similar patterns have been noted among first- or second-time user municipalities [7]. Willingness to recommend online voting to others is similarly strong: 98.2% of territorial respondents indicate they are 'definitely' or 'probably' likely to recommend online voting to others, compared to 95% of municipal voters. A slightly greater percentage of municipal online voters say they would 'definitely' recommend online voting. Again, it is not uncommon to see the percentage of respondents who would recommend online voting grow the longer it is offered. These results suggest that NWT voters are satisfied and feel somewhat favorable towards online voting, if they are willing to endorse its future use.

An interesting difference between the samples, however, is the percentage of voters who say they would not have voted otherwise had online ballots not been offered. Territorial voters are much less certain than Ontario municipal voters to say that they would have voted without the online option. Grouping together 'probably no' and 'definitely no' responses, we see that 42.8% of NWT online voters say they likely would not have voted without online voting compared to 13% of municipal voters. Earlier studies examining community-level elections in Canada have found that online voting can encourage a modest proportion of electors to cast a ballot [5, 7] by reducing the costs of voting [13]. Studies examining the City of Markham, Ontario showed that, in 2003, this percentage was as high as 25% and then decreased in each subsequent election, leveling off at around 10% to 13% [37]. Likewise, research with First Nations showed that 9% to 13% of respondents said they would not have voted without an online option [11]. The high percentage of NWT online voters that reported they may not have voted otherwise could be explained by the fact that respondents had to apply to vote online because they could not make it to an ordinary or advance poll. These responses suggest that extending this option to voters who need it can positively affect the participation of some. We explore this further by conducting a logistic regression.

5.3 Can Online Voting Engage Some Voters?

We performed a logistic regression to better understand the variables that may predict respondents saying whether they would/would not have voted without the online option. Our dependent variable is whether respondents would have voted without online voting (definitely no/probably no = 1, definitely yes/probably yes = 0). Our independent variables include age, disability, living outside of Yellowknife (NWT) or rurality (municipal sample), voting record, and frequency of internet use.[9] While not displayed here, we also carried out a confirmatory OLS regression. Table 1 presents the logistic regression results and includes two models: one for the NWT and a second drawing on the Ontario municipal data.[10]

Our results show that, for the NWT, living outside of Yellowknife and having an uncommitted voting record (reporting not voting in all elections) predict the likelihood of not having voted without the online option. More specifically, looking at the odds ratios, we see that if a voter is from outside of Yellowknife, there is a 128% increase in the odds that they would not have voted had online voting been unavailable to them. With respect to reporting an uncommitted voting record, the ability to predict not having voted without online voting is even greater. There is a 219% increase in the odds that a voter would not have cast a ballot otherwise.

---

[9] For the NWT model the reference category for community size is living outside of Yellowknife, while for the municipal model it is rural. For the voting record, respondents were asked to consider elections at all levels of government (First Nations, municipal, territorial, and federal) since they became eligible and whether they vote in 'all elections', 'most', 'few', or 'never before'. The reference category for voting record is uncommitted voter which groups the categories of voted in 'most' 'few' or no elections. Finally, the reference for internet use is 'several times a day'.

[10] Please note to interpret the odds ratios we use the following formula: % change in odds = [exp(B)-1] * 100.

Table 1. Factors predicting reported not voting without the online option.

Model 1 – NWT territorial (N=140)	Odds Ratio (SE)
Age	1.009 (0.011)
Disability	1.006 (0.522)
Internet use several times daily	1.215 (0.549)
Outside of Yellowknife	2.278 (0.392)**
Non-committed voter	3.193 (0.380)***
Constant	0.203 (0.907)*
Nagelkerke R^2	0.120

Model 2 – Ontario municipal (N=22,257)	
Age	0.842 (0.011)****
Disability	1.001 (.001)
Internet use several times daily	0.999 (0.044)
Rural	1.006 (0.088)
Non-committed voter	3.711 (0.043)****
Constant	0.170 (0.073)****
Nagelkerke R^2	0.112

*Denotes significance at 0.1 level, ** significance at 0.05 level; ***significance at 0.01 level; ****significance at 0.001 level

The fact that voters outside of Yellowknife have a greater likelihood of not voting without the online option may be explained by the fact that residents outside of the capital may have even less faith in the postal service. While some regional centres are relatively urban, they do not have the same infrastructure and services as Yellowknife. Certainly, for smaller communities, some of which are without main roads, timely access to ballots and the ability to have them promptly returned to be counted in the final tally may be a greater concern. A history of uncommitted voting among these respondents could reflect the additional barriers some face casting an absentee ballot. Online voting could reduce some of the perceived costs of casting an absentee ballot, making participation easier and therefore enabling persons who may not have voted otherwise [12, 13].

Conducting the same analysis with the Ontario municipal data for comparison, except that we use rural as the reference category instead of living outside of Yellowknife, we see a similarly strong result for past voting record. There is a 270% increase in the odds that voters with uncommitted voting records will vote because of the online option. While rurality is not significant in the municipal model, age is. We can interpret this to mean that for each additional year older a person is, the odds of having not voted without the online option decrease by 15.8%. This is an interesting result that future research could probe further. While older voters are the primary users of online voting municipally, young people typically report less committed voting histories. The reduced costs of casting an online ballot compared to a paper one (e.g., not having to travel to a poll location) could again reduce the net effort of casting a ballot and thus make voting more feasible.

Overall, while there are differences in the results across the samples - living outside of Yellowknife matters in the NWT sample, whereas age is significant in the Ontario municipal sample - reported voting history increases the odds of not having voted without online voting in both cases. This points to the potential of online voting to facilitate voter participation in both the context of absentee voters territorially and the full electorate municipally. While these findings do not directly comment on voter turnout per se, they are aligned with previous studies which show that online voting increases turnout among special groups of voters (i.e. expatriates and voters abroad) [26, 38] and that habitual voters are less likely to vote online [6].

6 Conclusion

This article has examined the first-ever collected data from online voters in a territorial election in Canada. Where possible, comparisons are made to data obtained from a survey of Ontario voters in the province's 2022 municipal elections. The study produces three main insights. First, it provides an understanding of who is opting to cast an online absentee ballot in territorial elections. This includes residents of all ages from a range of communities. A greater percentage of online voters are from the capital city of Yellowknife and proportionately young people aged 18 to 34 and 55 to 64 are more likely users of the voting mode. Absentee online voters in NWT have strong digital literacy[11] measured by reported access, frequency of use, and self-reported confidence in their ability to use the internet. Their digital profiles are stronger than municipal online voters despite living in one of the most rural and remote locations of Canada, where many areas have poor digital infrastructure.

Second, we find that territorial respondents are relatively supportive of online voting. They report being satisfied with the online voting process, are willing to recommend it to others, and while they have some concerns related to security and fraud, the largest proportion of respondents say they have no concerns. However, distinct from the Ontario municipal sample and previous findings on online voting use in local government [4, 9] and First Nations elections [14, 36], NWT respondents are much more likely to cite accessibility as their reason for voting online and correspondingly, are much less likely to attribute their use to convenience. In addition to differences in the rationale for use, another key distinction is the percentage of respondents who claim that they would not have voted if online voting was not an option. Previous research has found that, on average, about 10 to 13% of respondents indicate that they would not have voted otherwise. In the NWT sample, 43% say that they would not have voted without it. This suggests online voting has the potential to increase civic engagement among absentee voters in the territory.

To examine this further, we looked at which variables could predict this sentiment. We find that uncommitted voting records and living outside of Yellowknife predict the likelihood that respondents would not have voted otherwise. The Ontario municipal

---

[11] Recall from above that digital literacy refers to voters' capacity – or perceived capacity – to use online systems and/or digital technologies, including computers and other internet-enabled devices and platforms.

sample also finds that an uncommitted voting record is a significant predictor as well as age. This finding is consistent with previous research on municipal voters in Canada [6].

Taken together, these findings point to online voting being a positive voting channel for electors seeking to cast an absentee ballot in the NWT, especially since it can increase the likelihood of voting among residents whose districts are outside the capital and who may not have voted otherwise. Despite many differences between the territory and the centrally located province of Ontario, findings continue to point to support for online voting in areas it is used across Canada.

This study suggests several directions for future research. First, studies could examine why the digital profiles of online voters in the NWT are so strong despite having some of the weakest infrastructure and costliest internet services in the country. Where are the absentee voters with weaker digital access and skills? Are some potential voters being excluded based on internet availability, cost, or literacy? If so, what measures could be taken to enhance access? A second avenue for future research is to further investigate the extent to which online voting may motivate certain young people to vote. While research on online voting in Norway [39] and voting machines in the Netherlands [40] have documented that young people are less likely to cast an electronic ballot, does this differ based on voting record or intention to vote? Third, studies could examine the challenges of voting online in rural and remote communities. This could be especially interesting where online voting is not limited to certain subsets of the population. Finally, future work could consider the impact exogenous shocks such as the wildfires on online voting uptake [5].

Practitioners and policymakers consulting this work should not underestimate the potential of online voting to engage less committed voters outside of urban centres. As a best practice, election agencies and administrators should be open to working with academics to collect data on future deployments. Collecting data and probing the aforementioned questions could improve voter access to digital voting modes.

Acknowledgements. The authors are grateful to Jon Pammett for his comments on an earlier draft, and to the anonymous reviewers for their helpful feedback. Special thanks to Jared Boles for his exemplary research support. This research was financially supported by the Social Sciences and Humanities Research Council of Canada, Grant No. 430-2022-01059.

References

1. Goodman, N., Hayes, H. A., McGregor, R. M., Pruysers, S., Spicer, Z.: Voting Online: Technology and Democracy in Municipal Elections. McGill-Queen's Press-MQUP (2024)
2. Goodman, N., Spicer, Z.: Administering elections in a digital age: online voting in ontario municipalities. Can. Public Adm. **62**(3), 369–392 (2019)
3. Goodman, N., Harvey., B.: Internet Voting Study Report. St. Catharines: Brock University (2022)
4. Hayes, H.A., Goodman, N., McGregor, R.M., Spicer, Z., Pruysers, S.: The effect of exogenous shocks on the administration of online voting: evidence from Ontario, Canada. In: International Joint Conference on Electronic Voting, pp. 70–89. Cham, Springer International Publishing (September 2022)

5. Couture, J., Breux, S., Goodman, N.: La vote par Internet augmente-t-il la participation électorale? In: Loiseau H, Waldispuehl E (eds.). Cyberespace et science politique: De la méthode au terrain, du virtuel au réel, pp 123–148. Presses de l'Université du Québec, Quebec City (2017)

6. Environics Research.: Research on Telecommunications Services in Northern Canada (Final Report). Canadian-Radio-television and Telecommunications Commission (2023). https://epe.lac-bac.gc.ca/100/200/301/pwgsc-tpsgc/por-ef/crtc/2023/044-22-e/report.pdf

7. Goodman, N.J.: Internet voting in a local election in Canada. In: The internet and democracy in global perspective: Voters, candidates, parties, and social movements, pp. 7–24. Springer International Publishing, Cham (2014)

8. Goodman, N., Pyman, H.: Internet Voting Project Report. Centre for e-Democracy (2016). http://www.centreforedemocracy.com/internet-voting-project-report/

9. Berinsky, A.J., Burns, N., Traugott, M.W.: Who votes by mail? a dynamic model of the individual-level consequences of voting-by-mail systems. Public Opin. Q. **65**(2), 178–197 (2001)

10. Gabel, C., Goodman, N., Bird, K., Budd, B.: Indigenous adoption of internet voting: a case study of Whitefish River First Nation. Int. Indigenous Policy J. **7**(3) (2016)

11. Goodman, N., Gabel, C., Budd, B.: Online voting in Indigenous Communities: lessons from Canada. In: International Joint Conference on Electronic Voting, pp. 67–83. Cham: Springer International Publishing (September 2018). https://doi.org/10.1007/978-3-030-00419-4_5

12. Downs, A.: An economic theory of political action in a democracy. J. Polit. Econ. **65**(2), 135–150 (1957)

13. Goodman, N., Stokes, L.C.: Reducing the cost of voting: an evaluation of internet voting's effect on turnout. Br. J. Polit. Sci. **50**(3), 1155–1167 (2020)

14. Heller, A.L.: Public support for electoral reform: The role of electoral system experience. Elect. Stud. **72**, 102348 (2021)

15. Coppedge, M., Lindberg, S., Skaaning, S.E., Teorell, J.: Measuring high level democratic principles using the V-Dem data. Int. Polit. Sci. Rev. **37**(5), 580–593 (2016)

16. Germann, M., Serdült, U.: Internet voting and turnout: evidence from Switzerland. Elect. Stud. **47**, 1–12 (2017)

17. Norris, P.: Will new technology boost turnout? Evaluating experiments in UK local elections. In: Electronic Voting And Democracy: A Comparative Analysis, pp. 193–225. Palgrave Macmillan UK, London (2004)

18. Ciancio, A., Kämpfen, F.: The heterogeneous effects of internet voting. Eur. J. Polit. Econ. **79**, 102444 (2023)

19. Germann, M.: Internet voting increases expatriate voter turnout. Gov. Inf. Q. **38**(2), 101560 (2021)

20. Hall, T.: Internet voting: the state of the debate. In: Handbook of Digital Politics , pp. 103–117. Edward Elgar Publishing (2015)

21. Alvarez, R.M., Hall, T.E.: Point, Click, and Vote: The Future of Internet Voting. Rowman & Littlefield (2003)

22. Petitpas, A., Jaquet, J.M., Sciarini, P.: Does E-Voting matter for turnout, and to whom? Elect. Stud. **71**, 102245 (2021)

23. Solvak, M., Vassil, K.: Could internet voting halt declining electoral turnout? New evidence that e-voting is habit forming. Policy Internet **10**(1), 4–21 (2018)

24. Chevallier, M.: Internet voting, Turnout and deliberation: a Study. Electron. J. e-Gov. **7**(1), 71–86 (2009)

25. Trechsel, A. H., Vassil, K.: Internet voting in Estonia. Comp. Anal. Four Elections Since 20052010Rep. Counc. Eur. (2011)

26. Blais, A.: To Vote Or Not to Vote?: The Merits and Limits of Rational Choice Theory. University of Pittsburgh Press (2000)

27. Gronke, P., Galanes-Rosenbaum, E., Miller, P.A., Toffey, D.: Convenience voting. Annu. Rev. Polit. Sci. **11**, 437–455 (2008)
28. Goodman, N., Pammett, J.H., DeBardeleben, J.: Internet voting: the Canadian municipal experience. Can. Parliamentary Rev. **33**(3), 13–21 (2010)
29. Haspel, M., Knotts, H.G.: Location, location, location: precinct placement and the costs of voting. J. Polit. **67**(2), 560–573 (2005)
30. Dyck, J.J., Gimpel, J.G.: Distance, turnout, and the convenience of voting. Soc. Sci. Q. **86**(3), 531–548 (2005)
31. Northwest Territories Bureau of Statistics. Home Internet Access by Characteristic and Community [Excel File] (2019). https://www.statsnwt.ca/Housing/internet_usage.html
32. Carter, L., Bélanger, F.: Internet voting and political participation: an empirical comparison of technological and political factors. ACM SIGMIS Database: the DATABASE for Adv. Inf. Syst. **43**(3), 26–46 (2012)
33. Elections Northwest Territories.: Modernizing Election Administration in the Northwest Territories (2016). https://www.electionsnwt.ca/sites/electionsnwt/files/2016-05-20_ceo_rep ort_2015_general_election_en.pdf
34. Karp, J.A., Brockington, D.: Social desirability and response validity: a comparative analysis of overreporting voter turnout in five countries. J. Politics **67**(3), 825–840 (2005)
35. Elections Northwest Territories.: Report of the Chief Electoral Officer on the Administration of the 2023 Territorial General Election (2024). https://www.electionsnwt.ca/sites/elections nwt/files/2023_ceo_report-web_version.pdf
36. Budd, B., Gabel, C., Goodman, N.: Online voting in a First Nation in Canada: Implications for participation and governance. In: International Joint Conference on Electronic Voting, pp. 50–66. Cham: Springer International Publishing (September 2019). https://doi.org/10. 1007/978-3-030-30625-0_4
37. Goodman, N.: Online Voting in the City of Markham: Patterns & Trends 2003–2018. Report: City of Markham (2019)
38. Dandoy, R., Kernalegenn, T.: Internet voting from abroad: exploring turnout in the 2014 french consular elections. French Politics **19**(4), 421–439 (2021)
39. Segaard, S.B., Baldersheim, H., Saglie, J.: The Norwegian trial with Internet voting: Results and challenges. Rev. Gen. De Derecho Público Comparado **13**, 7 (2013)
40. Loeber, L.: The E-voting readiness index and the Netherlands. In: Electronic Voting: Third International Joint Conference, E-Vote-ID 2018, Bregenz, Austria, October 2–5, 2018, Proceedings 3, pp. 146–159. Springer International Publishing (2018). https://doi.org/10.1007/ 978-3-030-00419-4_10

ZK-SNARKs for Ballot Validity: A Feasibility Study

Nicolas Huber$^{(\boxtimes)}$, Ralf Küsters , Julian Liedtke , and Daniel Rausch

University of Stuttgart, Stuttgart, Germany
`firstname.secondname@sec.uni-stuttgart.de`

Abstract. Electronic voting (e-voting) systems have become more prevalent in recent years, but security concerns have also increased, especially regarding the privacy and verifiability of votes. As an essential ingredient for constructing secure e-voting systems, designers often employ zero-knowledge proofs (ZKPs), allowing voters to prove their votes are valid without revealing them. Invalid votes can then be discarded to protect verifiability without compromising the privacy of valid votes. General purpose zero-knowledge proofs (GPZKPs) such as ZK-SNARKs can be used to prove arbitrary statements, including ballot validity. While a specialized ZKP that is constructed only for a specific election type/voting method, ballot format, and encryption/commitment scheme can be more efficient than a GPZKP, the flexibility offered by GPZKPs would allow for quickly constructing e-voting systems for new voting methods and new ballot formats. So far, however, the viability of GPZKPs for showing ballot validity for various ballot formats, in particular, whether and in how far they are practical for voters to compute, has only recently been investigated for ballots that are computed as Pedersen vector commitments in an ACM CCS 2022 paper by Huber et al. Here, we continue this line of research by performing a feasibility study of GPZKPs for the more common case of ballots encrypted via Exponential ElGamal encryption. Specifically, building on the work by Huber et al., we describe how the Groth16 ZK-SNARK can be instantiated to show ballot validity for arbitrary election types and ballot formats encrypted via Exponential ElGamal. As our main contribution, we implement, benchmark, and compare several such instances for a wide range of voting methods and ballot formats. Our benchmarks not only establish a basis for protocol designers to make an educated choice for or against such a GPZKP, but also show that GPZKPs are actually viable for showing ballot validity in voting systems using Exponential ElGamal.

1 Introduction

A prominent approach for constructing secure e-voting systems is the homomorphic aggregation of ballots. In such systems, a vote/ballot is a vector of numbers, with one number per possible choice in the election. Typically, a choice corresponds to a candidate that the voter can give one or several votes/points, so

D. Duenas-Cid et al. (Eds.): E-Vote-ID 2024, LNCS 15014, pp. 107–123, 2025.
https://doi.org/10.1007/978-3-031-72244-8_7

in an election with n_{cand} candidates, a vote would be a vector of length n_{cand}. An additively homomorphic encryption or commitment scheme is then used to hide the vote. This scheme is typically applied component-wise, i.e., a vote vector of length n_{cand} results in an encrypted ballot[1] consisting of n_{cand} many ciphertexts/commitments. When using commitment schemes for hiding votes, voters have to send (shares of) an (encrypted) opening of their commitment. Currently, Exponential ElGamal (EEG) encryption is the most relevant option in practice [2,11]. To tally the election, all encrypted ballots are first homomorphically aggregated (component-wise) to obtain a single aggregated encrypted ballot that hides individual votes. This aggregated ballot is decrypted to obtain the *aggregated tally* consisting of a list of the total votes/points for each candidate.

Proofs for Ballot Validity. For the above approach of aggregation-based e-voting to be reasonable, one needs to ensure that all encrypted ballots used for aggregation are well-formed, i.e., that they contain a valid vote. The standard approach is to have voters use zero-knowledge proofs (ZKPs) to prove *ballot validity* during ballot submission.

A ZKP for ballot validity proves that the vote contained in an encrypted ballot belongs to the set of votes permitted by the current election. We call this set a *choice space* in the following. For instance, consider the straightforward case of single-vote elections, where a voter can cast a single vote for one out of n_{cand} candidates. A corresponding choice space can be defined as follows, where v_i denotes the number of votes given to candidate i in a ballot:

$$C_{\mathsf{single}} := \left\{ (v_1, \ldots, v_{n_{\mathsf{cand}}}) \middle| v_i \in \{0,1\}, \sum_{i=1}^{n_{\mathsf{cand}}} v_i \in \{0,1\} \right\}.$$

A voter is supposed to choose her ballot $\mathbf{b}$ as a vector from this set, i.e., $\mathbf{b} \in C_{\mathsf{single}}$. The voter then computes an encrypted ballot $\mathbf{c}$ from $\mathbf{b}$ and submits $\mathbf{c}$ alongside a ZKP which shows that $\mathbf{c}$ was obtained by encrypting a ballot $\mathbf{b} \in C_{\mathsf{single}}$. Ballots without valid ZKP are discarded by the voting system, ensuring that even malicious voters can contribute only one vote for one candidate.

State of the Art. A ZKP for ballot validity depends on the underlying choice space and the encryption/commitment scheme used to obtain $\mathbf{c}$. Therefore, ZKPs for ballot validity have usually been designed and proven secure only for specific combinations of choice spaces and (classes of) encryption/commitment schemes.

For example, Helios 2.0 [2] and Belenios [11,18] support C_{single} with component-wise EEG encryption. That is, $\mathbf{c}$ is a vector of EEG ciphertexts c_i, each encrypting one v_i. The ballot validity ZKPs in Helios and Belenios are based on disjunctive Chaum-Pedersen proofs [9,13], which show that an EEG ciphertext encrypts a value from a specific set S. Concretely, for C_{single} one considers the set $S = \{0,1\}$. Voters then compute a full proof for ballot validity by combining (i) one proof for each ciphertext c_i showing that the corresponding

---

[1] For simplicity of presentation, we will often only say "encrypted ballot" to refer to both cases, i.e., encryption or commitments.

plaintext v_i is from S, and (ii) one proof for the homomorphic sum of all n_{cand} ciphertexts c_i showing that the decryption lies in S. Generalizing single-vote, one can also use disjunctive Chaum-Pedersen proofs for showing ballot validity for multi-vote elections, where voters can assign up to n_{max} votes to candidates of their choice (up to a limit t for any individual candidate)[2, 11, 18]. However, for larger values of n_{max} (and t) this quickly becomes too inefficient. In such cases, one can replace disjunctive Chaum-Pedersen proofs with range-proofs [31].

Designing efficient ZKPs for ballot validity becomes an increasingly difficult task for more complex voting methods and ballot formats. As an example, consider the class of Borda count election methods, where points are assigned to candidates based on a ranking chosen by the voter. Such a ranking creates dependencies between points assigned to different candidates which cannot be captured by the above approach but requires different ZKPs. The ZKPs for Borda Ballots proposed in [21] only work when ties between candidates are not allowed. The proofs in [27] work for Borda ballots that allow ties at the last place. Both constructions are based on arguments for the correctness of a shuffle. To the best of our knowledge, the only work that has considered ZKPs for Borda ballots with ties at arbitrary positions is the Kryvos system [25], which uses GPZKPs (see below).

Condorcet methods are another class of elections that use very complex choice spaces and thus require advanced validity proofs. These ranked voting methods aim to determine a Condorcet winner who would win against every other candidate in a direct comparison. In [12], two ZKPs for validity of Condorcet ballots have been described. Both ZKPs are for ballots that are encrypted using EEG, but they differ in the ballot formats that are used to encode a vote.

Altogether, while efficient ZKPs for proving ballot validity exist for many election types, they are generally designed only for a specific voting method, ballot format/choice space, and (class of) encryption or commitment scheme. Designing an e-voting system for new types of elections with new ballot formats, therefore, usually entails constructing and proving the security of suitable ZKPs.

Using GPZKPs for Ballot Validity. A promising alternative which we investigate in this work are *general purpose zero-knowledge proofs (GPZKPs)*. GPZKPs can, in theory, show arbitrary statements, including ballot validity for any ballot and election. The main task left for a protocol designer using a GPZKP is to propose an optimized circuit for computing the statement that should be proven so that the resulting GPZKP instance is sufficiently efficient. Thus, GPZKPs have the potential to simplify the process of designing electronic election systems, enable faster prototyping if a new type of election with a different ballot format is implemented, and allow for supporting ballot formats that are so far out of reach of current *specialized ZKPs* which are constructed for showing a specific statement.

While GPZKPs such as ZK-SNARKs (zero-knowledge succinct non-interactive arguments of knowledge, called just SNARKs in the following) have recently gained traction in several areas such as blockchains [24], they have so far mostly gone unnoticed in the area of e-voting. In [15], techniques based on inner product arguments (which are commonly used for constructing GPZKPs [8]) are used for proving that a vector of ciphertexts encrypts bits. This can be used for proving validity of, e.g., single-vote ballots and can drastically outperform the Chaum-Pedersen-based approach we described above. The first (and so far the only) work that considered GPZKPs for more complex relations in encrypted ballots is the Kryvos system [25]. While not their primary focus, as a side result the authors of [25] were able to show that and how the state-of-the-art Groth16 SNARK [22] can be instantiated to obtain practical ballot validity proofs for a wide variety of common election types as long as encrypted ballots are computed by using Pedersen Vector Commitments (PVCs). Among others, and as mentioned above, using this GPZKP, they obtained the first (practical) ZKP for showing validity of Borda ballots that allow ties at arbitrary positions. However, the focus of the Kryvos system is the design of a publicly tally-hiding system rather than the design of ballot validity proofs. Hence, the authors did not further investigate the viability of GPZKPs for ballot validity beyond the uncommon case of PVCs.

It remains unclear if GPZKPs for ballot validity are practical beyond these specific settings, notably for complex ballots in the standard case of (component-wise) EEG. We note that specialized ZKPs, which have been constructed for and are tailored towards a specific election system, voting method, ballot format/choice space, and encryption/commitment scheme, can, of course, be more optimized and hence more efficient than GPZKPs. The advantage of GPZKPs lies in their generality, which, if shown to be practical in at least some settings, would open up a simple and generic approach to building new e-voting systems.

Contributions. In this work we perform a feasibility study that investigates viability and limits of GPZKPs for ballot validity for many ballot formats in commonly used EEG-based e-voting systems. On a technical level, we build on the techniques for instantiating the Groth16 SNARK established in Kryvos [25] and explain how they can, in principle, be used for proving ballot validity when ballots are encrypted component-wise via EEG. As part of this, we also provide a detailed description of their techniques for proving ballot validity, which had only been briefly sketched in [25] with most information left to their implementation.

As the main contribution of our feasibility study, we have implemented several circuits and benchmarked and compared the corresponding Groth16 SNARK instances for showing ballot validity for EEG encryption for a wide range of voting methods and corresponding choice spaces.[2] This includes not only major existing ones: Single- and Multi-Vote, Borda Count, and Condorcet methods. To investigate the potential and limits of GPZKPs for developing and supporting new voting methods and systems, we also consider two new variants of Multi-Vote. These variants introduce non-trivial conditions on ballot formats and mainly serve demonstration purposes. We are not aware that they are currently used in real elections.

To summarize our findings, our benchmarks show that all of these instances are actually practical, both for simple and complex voting methods and choice spaces. Performance depends mainly on the number of candidates. Interestingly,

---

[2] All of our implementations are available at [26].

however, the performance of these Groth16 instances is otherwise essentially independent of the complexity of the underlying choice space. That is, introducing and proving additional conditions on the format of ballots, even multiple highly complex ones, barely changes overall performance.

Altogether *our work establishes for the first time that current GPZKPs are a viable option even for complex ballot formats for commonly used Exponetial ElGamal-based e-voting systems*, which opens up new options for supporting different voting methods. Our benchmarks further provide a basis for protocol designers to make an educated choice for or against a Groth16-based ballot validity ZKPs.

2   Preliminaries: GPZKPs, SNARKs, Groth16

A general purpose zero-knowledge proof (GPZKP) system takes as input an arbitrary indicator function $f_R : \{0,1\}^* \times \{0,1\}^* \to \{0,1\}$ for some binary relation R such that $f_R(x,w) = 1$ iff $(x,w) \in R$ for a public *statement* x and a secret *witness* w. It then allows for computing a zero-knowledge proof (ZKP) which shows the existence/knowledge of w such that $f_R(x,w) = 1$. In the following, we only consider proofs of knowledge as typically needed in e-voting [30].

To be practical for showing ballot validity, good prover efficiency and small proof sizes are crucial: Impatient voters have to be able to compute and then transmit the GPZKP using their own personal devices within reasonable time and possibly having only little bandwidth available. While election verification is less time critical, verification speed should at least be moderately fast and, again, proof sizes should be small since proofs from all voters need to be downloaded.

Of the various GPZKP systems [3,6,10,17,20,22,29], SNARKs fit these requirements best. Following [25], we use the highly efficient state-of-the-art Groth16 SNARK [22] that offers constant small proof size of less than 1 kilobyte with (almost) constant verification time of about a few milliseconds on a standard PC[3] - independently of the function f_R. It further achieves fast polynomial proving time and thus scales well even for highly complex functions f_R. The Groth16 SNARK is therefore an ideal candidate for showing ballot validity.

A bit simplified, Groth16 consists of three algorithms: Setup, Prove, and Verify. The Setup(f_R) algorithm generates two common reference strings, CRS_{EK} (*evaluation key* CRS) and CRS_{VK} (*verification key* CRS) that depend on f_R. CRS_{VK} is a much smaller substring of CRS_{EK}. This creates an instance of Groth16 that is specific to the function f_R.[4] The CRS_{EK} can be used by anyone to create a proof $\pi \xleftarrow{\$} \mathsf{Prove}(CRS_{EK}, x, w)$ for $f_R(x,w) = 1$. One can use $\mathsf{Verify}(CRS_{VK}, x, \pi)$ to verify the proof, which requires only the smaller CRS_{VK}. Groth16 SNARKs are based on pairing groups of elliptic curves; a proof consists of 3 group elements.

---

[3] All of our benchmarks were obtained on an ESPRIMO Q957 (64-bit, i5-7500T CPU @ 2.70GHz, 16 GB RAM).

[4] Some other SNARK constructions, such as [17] have a universal setup ceremony, i.e., the CRS only needs to be generated once and can then be updated for different indicator functions. This comes at the cost of increasing proof size and proving times.

We use the common curve BN254, which is defined over a base field of size $\sim 2^{254}$ and provides ~ 100 bits of security. Concretely, and following [25, 28], we use the libsnark implementation [34] of Groth16 for obtaining our benchmarks. Other implementations [4, 19] support curves for higher security levels, such as BLS12-381 or BLS24-317 for $128 - 160$ bits of security.

Groth16 uses the language of quadratic arithmetic programs (QAPs) to specify the indicator function f_R and hence the underlying relation R. Typically, in order to obtain a QAP, $f_R(x, w)$ is first expressed as an arithmetic circuit where each input/output/internal wire is represented either by a variable or a constant. The public input x is a list of values assigned to some wire variables (not necessarily only input wires). A valid witness w then consists of values assigned to all remaining wire variables such that all of these values, together with constants, describe a correct computation of the circuit.[5] This circuit is then converted to a set of so-called constraints that can in turn be compiled into a QAP instance, which we will not discuss further in this paper. A constraint over n variables $a_1, \ldots, a_n$ is an equation $\sum_{i=1}^{n} a_i u_i \cdot \sum_{i=1}^{n} a_i v_i = \sum_{i=1}^{n} a_i w_i$, where u_i, v_i and w_i are constants defining the constraint. For describing instantiations of concrete indicator functions f_R one can thus use both arithmetic circuits and constraints mostly interchangeably. We will usually describe an instantiation as a circuit yielding a certain number of constraints.

The time required to create a proof and the size of $\mathsf{CRS_{EK}}$ of a Groth16 SNARK instance depend linearly on the number of inputs and the number of constraints, i.e., the size of the circuit. Concretely, $\mathsf{CRS_{EK}}$ consists of $3\nu + \mu + 6$ group elements, where ν denotes the number of constraints and μ denotes the number of inputs. As the number of inputs only has a minor effect on these benchmarks, typically only the number of constraints is considered. To get an idea, here are some figures using the libsnark instantiation over BN254 for a standard PC (cf. Footnote 3): For $100,000$, $500,000$, and $1,250,000$ constraints, the size of the $\mathsf{CRS_{EK}}$ is about 162 MB, 810 MB, and 2 GB, respectively. Note that these $\mathsf{CRS_{EK}}$ sizes are uncompressed sizes and can usually be reduced by a factor of at least 2 via standard compression methods. Proofs can be computed in about 4.46, 22.3, and 55.75 seconds, respectively. As mentioned above, proof size and verification time are small and independent of the circuit while $\mathsf{CRS_{VK}}$ is a small subset of $\mathsf{CRS_{EK}}$ which only contains $\ell + 4$ group elements, where ℓ is the number of wires assigned to the public input (e.g., for $3,000$ such wires - far more than we will need - $\mathsf{CRS_{VK}}$ is smaller than 500 KB). In this paper we therefore mainly focus on determining and optimizing prover runtime and size of $\mathsf{CRS_{EK}}$.

CRS Generation and Soundness. We note that soundness of our ZKPs breaks down if the CRSs are not generated honestly. One can mitigate this issue by computing the CRSs in a distributed fashion before an election; see, e.g., [1, 5, 7]. We note that it is of course desirable to minimize trust assumptions for verifiability. However, in practice one often still has some trust assumptions,

---

[5] Usually, a valid w is described only in terms of input wire variables as this already fully defines the remaining witness values for internal and output wire variables.

e.g., trusted bulletin boards, authentication/registration servers, or a trusted PKI. Alternatively, there are other GPZKPs, such as [3,8], which do not require a trusted CRS generation and are in principle compatible with our constructions, as they use a similar underlying language as Groth16, while being less efficient in terms of computation and proof size.

3   Proving Ballot Validity Using Groth16

To construct ballot validity proofs using Groth16, we follow the approach from Kryvos [25] for PVC-based encrypted ballots. In this section, we give a complete overview of their approach, explain how the same techniques can be used for EEG-based ballots, and provide the first benchmarks for several subcomponents. Our benchmarks for complete ballot validity proofs are then given in Sect. 4.

Recall that voters choose their plain ballot $\mathbf{b}$ as a length-N-vector from some choice space C and then use an (additively) homomorphic encryption or commitment scheme $\mathsf{Enc}(\cdot)$ to obtain an encrypted ballot $c \leftarrow \mathsf{Enc}(\mathbf{b})$. To show ballot validity via a GPZKP such as Groth16, a voter uses the following indicator function $f_R(x, w)$: the public statement x contains the encrypted ballot c. The witness w contains a plain ballot $\mathbf{b}$ and randomness $\mathfrak{r}_w$ such that $f_R(x, w) = 1$ iff $\mathsf{Enc}(\mathbf{b}, \mathfrak{r}_w) = c$ and $\mathbf{b} \in C$.

We construct a corresponding arithmetic circuit $\mathfrak{C}$ for ballot validity from two separate sub-circuits as shown in Fig. 1. The *encryption* subcircuit $\mathfrak{C}_{\mathsf{Enc}}$ re-computes the encrypted ballot from the plain ballot $\mathbf{b}$ and randomness $\mathfrak{r}_w$ contained in the witness w and from the public encryption key contained in a public input $\mathsf{aux}_{\mathsf{Enc}}$. The public encrypted ballot c is assigned to the output wires of $\mathfrak{C}_{\mathsf{Enc}}$, which implies that $\mathsf{Enc}(\mathbf{b}, \mathfrak{r}_w) = c$ holds in a valid proof for this circuit. The *voting* subcircuit $\mathfrak{C}_{\mathsf{Voting}}$ takes as input the plain ballot $\mathbf{b}$ from the input witness w and then outputs a bit indicating whether $\mathbf{b} \in C$. The constant 1 is assigned to the output wire of $\mathfrak{C}_{\mathsf{Voting}}$, which implies that $\mathbf{b} \in C$ holds for valid proofs. Both subcircuits might take additional auxiliary public and witness values as input which can be used to improve efficiency or to generalize circuits.

This modular design of $\mathfrak{C}$ simplifies circuit design and optimization while enabling the re-use of components shared by circuits for different voting methods, most notably $\mathfrak{C}_{\mathsf{Enc}}$, which does not depend on C (except for the length of the vote vector). In the following subsections, we will explain how we construct both subcircuits while keeping the number of constraints small. We note that the overall number of constraints and, hence, the overall performance of $\mathfrak{C}$ is essentially the sum of $\mathfrak{C}_{\mathsf{Enc}}$ and $\mathfrak{C}_{\mathsf{Voting}}$. To compare their relative impact we therefore also provide benchmarks for all subcomponents.

3.1   Constructing and Optimizing $\mathfrak{C}_{\mathsf{Enc}}$

Due to the complexity of encryption/commitment schemes, designing an efficient $\mathfrak{C}_{\mathsf{Enc}}$ with a small and hence practical number of constraints is a highly non-trivial task that makes or breaks the practicality of the overall ballot validity proof. The authors of Kryvos [25] spent much effort on designing a highly optimized $\mathfrak{C}_{\mathsf{Enc}}^{\mathsf{PVC}}$ for PVCs which we will first recall and then show how it can be transformed into a circuit $\mathfrak{C}_{\mathsf{Enc}}^{\mathsf{EEG}}$ for EEG. This transformation is mostly straightforward on a technical level as both primitives use the same operations. The main question we investigate rather is the resulting performance and practicality, which is unclear for $\mathfrak{C}_{\mathsf{Enc}}^{\mathsf{EEG}}$ due to the reasons detailed at the end of the next paragraph.

Existing Building Blocks for PVCs from [25]. Let $\mathcal{G}$ be a (multiplicative) group of prime order q and let $h, g_1, \ldots, g_N$ be generators of $\mathcal{G}$ such that no relation between these generators is known. A PVC on a plaintext vector $\boldsymbol{v} = (v_1, \ldots, v_N) \in \mathbb{Z}_q^N$ is defined as $c =, (\boldsymbol{v}, r) = g_1^{v_1} \cdot \ldots \cdot g_N^{v_N} \cdot h^r \in \mathcal{G}$ for (uniform) randomness $r \xleftarrow{\$} \mathbb{Z}_q$. The case $N = 1$ gives a standard Pedersen commitment.

A major factor for the size and hence performance of $\mathfrak{C}_{\mathsf{Enc}}^{\mathsf{PVC}}$ is exponentiation. Building on results from [28], Kryvos uses an instantiation of the common Montgomery elliptic curve Curve25591 over the scalar field of BN254 (the curve used for Groth16 by libsnark [34], see Sect. 2), which allows for an efficient implementation of exponentiation via the Montgomery ladder algorithm.[6] More precisely, as described in [28], we set $\mathcal{G}$ to be the large prime-order subgroup of this curve, which has size $q \approx 2^{251}$. A group element is a curve point that can be represented in affine or equivalently projective coordinates consisting of two resp. three coordinates in $\mathbb{Z}_q$. In $\mathfrak{C}_{\mathsf{Enc}}^{\mathsf{PVC}}$, a point is represented by one wire per coordinate. For affine coordinates, a third wire is used to indicate whether the given point is the special point at infinity. The number of constraints needed for implementing the Montgomery ladder algorithm then depends on the (maximal) size of the exponent. According to [25], an exponentiation with an arbitrary 255 bit randomness r requires 5,084 constraints. However, valid votes $\boldsymbol{v}$ usually have much smaller entries v_i, typically just a few bits (depending on the choice space). Kryvos bounds the size of a (valid) v_i by 32 bits, which covers all interesting choice spaces and requires only 624 constraints for one exponentiation.

Based on this choice of $\mathcal{G}$, Kryvos designed and reported constraint numbers for the following subcircuits: (i) The aforementioned circuit for computing an exponentiation g^m of an elliptic curve point g with $m \le q$ using Montgomery's ladder. This only gives the (projective) X- and Z-coordinate of g^m. (ii) A circuit for computing the (projective) Y-coordinate from output of the Montgomery ladder and the (projective) Y-coordinate of g following Okea and Sakurai [32] (39 constraints). (iii) A circuit for converting projective to affine coordinates (15 constraints). (iv) A circuit for multiplying two points given in affine coordinates (86 constraints). These subcircuits are then combined to obtain $\mathfrak{C}_{\mathsf{Enc}}^{\mathsf{PVC}}$.

Observe that the exponentiation with large randomness is by far the most expensive step. This is why this approach scales particularly well for PVCs: For committing to a vector of size N, only a single expensive exponentiation (h^r) is needed ($N+1$ exponentiations overall). In contrast, EEG requires more exponentiations ($3N$) for encrypting a vector of size N and $2N$ of those exponentiations are for the large randomness. So this raises the question whether we can obtain reasonably efficient ballot validity SNARKS for EEG.

---

[6] We stick with multiplicative notion of the group law also for elliptic curve groups.

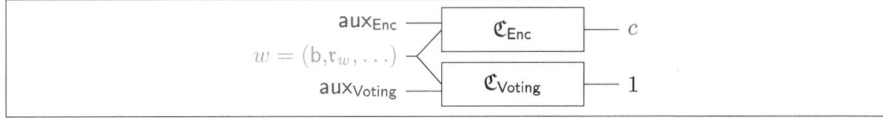

Fig. 1. The arithmetic circuit $\mathfrak{C}$ for proving ballot validity. Secret/witness values are shown in orange, public values are blue, and constants are black. (Color figure online)

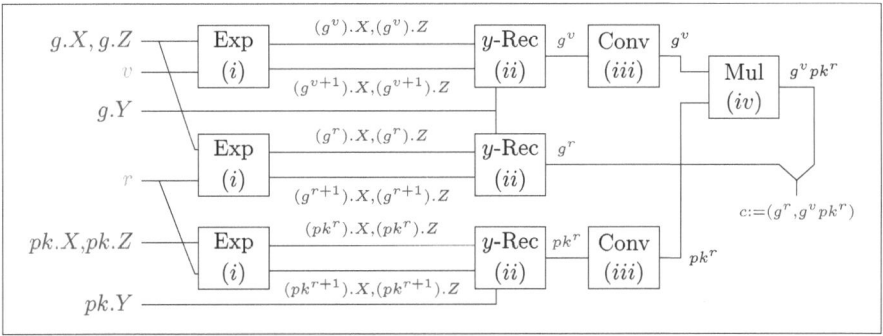

Fig. 2. Circuit $\mathfrak{C}_{\mathsf{Enc}}$ for computing an EEG ciphertext c from plaintext v with randomness r. The secret witness (marked in orange) is $w := (v, r)$. The public statements (marked in blue) are the ciphertext $c = (g^r, g^v pk^r)$ and $\mathsf{aux}_{\mathsf{Enc}}$, which contains the public key pk and the generator g. Where important, we show wires with individual coordinates, e.g., $g.X$ denotes the projective X-coordinate of g. We also use purple/black color for projective/affine coordinates. When no individual coordinate but just a point is given, e.g., g^v, then this represents the three wires for that point's coordinates. The numbers $(i) - (iv)$ refer to the sub-circuits from Sect. 3.1. (Color figure online)

Proving Plaintext Knowledge for a Vector of EEG Ciphertexts. Again, let $\mathcal{G}$ be a (multiplicative) group of prime order q and generator g. An EEG ciphertext for a plaintext $v \in \mathbb{Z}_q$ and a given public key $pk \in \mathcal{G}$ is obtained by sampling a randomness $r \xleftarrow{\$} \mathbb{Z}_q$ and returning $c = (c_0, c_1) = (g^r, g^v \cdot pk^r)$.

We constructed a circuit $\mathfrak{C}_{\mathsf{Enc}}^{\mathsf{EEG}}$ for computing N such ciphertexts from N plaintexts v_i, N randomnesses r_i, and a public key pk from the subcircuits established in Kryvos. We depict the resulting circuit in Fig. 2 for the case $N = 1$. For $N > 1$, this circuit is copied N times with separate input and output wires, except for the input wires corresponding to pk and g which are shared by all copies.

Benchmarks and Comparison. After implementing our new circuit $\mathfrak{C}_{\mathsf{Enc}}^{\mathsf{EEG}}$ for EEG ciphertexts, we have benchmarked the performance of Groth16 for this circuit and various sizes N of the plaintext vector, as well as various upper bounds on the bit length of individual plaintexts. We have also benchmarked the existing implementation of $\mathfrak{C}_{\mathsf{Enc}}^{\mathsf{PVC}}$ for PVCs on the same machine (see Footnote 3 on Page 111) to obtain a fair comparison, with all results shown in Fig. 3.

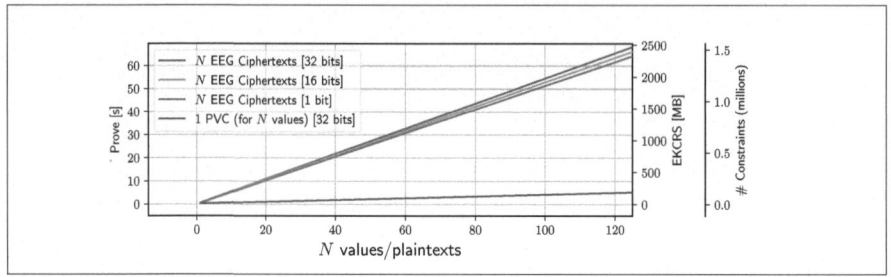

Fig. 3. Prover runtime, $\mathsf{CRS_{EK}}$ size, and constraints for $\mathfrak{C}_{\mathsf{Enc}}^{\mathsf{EEG}}$ and $\mathfrak{C}_{\mathsf{Enc}}^{\mathsf{PVC}}$

As expected, creating a SNARK proof for validating a vector of EEG ciphertexts instead of a PVC is much less efficient for large vector lengths N. However, and perhaps unexpected, even for a vector consisting of 50 EEG ciphertexts a voter can still compute a proof in less than 30 seconds using a $\mathsf{CRS_{EK}}$ of about 1 GB, which is already good enough to be viable in a wide range of settings and election types. For a more detailed discussion of practicality in various situations, see Sect. 4.

Interestingly, our prover runtimes for $\mathfrak{C}_{\mathsf{Enc}}^{\mathsf{PVC}}$ significantly outperformed the ones that we obtained in [25] by a factor of 2 to 3 on a comparable machine. After investigating the issue, it turns out that in [25], we accidentally used a custom version of the libsnark library that performs additional computations for debugging purposes and hence is much slower.

3.2 Constructing and Optimizing $\mathfrak{C}_{\mathsf{Voting}}$

Since the subcircuit $\mathfrak{C}_{\mathsf{Voting}}$ checks that a (plain) ballot belongs to a given choice space, its design depends on the voting method/choice space. Here, we describe and benchmark circuits for the following common voting methods/choice spaces: Single-Vote, Multi-Vote, Borda Count, and Condorcet. To investigate the potential and limits of GPZKPs for developing and supporting new voting methods and systems, we further construct and benchmark circuits for two additional (somewhat artificial) complex choice spaces - both variants of Multi-Vote, which we call *Line-Vote* and *Multi-Vote with Rules*. We provide the benchmarks for $\mathfrak{C}_{\mathsf{Voting}}$ for all of our choice spaces in Fig. 4.

Since $\mathfrak{C}_{\mathsf{Voting}}$ is independent of the method used for encrypting ballots - thanks to the modularity of $\mathfrak{C}$ - we can reuse the existing sub-circuits for Single-Vote, Multi-Vote, Borda Count, and Condorcet from [25] with some minor optimizations and extensions. We briefly recall their designs for completeness and provide some additional details, such as constraint numbers. We also provide the first benchmarks for these subcircuits, which were not benchmarked separately in [25].

Single-Vote. Recall that in a single-vote election, a voter can give only one vote for their preferred candidate, with the corresponding choice space C_{single}

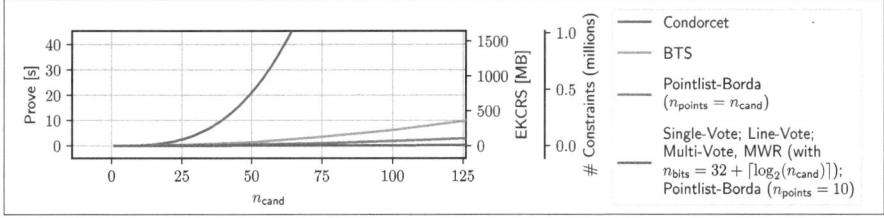

Fig. 4. Prover runtime, $\mathsf{CRS_{EK}}$ size, and constraints of $\mathfrak{C}_{\mathsf{Voting}}$ for several voting methods. For Pointlist-Borda, we use $\mathcal{L} = \{1, \ldots, n_{\mathsf{points}}\}$, for Multi-Vote and MWR, we use $t = 2^{32} - 1$ and $n_{\mathsf{max}} = n_{\mathsf{cand}} \cdot t$.

defined in Sect. 1. Checking that $b \in C_{\mathsf{single}}$ entails two substeps: (i) Checking that each ballot entry is a bit, which requires one constraint per candidate, and (ii) checking that the sum of all ballot entries equals 1, which requires one constraint. To allow abstention by casting a ballot without a vote, one can instead check that the sum is a bit, which also requires one constraint.

For n_{cand} candidates, $\mathfrak{C}_{\mathsf{Voting}}^{\mathsf{single}}$ thus consists of $n_{\mathsf{cand}} + 1$ constraints. This yields a very small $\mathsf{CRS_{EK}}$ of less than 1 MB and proof times of less than 0.05 seconds for any realistic number of candidates (see Fig. 4).

Multi-vote. Multi-vote generalizes single-vote by letting voters allocate up to n_{max} votes among n_{cand} candidates, with a maximum of t votes assigned to any candidate. Analogous to C_{single}, we define the following choice space:

$$C_{\mathsf{multi}}(n_{\mathsf{max}}, t) := \left\{ (v_1, \ldots, v_{n_{\mathsf{cand}}}) \mid \forall i : v_i \in \{0, 1, \ldots, t\} \wedge 0 \leq \sum_{i=1}^{n_{\mathsf{cand}}} v_i \leq n_{\mathsf{max}} \right\}.$$

The circuit $\mathfrak{C}_{\mathsf{Voting}}^{\mathsf{multi}}$ for C_{multi} then checks that each v_i is in the allowed range (between 0 and t) and that the sum of all v_i is in the correct range (between 0 and n_{max}). Such range checks require converting the respective value into individual bits. Therefore, the number of constraints depends on the maximal possible bit size n_{bits} of $\sum_{i=1}^{n_{\mathsf{cand}}} v_i$ which is, in turn, determined by the bit sizes of t and n_{max}. The complete circuit requires about $(n_{\mathsf{bits}} + 1) \cdot (n_{\mathsf{cand}} + 1)$ constraints (the exact number depends on t and n_{max}), which - even for unrealistically high values of n_{bits} such as $n_{\mathsf{bits}} = 41$ - is still very small for any realistic number of candidates. Hence, performance of $\mathfrak{C}_{\mathsf{Voting}}^{\mathsf{multi}}$ is essentially the same as for $\mathfrak{C}_{\mathsf{Voting}}^{\mathsf{single}}$ (see Fig. 4).

Supporting New Choice Spaces: Line-Vote and Multi-Vote with Rules. We consider two modifications of multi-vote that are somewhat artificial but represent cases where one might want to use GPZKPs: they are novel choice spaces, so no ballot validity ZKPs exist, and as they are obtained by adding non-trivial interdependencies between the votes for individual candidates, it is hard to construct new specialized ZKPs.

Line-Vote: In Line-Vote, voters are given n_{cand} many (ordered) options to vote YES or NO. Voters can vote YES for any number of those options subject to the restriction that all YES-votes must form a continuous line, i.e., if two options receive a YES-vote, then all options in-between must receive a YES-vote as well. The choice space can be formalized as follows:

$$C_{\text{line}} := \{(v_1, \ldots, v_{n_{\text{cand}}}) \mid v_i \in \{0, 1\} \land (i < j \land v_i, v_j = 1 \Rightarrow \forall i < k < j : v_k = 1)\}.$$

A corresponding circuit $\mathfrak{C}_{\text{Voting}}^{\text{line}}$ can be built easily analogous to $\mathfrak{C}_{\text{Voting}}^{\text{multi}}$: $\mathfrak{C}_{\text{Voting}}^{\text{line}}$ uses an additional "helper" wire which is first set to v_1 and is then incremented for all non-zero v_i that occur directly after a zero entry v_{i-1}. A ballot is then valid iff all v_i and the helper wire are bits. This circuit consists of $2n_{\text{cand}}$ constraints.

Multi-Vote with Rules (MWR): In MWR, we consider multi-vote ballots whose entries are subject to additional arithmetic rule(s). One can add arbitrary (numbers of) rules. As a concrete example, we consider a rule where the product of the second and the third ballot entry equals the first one:

$$C_{\text{MWR}}(n_{\text{max}}, t) := \{b = (v_1, \ldots, v_{n_{\text{cand}}}) \in C_{\text{multi}}(n_{\text{max}}, t) \mid v_1 = v_2 \cdot v_3\}.$$

The corresponding circuit $\mathfrak{C}_{\text{Voting}}^{\text{MWR}}$ is again easy to construct: use $\mathfrak{C}_{\text{Voting}}^{\text{multi}}$ as a basis and add additional constraints for each rule. In the above example, just 2 additional constraints are needed.

Altogether, both examples confirm that it is indeed simple to support new choice spaces via GPZKPs and that, depending on the additional conditions imposed on the v_i, this might not even come at a noticeable cost (see Fig. 4).

Pointlist-Borda and Borda Tournament Style (BTS). Borda is a ranked election method where voters rank the candidates according to their preference and, based on this ranking, points are assigned to each candidate. Variants of Borda are used, e.g., for parliamentary elections in Nauru [33] and the Eurovision Song Contest (ESC) [16]. As suggested in [25], such variants used in practice can be captured as instances of what they call *Pointlist-Borda*. A Pointlist-Borda instance is defined via a fixed point list $\mathcal{L}$ that contains n_{points} many distinct positive numbers. Voters then construct their ballots by assigning each number in $\mathcal{L}$ to one candidate and, if $n_{\text{points}} < n_{\text{cand}}$, 0 points to all remaining candidates. Observe that this represents a ranking where the highest-ranked candidate receives the most points and so on with $n_{\text{cand}} - n_{\text{points}}$ candidates tied for the last place. Formally, the choice space is as follows:

$$C_{\text{BordaPointList}}(\mathcal{L}) := \Big\{(v_1, \ldots, v_{n_{\text{cand}}}) \Big| (\forall p \in \mathcal{L} \, \exists i : v_i = p)$$
$$\land \, |\{i \in [1, n_{\text{cand}}] \mid v_i = 0\}| = n_{\text{cand}} - n_{\text{points}}\Big\}.$$

The size of $\mathfrak{C}_{\text{Voting}}^{\text{BordaPointList}}$ depends on $n_{\text{points}} = |\mathcal{L}|$ but is not affected by the concrete values in $\mathcal{L}$ (hence, we simply take $\mathcal{L} = [1, n_{\text{points}}]$ for benchmarking). For small constants, such as $n_{\text{points}} = 10$, the size of $\mathfrak{C}_{\text{Voting}}^{\text{BordaPointList}}$ scales linearly in n_{cand}, similar to single-/multi-vote. The worst case is $n_{\text{points}} = n_{\text{cand}}$, which scales quadratically in n_{cand} but remains practical. For example, in an extreme case of $n_{\text{points}} = n_{\text{cand}} = 100$, computing a proof still only requires less than 2 seconds and a CRS_{EK} of less than 100 MB (see Fig. 4 for both cases).

There are many ways to design generalized (academical) Borda variants that allow for ties between candidates at arbitrary positions. For example, [25]considers an even more complex Borda variant they call *Borda tournament style (BTS)* which we include in our benchmarks using their circuit $\mathfrak{C}_{\text{Voting}}^{\text{BTS}}$ (see Fig. 4). Due to space limitations, we refer to [25] for details of BTS.

Condorcet Methods. In Condorcet methods, which are, e.g., used for internal elections of the Debian project [14], a voter submits a ranking of candidates. Condorcet methods differ in how they determine the winner but, if such a candidate exists, they will return the candidate who wins against all other candidates in a direct comparison. To make rankings compatible with aggregation of ballots, they are typically represented as comparison matrices [12, 23, 25].

Specifically, given a ranking $r = (r_1, \dots, r_{n_{\text{cand}}}) \in \mathbb{N}^{n_{\text{cand}}}$ of candidates (where $r_i > r_j$ means that candidate i is ranked worse than candidate j), a voter constructs her ballot as an $n_{\text{cand}} \times n_{\text{cand}}$ matrix A with 1 at position (i, j) if candidate i is ranked better than candidate j and 0 otherwise. Note that hence n_{cand}^2 many values are used for a ballot, unlike all aforementioned voting methods that used one value per candidate. Also note that, if candidates are tied, then this is represented by A_{ij} and A_{ji} both being 0, i.e., a ballot is a *positive preference matrix* as defined in [12]. The choice space then is:

$$C_{\text{Condorcet}} = \left\{ A \in \{0, 1\}^{n_{\text{cand}} \times n_{\text{cand}}} \middle| \exists (\ r_1, \dots, r_{n_{\text{cand}}}) \in \mathbb{N}^{n_{\text{cand}}} \text{ s.t. } \forall i, j \in [1, n_{\text{cand}}] : \right.$$

$$r_i > r_j \Rightarrow A_{ij} = 0, A_{ji} = 1 \ \wedge$$

$$\left. r_i = r_j \Rightarrow A_{ij} = A_{ji} = 0 \right\}$$

The circuit $\mathfrak{C}_{\text{Voting}}^{\text{Condorcet}}$ extends the one proposed in [25], which did not support ties. It first checks that all matrix entries are bits and that for $i \neq j$ also $A_{ij} + A_{ji}$ is a bit.[7] It remains to check transitivity (i.e., that, for any triple (i, j, k) of distinct candidates, it holds that $r_i \leq r_j$ and $r_j \leq r_k$ imply $r_i \leq r_k$, with $r_i = r_k$ iff $r_i = r_j$ and $r_j = r_k$). Checking both cases, i.e., $\leq$ and $=$, turns out to be easier if ties through 1-entries instead of 0-entries. For this, $\mathfrak{C}_{\text{Voting}}$ computes a "check matrix" B with $B_{ij} := 1 - A_{ji}$, which does not require any new constraints. Note that B equals A everywhere except that 1-entries replace the 0-entries that represent ties in A. Then, the circuit checks whether $B_{ij} \cdot B_{jk} \cdot (1 - B_{ik}) = 0$, which is true iff A is transitive (observe that this check indeed covers both the $\leq$ and the $=$ case). The resulting circuit scales cubically in the number of candidates, where, e.g., 25 candidates require a CRS_{EK} of about 90 MB and a proof time of about 2.5 seconds (see Fig. 4).

---

[7] One can instead check that $A_{ij} + A_{ji} = 1$ to prevent ties as proposed in [25]. This yields the same number of constraints.

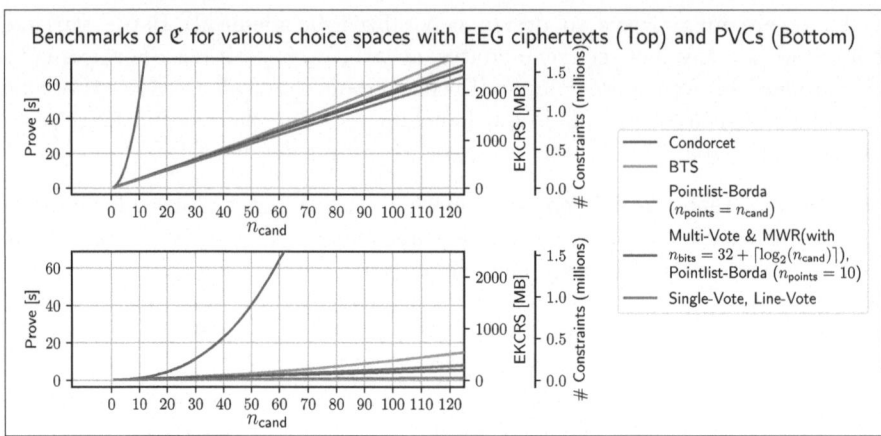

Fig. 5. Comparison of full ballot validity proofs. Condorcet, Single-, and Line-Vote use $\mathfrak{C}_{\mathsf{Enc}}$ with 1-bit plaintexts; all other choice spaces use 32-bit plaintexts.

4   Overall Benchmarks for Proving Ballot Validity

Following the outline given in Sect. 3, we can now combine the encryption subcircuit $\mathfrak{C}_{\mathsf{Enc}}$ with a suitable plaintext bit size from Sect. 3.1 and a voting subcircuit $\mathfrak{C}_{\mathsf{Voting}}$ from Sect. 3.2 to obtain complete circuits $\mathfrak{C}$ for proving ballot validity. Our benchmarks of prover runtime, $\mathsf{CRS}_{\mathsf{EK}}$ size, and constraints for these circuits using EEG encryption and depending on the number of candidates n_{cand} are given in the top half of Fig. 5. For comparison, in the bottom half of Fig. 5 we provide our benchmarks for ballots computed as PVCs using the constructions of [25]. As mentioned in Sect. 2, the proof size is less than 1 KB, and verification requires only about 7 ms as both are mostly independent of the circuit. Since the $\mathsf{CRS}_{\mathsf{VK}}$ is a subset of $\mathsf{CRS}_{\mathsf{EK}}$ we do not provide separate benchmarks, but its size is always in the order of ~ 20 KB and hence negligible.

The performance of the Groth16 proof for the combined circuit $\mathfrak{C}$ is essentially the sum of the subcircuits $\mathfrak{C}_{\mathsf{Enc}}$ and $\mathfrak{C}_{\mathsf{Voting}}$ and thus dominated by the much slower $\mathfrak{C}_{\mathsf{Enc}}$. Note that the performance of $\mathfrak{C}_{\mathsf{Enc}}$ in Fig. 3 was given depending on the number N of plaintexts, while for the combined circuit $\mathfrak{C}$ we consider performance depending on number n_{cand} of candidates. All but one choice space use one plaintext per candidate, i.e., $N = n_{\mathsf{cand}}$, so the benchmarks given in Fig. 5 mostly retain the linear behavior of $\mathfrak{C}_{\mathsf{Enc}}$, potentially plus some small non-linear overhead caused by $\mathfrak{C}_{\mathsf{Voting}}$. The exception are Condorcet ballots, where $N = n_{\mathsf{cand}}^2$. This causes visibly quadratic behavior in the combined circuit due to $\mathfrak{C}_{\mathsf{Enc}}$ (plus some much smaller cubic overhead due to $\mathfrak{C}_{\mathsf{Voting}}^{\mathsf{Condorcet}}$).

To summarize our benchmarks, for most election types with EEG, Groth16 ballot validity proofs can be computed by voters within a reasonable time on standard PCs, even for large numbers of candidates. Since runtime is dominated by $\mathfrak{C}_{\mathsf{Enc}}$, it stays mostly the same even for new ballot formats with potentially very complex validity rules, as shown by Line-Vote, MWR, and BTS. The only outlier is Condorcet, for which computing a proof quickly becomes impractical due to the quadratic number of ciphertexts. We note, however, that real-world Condorcet elections, such as [14], rarely have more than 10 candidates. For such cases, a proof of ballot validity can still be computed in less than a minute. As for the size of $\mathsf{CRS_{EK}}$, it is non-negligible in all cases but still within ranges that can reasonably be downloaded once as part of the election software. Also, recall that the presented $\mathsf{CRS_{EK}}$ sizes are uncompressed sizes. We also note that the same CRS can then be re-used for multiple elections.

In conclusion, our results establish that Groth16 and, hence, GPZKPs are a viable option for showing ballot validity in EEG-based voting systems. We have further shown the potential of GPZKPs for supporting new voting methods with novel complex ballot formats. While specialized ZKPs, where available, can still be preferable to GPZKPs, e.g., due to better efficiency, our results show that GPZKPs can be a viable and, importantly, quite generic and uniform option. A detailed performance comparison between GPZKPs and specialized ZKPs for various ballot formats and group choices would be an interesting future work.

Acknowledgements. This research was funded in part by the Deutsche Forschungs-gemeinschaft (DFG, German Research Foundation), grant 411720488.

References

1. Abdolmaleki, B., et al.: UC-Secure CRS Generation for SNARKs. In: AFRICACRYPT 2019, Proceedings. LNCS, vol. 11627, pp. 99–117. Springer (2019)
2. Adida, B., et al.: Electing a university president using open-audit voting: analysis of real-world use of helios. In: USENIX/ACCURATE Electronic Voting Technology (EVT 2009) (2009)
3. Ames, S., et al.: Ligero: lightweight sublinear arguments without a trusted setup. In: ACM CCS 2017, pp. 2087–2104 (2017)
4. Bellés-Muñoz, M., et al.: Circom: a circuit description language for building zero-knowledge applications. IEEE Trans. Dependable Secur. Comput. **20**(6), 4733–4751 (2023)
5. Ben-Sasson, E., et al.: Secure sampling of public parameters for succinct zero knowledge proofs. In: IEEE SP 2015, pp. 287–304. IEEE Computer Society (2015)
6. Ben-Sasson, E., et al.: Scalable, transparent, and post-quantum secure computational integrity. IACR Cryptology ePrint Archive **2018**, 46 (2018)
7. Bowe, S., Gabizon, A., Miers, I.: Scalable multi-party computation for zk-SNARK parameters in the random beacon model. IACR Cryptol. ePrint Arch. **2017**, 1050 (2017)
8. Bünz, B., et al.: Bulletproofs: short proofs for confidential transactions and more. In: SP 2018, pp. 315–334 (2018)
9. Chaum, D., Pedersen, T.P.: Wallet databases with observers. In: CRYPTO '92. LNCS, vol. 740, pp. 89–105. Springer (1992)
10. Chiesa, A., Ojha, D., Spooner, N.: Fractal: post-quantum and transparent recursive proofs from holography. In: EUROCRYPT 2020, pp. 769–793 (2020)

11. Cortier, V., Gaudry, P., Glondu, S.: Belenios: a simple private and verifiable electronic voting system. In: Guttman, J.D., Landwehr, C.E., Meseguer, J., Pavlovic, D. (eds.) Foundations of Security, Protocols, and Equational Reasoning. LNCS, vol. 11565, pp. 214–238. Springer, Cham (2019). https://doi.org/10.1007/978-3-030-19052-1_14

12. Cortier, V., Gaudry, P., Yang, Q.: A toolbox for verifiable tally-hiding e-voting systems. In: ESORICS 2022. LNCS, vol. 13555, pp. 631–652. Springer (2022)

13. Cramer, R., Damgård, I., Schoenmakers, B.: Proofs of partial knowledge and simplified design of witness hiding protocols. In: CRYPTO 1994, pp.174–187. Springer (1994)

14. Debian Project: Debian Voting Information (2024). https://www.debian.org/vote/

15. Devillez, H., Pereira, O., Peters, T.: How to verifiably encrypt many bits for an election? In: ESORICS 2022. LNCS, vol. 13555, pp. 653–671. Springer (2022)

16. European Broadcasting Union: Eurovision Song Contest - How it works (2024). https://eurovision.tv/about/how-it-works

17. Gabizon, A., Williamson, Z.J., Ciobotaru, O.: Plonk: permutations over lagrange-bases for oecumenical noninteractive arguments of knowledge. IACR Cryptol. ePrint Arch. **2019**, 953 (2019)

18. Gaudry, P.: Some ZK security proofs for belenios (2017)

19. Gautam Botrel and Others: Consensys/gnark: v0.10.0 (2024). https://doi.org/10.5281/zenodo.11034183

20. Giacomelli, I., Madsen, J., Orlandi, C.: ZKBoo: faster Zero-Knowledge for boolean circuits. In: USENIX Security Symposium 2016, pp. 1069–1083. USENIX Association (2016)

21. Groth, J.: Non-interactive zero-knowledge arguments for voting. In: ACNS 2005. LNCS, vol. 3531, pp. 467–482 (2005)

22. Groth, J.: On the size of pairing-based non-interactive arguments. In: EUROCRYPT 2016. LNCS, vol. 9666, pp. 305–326. Springer (2016)

23. Hertel, F., et al.: Extending the tally-hiding ordinos system: implementations for borda, hare-niemeyer, condorcet, and instant-runoff voting. In: E-Vote-ID 2021, pp. 269–284. University of Tartu Press (2021)

24. Hopwood, D.E., et al.: Zcash Protocol Specification (2024). https://zips.z.cash/protocol/protocol.pdf

25. Huber, N., et al.: Kryvos: publicly tally-hiding verifiable e-voting. In: CCS 2022, pp. 1443–1457. ACM (2022)

26. Huber, N., et al.: Implementation of our Circuits (2024). https://github.com/HicolasNuber/ballotsnarks

27. Joaquim, R.: How to prove the validity of a complex ballot encryption to the voter and the public. JISA **19**(2), 130–142 (2014)

28. Kosba, A., et al.: CØCØ: A framework for building composable zero-knowledge proofs. Cryptology ePrint Archive (2015)

29. Maller, M., et al.: Sonic: zero-knowledge SNARKs from linear-size universal and updatable structured reference strings. In: Proceedings of the 2019 ACM CCS, pp. 2111–2128 (2019)

30. Mestel, D., Müller, J., Reisert, P.: How efficient are replay attacks against vote privacy? A formal quantitative analysis. J. Comput. Secur. **31**(5), 421–467 (2023)

31. Morais, E., Koens, T., van Wijk, C., Koren, A.: A survey on zero knowledge range proofs and applications. SN Appl. Sci. **1**(8), 1–17 (2019). https://doi.org/10.1007/s42452-019-0989-z

32. Okeya, K., Sakurai, K.: Efficient elliptic curve cryptosystems from a scalar multiplication algorithm with recovery of the y-coordinate on a montgomery-form elliptic curve. In: Koç, Ç.K., Naccache, D., Paar, C. (eds.) CHES 2001. LNCS, vol. 2162, pp. 126–141. Springer, Heidelberg (2001). https://doi.org/10.1007/3-540-44709-1_12

33. Republic of Nauru: Electoral Act No. 15 (2024). http://ronlaw.gov.nr/nauru_lpms/files/acts/d83250a1ebdc56c1701fa7aa245af5b1.pdf

34. scipr-lab: libsnark (2024). https://github.com/scipr-lab/libsnark

Direct and Transparent Voter Verification with Everlasting Receipt-Freeness

Rafieh Mosaheb[1]([✉]), Peter B. Rønne[1], Peter Y A Ryan[1],
and Sara Sarfaraz[2]

[1] University of Luxembourg, Esch-sur-Alzette, Luxembourg
{rafieh.mosaheb,peter.roenne,peter.ryan}@uni.lu
[2] University of Waterloo, Waterloo, Canada
sarasarfaraz@uwaterloo.ca

Abstract. We present a new verifiable voting scheme based on the Hyperion scheme but providing everlasting privacy and receipt-freeness. As with Selene and Hyperion, it provides a direct form of E2E verifiability: voters verify the presence of their votes in plaintext in the tally. However, in contrast to Selene or Hyperion, the privacy of this protocol is everlasting. In addition, our protocol offers the novel feature of everlasting receipt-freeness and coercion mitigation.

Keywords: Verifiable elections · Everlasting privacy · Coercion mitigation

1 Introduction

A key challenge in electronic voting is to provide verifiability and coercion resistance at the same time. The goal of end-to-end verifiable (E2E V) electronic voting systems is to provide evidence to voters that their vote is correctly counted while giving them the ability to deny their real vote in the presence of a coercer. In addition, for many elections, it is critical to maintain privacy of voters in the future. Considering the pace of advances in computational power and quantum computing, it is necessary to protect privacy against future adversaries with more powerful computational resources. The term everlasting privacy was coined by Moran and Naor [14] to address this concern by guaranteeing privacy against computationally unbounded adversaries. A more realistic version of everlasting privacy, called practical everlasting privacy was then introduced in [1], limiting the amount of the information a future adversary can access, i.e. to information posted on the bulletin board to enable the verification of the tally.

In this paper, we propose a protocol that simultaneously provides verifiability, everlasting privacy, and coercion mitigation against a computationally unbounded coercer. The protocol is based on Hyperion [8], which provides highly transparent verifiability and coercion mitigation against a limited coercer but does not offer everlasting privacy. Furthermore, we increase the coercer's power

D. Duenas-Cid et al. (Eds.): E-Vote-ID 2024, LNCS 15014, pp. 124–140, 2025.
https://doi.org/10.1007/978-3-031-72244-8_8

to interact with the voter at anytime even before the beginning of casting phase to ensure higher levels of coercion resistance.

The main changes applied to Hyperion is the use of a perfectly private audit trail using perfectly hiding commitments [7], while making sure the Hyperion terms are likewise perfectly hiding, and the use of re-randomisation of the published terms to achieve receipt-freeness, with the Hyperion style verification ensuring verifiability of the election result.

Related Works Recently, an extensive survey by Haines et al. [13] on e-voting systems with everlasting privacy (EP), identified designing a system which satisfies both EP and receipt-freeness without the use of anonymous submission channels as an open challenge. This is important since according to Haines et al. the approaches that achieve EP based on privacy-preserving techniques are superior to the ones based on anonymous channels. In [9] they solve this problem by designing the first universally verifiable e-voting system with EP and receipt-freeness using the perfectly private audit trail (PPAT) technique in [7]. According to [13], the PPAT approach is a reasonable solution for achieving EP. In this work we also use the superior approach by employing the PPAT technique not only to achieve EP but also everlasting receipt-freeness.

Structure of the Paper In the next section, we introduce the preliminaries to provide a better understanding of our scheme. We describe the voter's perspective of our proposed e-voting system in Sect. 3 and the protocol in detail in Sect. 4. In Sect. 5, we provide proof of the security properties.

2   Preliminaries

This section begins by presenting the notation utilized throughout the paper, followed by an overview of the parties engaged in the protocol, and concludes with an explanation of the cryptographic primitives employed in the voting protocol.

Notation We use bold letters to denote vectors, e.g., $\mathbf{e}, \mathbf{E}$, and sans-serif letters to denote algorithms, e.g., Shuffle. The bold letter $\mathbf{G}$ denotes a cyclic group of prime order q, such as $\mathbf{G}_1$, $\mathbf{G}_2$, and $\mathbf{G}_T$. Group generators are denoted as $g \in \mathbf{G}_1$ and $h \in \mathbf{G}_2$. Public and secret keys are denoted pk and sk, and may include an index to indicate the key holder. The set of all permutations of size n is denoted by $\mathcal{S}_n$, with a specific permutation is represented by π and its inverse by π^{-1}. We denote a zero-knowledge proof by Π, a Commitment Consistent proof by P (see Sect. 2), and the voter's signature by σ.

Parties The voting protocol is run between the following parties.

Voters (V): n voters $\mathsf{V}_1, \mathsf{V}_2, \ldots, \mathsf{V}_n$ with identities $\mathsf{ID}_1, \mathsf{ID}_2, \ldots, \mathsf{ID}_n$.

Election Authority (EA): responsible for generating the election parameters.

Talliers (T): k talliers $T_1, T_2, \ldots, T_k$ who threshold share the secret key and cooperate to decrypt the ciphertexts.

Mix-servers (M): N mix servers $M_1, M_2, \ldots, M_N$ responsible for the mixing part of the tally phase.

Bulletin Board (**PBB and SBB**): similar to [7], we assume two secure broadcast channels: PBB is the public board for all participants and SBB is the secret board shared with the T and M. All designated participants share the same view of each board.

Election Admin(Adm): responsible for checking the validity of submitted ciphertexts by V, and relaying information between V and SBB.

Cryptographic Primitives In the electronic voting protocol proposed in Sect. 4, we use the following cryptographic primitives.

Signature. Any secure public key signature scheme is suitable for our needs. We use $\mathsf{Sign}_{sk}(m)$ to demonstrate the signature on message m using the secret signing key sk and verification of signature σ_m with verification key vk as $\mathsf{Verify}_{vk}(\sigma_m)$.

Elliptic Curve. Similar to [7], a bilinear map in SXDH[1] setting is denoted by $e : \mathbf{G}_1 \times \mathbf{G}_2 \rightarrow \mathbf{G}_T$ where there are no efficiently computable homomorphisms between $\mathbf{G}_1$ and $\mathbf{G}_2$. In this setting, the two following problems are computationally intractable in both groups $\mathbf{G}_1, \mathbf{G}_2$. The security of our protocol relies on this assumption.

- Decisional Diffie-Hellman (DDH): given g^{x_1} and g^{x_2} for uniformly indepdently chosen $x_1, x_2 \in \mathbb{Z}_q$, $g^{x_1 x_2}$ is indistinguishable from a random value in $\mathbf{G}$.
- Computational 1-Diffie-Hellman Inversion (1-DHI): given $g^x \in \mathbf{G}$ with $x \in \mathbb{Z}_q$, it is intractable to compute $g^{1/x}$.

Threshold ElGamal Encryption (TEG). We use the IND-CPA threshold ElGamal encryption system in [6,11] to encrypt a message m in group $\mathbf{G}_1$ with generator g. Let sk be the encryption secret key and $pk := g^{sk}$ the public key. Using the (t, k)−threshold Shamir secret sharing (SSS) scheme, we split sk into k shares: $\mathsf{SSS}(sk) = (sk_i)_{i=1}^k$, distributing them among the shareholders T_i. Each T_i then computes their verification key $vk_i := g^{sk_i}$. The Enc and Dec algorithms work as follows:

---

[1] Symmetric External Diffie-Hellman (SXDH) assumption: when DDH assumption, explained in the text, holds in both groups $\mathbf{G}_1$ and $\mathbf{G}_2$.

- $\mathsf{Enc}_{pk}(m;r) = (m \cdot pk^r, g^r)$, with $r \in \mathbb{Z}_q$.
- To decrypt a ciphertext $(a, b) \in \mathbf{G}_1^2$, each T_i takes the following steps: 1) Compute $b_i := b^{sk_i}$. 2) Use vk_i to prove $\log_g^{vk_i} = \log_b^{b_i}$. 3) Without loss of generality assume the log equality holds for any i in $S_t := \{1, \ldots, t\}$. 4) Compute Lagrange coefficients in Lagrange interpolation $sk = \sum_{i=1}^{t} sk_i \cdot \lambda_{0,i}^{S_t}$ as $\lambda_{0,i}^{S_t} = \prod_{j \in S_t \setminus \{i\}} \frac{j}{j-i}$. 5) Compute $\prod_{i \in S_t} b_i^{\lambda_{0,i}^{S_t}} = \prod_{i \in S_t} b^{sk_i \cdot \lambda_{0,i}^{S_t}} = b^{sk}$. 6) Derive $\mathsf{Dec}_{sk}(a, b) = a/b^{sk} \bmod q$.

Commitment Consistent Encryption (CCE). We use the Perfectly Private Audit Trail for Complex ballots (PPATC), which is the mix-net version of CCE proposed in [7]. Let $m \in \mathbf{G}_1$ be a message and pk_T be the talliers' joint public key. Given a ciphertext $e = \mathsf{Enc}_{pk_T}(m)$, the goal is to derive a commitment $c = \mathsf{Com}(m; r)$ with a randomness $r \in \mathbb{Z}_q$ to the same encrypted message m. As explained in [7], for simplicity the opening value of the commitment is considered to be r instead of (m, r). To clarify, consider the talliers hold the following keys: $sk_T = (x_1, x_2) \in \mathbb{Z}_q^2$ and $pk_T = (g_1 := g^{x_1}, g_2 := g^{x_2}) \in \mathbf{G}_1^2$. The public set of parameters is $prm := \{q, \mathbf{G}_1, \mathbf{G}_2, g, h, h_1\}$ where g and h are the generators of $\mathbf{G}_1$ and $\mathbf{G}_2$ respectively and $h_1 \in \mathbf{G}_2$. Let $\mathbf{r} = (r, r_1, r_2) \in_R \mathbb{Z}_q^3$ be the randomness. The CCE ciphertext, shown by $\mathsf{CCE}(prm, m; \mathbf{r})$ is a tuple $(\mathbf{e}, \mathbf{c}) = (e_1, e_2, e_3, c_1, c_2)$ where $e_1 := g^{r_1}$, $e_2 := g^{r_2}$, $e_3 := g_1^r g_2^{r_2}$ and $c_1 := h^r h_1^{r_1}$, $c_2 := mg_1^{r_1}$. In fact, $\mathbf{e}$ is the TEG encryption of the opening value $\mathbf{r}$, and $\mathbf{c}$ is the desired commitment to the message m. Throughout this paper, for the sake of simplicity, we sometimes use $\mathbf{cce}$ instead of $(\mathbf{e}, \mathbf{c})$.

In our protocol, we use three more algorithms from [7] for the CCE ciphertext: Dec, Open, and Verify. These algorithms work as follows: $\mathsf{Dec}_{sk_T}(\mathbf{cce}) := c_2/e_1^{x_1}$, $\mathsf{Open}(sk_T, \mathbf{cce}) := e_3/e_2^{x_2}$, $\mathsf{Verify}(pk_T, c_1, c_2, m, o) := 1$ if $e(g_1, c_1) = e(o, h)e(c_2/m, h_1)$ and 0 otherwise, with o being the opening value of $\mathbf{cce}$.

Sigma Protocol. We use the validity proof of CCE in [7] but in an interactive manner: here, the verifier generates the challenge ch randomly. More precisely, let $(\mathbf{e}, \mathbf{c}) = (e_1, e_2, e_3, c_1, c_2)$. We build a Sigma (Σ) protocol with the transcript $(\mathbf{a}, ch, \mathbf{z})$ for the relation $\mathcal{R} = \{((prm, (\mathbf{e}, \mathbf{c})), (m, \mathbf{r})) : \mathsf{CCE}(prm, m; \mathbf{r}) = (\mathbf{e}, \mathbf{c})\}$ as follows: the prover generates random values $s, s_1, s_2 \in_R \mathbb{Z}_q$ and computes $(e_1', e_2', e_3', c_1') := (g^{s_1}, g^{s_2}, g_1^s g_2^{s_2}, h^s h_1^{s_1})$. Then, she sends (e_1', e_2', e_3', c_1') as $\mathbf{a}$ to the verifier. The verifier generates and sends a uniformly random challenge ch to the prover. The prover computes the response $\mathbf{z} = (z, z_1, z_2)$ with $z := s + ch \cdot r$, $z_1 := s_1 + ch \cdot r_1$, $z_2 := s_2 + ch \cdot r_2$ and sends $\mathbf{z}$ to the verifier. The verifier computes $e_1'' := \frac{g^{z_1}}{e_1^{ch}}$, $e_2'' := \frac{g^{z_2}}{e_2^{ch}}$, $e_3'' := \frac{g_1^z g_2^{z_2}}{e_3^{ch}}$, $c_1'' := \frac{h^z h_1^{z_1}}{c_1^{ch}}$. If all equalities $e_1'' = e_1'$, $e_2'' = e_2'$, $e_3'' = e_3'$ and $c_1'' = c_1'$ hold, she returns 1; otherwise, 0.

In [7] this is transformed into a non-interactive proof using the Fiat-Shamir transformation. In our case, it is important that the proof is fresh, especially we don't want a coercer to forward a ciphertext with an unknown vote to the voter and ask her to submit this. To avoid this, we can use the non-interactive proof mentioned above which will be extractable in the plaintext message. Alternatively, one can make a two-move protocol, where the authorities first send a challenge to the voter, and the voter includes this challenge in the hash used for the Fiat-Shamir transformation.

Non-interactive Zero Knowledge Proof of Knowledge (NIZKPoK). To prove knowledge of a secret s, we use Schnorr proof [15] and combine it with (strong) Fiat-Shamir transformation [3] to achieve a non-interactive proof system. We then use the notation NIZKPoK(s) for the combination.

Re-randomization (ReRand). We use this primitive to re-randomize a CCE ciphertext, a TEG ciphertext and a public key of the form g^x. For $\mathbf{cce} = \mathsf{CCE}(prm, m; \mathbf{r})$ with $\mathbf{r} \in_R \mathbb{Z}_q^3$, we multiply the ciphertext by encryption of the unity element $1 \in \mathbf{G}_1$ with a random. For $\mathbf{E} = \mathsf{Enc}_{pk}(m; r) = (m \cdot pk^r, g^r)$ with $r \in \mathbb{Z}_q$, we exponentiate the ciphertext by a first random value and re-randomize it by a second random value. Lastly, for the public key we exponentiate it by a randomness:

- $\mathsf{ReRand}(\mathbf{cce}, \mathbf{r}') := \mathbf{cce} \cdot \mathsf{CCE}(prm, 1; \mathbf{r}') = \mathsf{CCE}(prm, m; \mathbf{r}'')$ with $\mathbf{r}' \in_R \mathbb{Z}_q^3$ and $\mathbf{r}'' = \mathbf{r} + \mathbf{r}'$.
- $\mathsf{ReRand}(\mathbf{E}, s, r') := \mathsf{ReRand}(\mathsf{Exp}(\mathbf{E}, s), r') = \mathsf{Enc}_{pk}(m^s; rs + r')$ with $\mathsf{Exp}(\mathbf{E}, s) := ((m \cdot pk^r)^s, (g^r)^s)$ and $s, r' \in \mathbb{Z}_q$.
- $\mathsf{ReRand}(pk, s) := (g^x)^s$ for $s \in \mathbb{Z}_q$.

For the sake of brevity, we write $\mathsf{ReRand}\{(\mathbf{cce}, \mathbf{r}'), (\mathbf{E}, s, r'), (pk, s)\}$ instead of $\{\mathsf{ReRand}(\mathbf{cce}, \mathbf{r}'), \mathsf{ReRand}(\mathbf{E}, s, r'), \mathsf{ReRand}(pk, s)\}$. Moreover, we omit the randomness when it is not needed for further computations.

Shuffle. Each mix server M_j, $j \in \{1, \cdots, N\}$, uses the Shuffle algorithm to permute and re-randomize the CCE ciphertexts together with the ElGamal encryption $\mathbf{E}$ of a verification term, and the voters' public keys of the form g^x for a secret x. More precisely, assume we have a list of size n as $\{(\mathbf{e}_i, \mathbf{c}_i), \mathbf{E}_i, pk_i\}_{i \in \{1, \dots, n\}}$ before mixing, where $(\mathbf{e}_i, \mathbf{c}_i) := \mathsf{CCE}(prm, m_i; \mathbf{r}_i)$ and $\mathbf{E}_i := \mathsf{Enc}_{pk_T}(g; 0) = (g, 1)$ which is the same value for each V_i in the beginning. The mix server M_j generates a random permutation $\pi^j \in \mathcal{S}_n$, and for each voter V_i generates a random vector $\mathbf{r}_i^j \in \mathbb{Z}_q^3$, and two random values $r_i^j, s_i^j \in \mathbb{Z}_q$. Assume $\{(\mathbf{e}_i^{j-1}, \mathbf{c}_i^{j-1}), \mathbf{E}_i^{j-1}, pk_i^{j-1}\}_i$ is the output of M_{j-1}.[2] Then, M_j runs the Shuffle algorithm as follows.

$$\mathsf{Shuffle}\left(\{(\mathbf{e}_i^{j-1}, \mathbf{c}_i^{j-1}), \mathbf{E}_i^{j-1}, pk_i^{j-1}\}_i, \{\mathbf{r}_i^j, s_i^j, r_i^j\}_i, \pi^j\right) :=$$

$$\{\mathsf{ReRand}\{((\mathbf{e}_{\pi^j(i)}^{j-1}, \mathbf{c}_{\pi^j(i)}^{j-1}), \mathbf{r}_{\pi^j(i)}^j), (\mathbf{E}_{\pi^j(i)}^{j-1}, s_{\pi^j(i)}^{j-1}, r_{\pi^j(i)}^{j-1}), (pk_{\pi^j(i)}^{j-1}, s_{\pi^j(i)}^{j-1})\}\}_i$$

This will be the output of M_j that we show by $\{(\mathbf{e}_i^j, \mathbf{c}_i^j), \mathbf{E}_i^j, pk_i^j\}_i$. Let's define $\mathbf{cce}^j := (\mathbf{e}^j, \mathbf{c}^j)$. Similar to [7], M_j computes two commitment consistent proofs of shuffle with respect to π^j: $\mathsf{P}_{\mathbf{cce}}^j$ and $\mathsf{P}_{\mathbf{c}}^j$. The first proof demonstrates that $\mathbf{cce}^j$ is a shuffle of $\mathbf{cce}^{j-1}$ and the second proof demonstrates that $\mathbf{c}^j$ is a shuffle

---

[2] The first mix server M_1 has to use the original values that we mentioned before mixing.

of $\mathbf{c}^{j-1}$. In our case, M_j extends this proof to also show that first, $\mathbf{E}^j$ and pk^j are shuffled in parallel with the same permutation π^j, second $\mathbf{E}^j$ is exponentiated with the same randomness s^j as in pk^j[3], and lastly, proof of knowledge of s^j s.t. $\mathsf{ReRand}(pk, s^j) = pk^j$. We show the extended proofs by $\mathrm{P}^j_{\mathbf{cce},\mathbf{E},pk}$ and $\mathrm{P}^j_{\mathbf{c},\mathbf{E},pk}$.

In [12] the authors present an efficient mixnet for the PPATC scheme including a machine-verified proof of the protocol. The current mixnet is a straightforward extension, in particular each mixnode commits to their permutation which can be reused for the extra terms being mixed in parallel. Note that we deliberately kept the public key of the voter and the encryption $\mathbf{E}$ in the same group.

3   The Voter Experience

In this section, we describe the voter's view of our protocol, firstly in the absence of coercion. Then we describe the actions required in the presence of a coercer. We assume that each voter has a pair of signing keys (vk_i, sk_i) and that each voter's device generates an ephemeral trapdoor key pair when they join.

3.1   The Base Protocol

- The voter inputs her vote and her device generates the commitment to this vote and signs the result.
- The voter's device signs her public trapdoor key and sends it to the Election Admin along with the signed commitment on the vote and voter's ID.

The voter's commitment will be re-randomized and published on PBB along with her trapdoor public key and ID. Subsequently, information on the PBB will be shuffled and re-randomized with each step being displayed on the PBB. Finally, the voter will be invited to check PBB.

- After a certain period, the voter will receive a notification term denoted α which she inputs to her device to extract her unique tracking number. She will then use this tracking number to verify that her vote appears correctly in the tally on the PBB.

3.2   The Protocol in the Event of Coercion

In the event of coercion, the voter needs to take some additional steps to evade the coercer. The vote casting steps are identical.

- Once the tally to published the voter visits PBB and finds an alternative tracking number appearing against the coercer's required vote and saves that in her device.

---

[3] One can use a simple proof of dicrete log equality.

- Voter's device computes a fake α term (which raised to the power of voter's secret trapdoor key and results in the alternative tracking). This step requires the voter's secret trapdoor key.
- After a certain period, the voter receives a notification containing the real α term, inputs it into her device to extract her unique tracking number, and uses this tracking number to verify her vote on PBB.
- In case the coercer asks for the tracking number or α term, she can provide him with the fake ones that were computed by her device.

4   Details of Our Scheme

This section outlines the various stages of our e-voting protocol, encompassing setup, submission, tally, and verification phases. The parties involved and the cryptographic primitives used in these phases are explained in detail in Sects. 2 and 2 respectively.

4.1   Setup Phase

During this phase, the EA generates the election parameters prm, determining the voting method, defining the set of candidates, and providing any other necessary information. This also includes encryption of the public value g under talliers public key pk_T as $E_g := \mathsf{Enc}_{pk_T}(g; 0) = (g, 1)$. This value is the same in the beginning for all voters V_i but will change later. However, we refer to it as E_i from the beginning. EA creates a vector $\mathbf{E} = \{E_i\}_i$ and sends $\mathbf{E}$ to SBB. We also assume that each voter V_i has a signing key pair (vk_i, sk_i).

4.2   Submission Phase

This phase consists of two parts. In the first part, each voter V_i prepares their ballot and sends it privately to the Adm. In the second part, the Adm is responsible for checking the validity of the submitted CCE by V_i.

Ballot preparation

1. Similar to Hyperion [8], V_i generates an ephemeral trapdoor key $x_i \in \mathbb{Z}_q$ and compute the public trapdoor key $pk_i := g^{x_i}$ using her device. Next, V_i signs pk_i as $\sigma_{i1} := \mathsf{Sign}_{sk_i}(pk_i)$ and computes the proof $\Pi_i :=$NIZKPoK(x_i). Π_i should be non-malleable and bound to the identity of the voter.
2. V_i commits to her vote v_i using the CCE scheme explained in the Sect. 2 by computing the ciphertext $\mathbf{cce}_i := (\mathbf{e}_i, \mathbf{c}_i) = \mathsf{CCE}(prm, v_i; \mathbf{r}_i)$ with $\mathbf{r}_i \in_R \mathbb{Z}_q^3$. Then, she signs it as $\sigma_{i2} := \mathsf{Sign}_{sk_i}(\mathbf{cce}_i)$.

Now, the voter V_i sends $\{\mathsf{ID}_i,\ pk_i, \sigma_{i1},\ \Pi_i,\ \mathbf{cce}_i,\ \sigma_{i2}\}$ privately to the Adm.

4.3 Validity Check

The voter V_i as the prover and the Adm as the verifier run the Sigma protocol Σ_i for the Adm to check whether cce_i is a valid CCE or not. If it is, then the Adm proceeds by re-randomizing it as $cce'_i := (e'_i, c'_i) = \mathsf{ReRand}(e_i, c_i)$. Finally, Adm sends cce_i and cce'_i together with a proof of correct re-randomization (Π^*_i) to SBB and publishes $\{ID_i, pk_i, \sigma_{i1}, c'_i\}$ on PBB.

4.4 Tally Phase

In this phase, first the mix servers have to run the Shuffle algorithm one by one and publish the commitments on PBB and the encryption of the opening values on SBB. Then, the mix-servers have to run the mix-net backwards on the term E^N, output by M_N, to get the correct term for the voter V_i. Finally, the talliers have to decrypt the output of the reverse mixing and send it to the Adm. Adm sends this back to the voter. More precisely, the tally phase works as follows.

Mixing
First, M_1 generates a random permutation $\pi^1 \in \mathcal{S}_n$, and for each V_i generates a random vector $\mathbf{r}_i^1 \in \mathbb{Z}_q^3$, and two random values $r_i^1, s_i^1 \in \mathbb{Z}_q$ and runs the shuffle algorithm as $\mathsf{Shuffle}\left(\{(e'_i, c'_i), E_i, pk_i\}_i, \{\mathbf{r}_i^1, s_j^1, r_i^1\}, \pi^j\right)$. Let's call the output $\{(e_i^1, c_i^1), E_i^1, pk_i^1\}_i$. As explained in Sect. 2, M_1 generates $\mathsf{P}^1_{cce,E,pk}$ and $\mathsf{P}^1_{c,E,pk}$. Then, she sends $\{c_i^1, pk_i^1\}_i$ and $\mathsf{P}^1_{c,E,pk}$ to PBB and sends $\{e_i^1, E_i^1\}_i$ and $\mathsf{P}^1_{cce,E,pk}$ to SBB. The output of M_1 is the input of the next mix server M_2 and so on. Lastly, the final output of the mix-net that M_N generates is $\{(e_i^N, c_i^N), E_i^N, pk_i^N\}_i$. Similar to M_1, M_N sends $\{c_i^N, pk_i^N\}_i$ and $\mathsf{P}^N_{c,E,pk}$ to PBB and sends $\{e_i^N, E_i^N\}_i$ and $\mathsf{P}^N_{cce,E,pk}$ to SBB.

Reverse Mixing. Define $s^{total} := s_{\pi^1\pi^2\cdots\pi^N(i)}^1 s_{\pi^2\cdots\pi^N(i)}^2 \cdots s_{\pi^N(i)}^N$ [4]. The output E_i^N by M_N is indeed $\mathsf{Enc}_{pk_T}(g^{s^{total}})$. The value $g^{s^{total}}$ does not belong to V_i, but to $V_{\pi^1\pi^2\cdots\pi^N(i)}$. Hence, the mixnet servers have to run the mixnet backward: M_N uses $(\pi^N)^{-1}$ to shuffle and a fresh randomness $r_i'^N$ to re-randomize (without exponentiation) E_i^N. M_N sends the result $E_i'^N$ with $\Pi^N := \mathsf{NIZKPoK}((\pi^N)^{-1}, r_i'^N)$ to SBB. M_{N-1} proceeds with $E_i'^N$ with the inverse permutation $(\pi^{N-1})^{-1}$. $E_i'^1$ which is the final value and the output of M_1 will be posted on SBB.

Decryption of Opening and Verification Terms.
- Talliers using sk_T decrypt each ciphertext $cce_i^N = (e_i^N, c_i^N)$ as $vote_i := \mathsf{Dec}_{sk_T}(cce_i^N)$. Then, they run the Open algorithm to obtain $o_i := \mathsf{Open}(sk_T, cce_i^N)$. They publish $vote_i, o_i$ on PBB together with a proof of correct decryption Π_T.

---

[4] The index $\pi^1\pi^2\cdots\pi^N(i)$ is composition of the permutations in group $\mathcal{S}_n$ with the same order: $\pi^1\left(\pi^2\left(\cdots\left(\pi^N(i)\right)\right)\right)$

- Talliers using their secret keys compute their decryption shares of the TEG encryption $E_i'^1$ and send it to the Adm with a proof of correct decryption Π_T^*. Then, Adm sends the decryption result as α_i to the voter V_i.

4.5 Verification Phase

The voter V_i raises α_i to the power of her secret x_i. Then, V_i can verify her vote by finding the row which contains $\alpha_i^{x_i}$ as the shuffled public key, i.e. pk_i^N.

5   Analysis

In our e-voting protocol, the vote of V_i lies in $\mathbf{G}_1$, which means it handles complex ballots in contrast to the homomorphic tally approaches. However, here, despite using a mix tally, we require V_i to run an interactive $\Sigma-$protocol with the Adm to prove v_i lies in the correct space of candidates in case that the number of candidates does not match size of $\mathbf{G}_1$ which is q. This provides accountability in the submission phase in case of a dispute between V_i and Adm.

5.1   Verifiability

The everlasting Hyperion scheme's verifiability is similar to Selene's as proven in [10]. Universal verifiability holds due to the soundness of the NIZKs for the mixnet and the DDH assumption for the binding property of the commitment opening. The EUF-CMA signatures from voters prevent ballot stuffing.

The soundness of the individual verifiability follows from the 1-DHI assumption using the extractability of the exponents x_i in the submitted public keys and of s_i in the final terms $pk_i^{s_i} = g^{x_i s_i}$ next to the plaintext votes. The reason is that if Adm could send an α to V_i such that $(\alpha)^{x_i} = pk_j^{s_j} = g^{x_j s_j}$ for some j, it would imply $g^{1/x_i} = \alpha^{1/(s_j x_j)}$.

5.2   Ballot Privacy

In this section we prove ballot privacy in a strong adversary model where the adversary can control the submitted vote ballots and the tally procedure, i.e. against a malicious board. We use the definition du–mb–BPRIV from [10] which is a version of the mb–BPRIV definition from [5] which allows late verification after the tally, as we have in Hyperion (see details in [10]). This definition is in terms of an experiment $\mathsf{Exp}_{\mathcal{A},\mathcal{V},\mathsf{Sim}}^{\mathsf{du-mb-BPRIV,Recover},\beta}(\lambda)$ detailed in Fig. 1 , where the adversary wins if it correctly guesses whether it sees a real or a simulated world ($\beta = 0, 1$). The adversary has access to the ballots cast by honest voters using the $\mathcal{O}$board where publish in our case simply gives both the private and public board input to the adversary.

In our case the adversary will be allowed to control both the public and private bulletin board (BB in the game), but we assume both will be honestly verified – the internal by the election authorities and the public by voters or any third party. This is captured by ValidBoard in Line 10 of the game, and will include checking all proofs on the submitted ballots (also if these are interactive).

The voters are divided into honest H and dishonest D voters, with honestly generated public credentials PU (Line 5-6) and corresponding secret credentials U. The adversary will get access to the secret credentials of the dishonest voters (Line 7). This means that the adversary cannot modify the signing keys and the Hyperion keys of the voters when altering the boards, which would also immediately lead to attacks. In practice, this is enforced by the signatures in the protocol. Since the definition assumes honestly generated keys, this is not the strongest possible definition. We plan to improve on this in future work, but for now we use this peer-reviewed definition.

The adversary can also output the result and tally of the election, denoted by (r^*, π^*) in Line 13. This entails the full mixnet output and proofs. This is verified using VerifyTally in Line 14 which will verify all ZKPs. Further, the voters can make individual verification of this tally result using the Hyperion mechanism. In the definition H_{check} defines those (honest) voters who have to verify, Checked those who actually verified, and Happy will be those who verified successfully. The adversary decides who verifies using the $\mathcal{O}$verify oracle, but will be punished if not all voters in H_{check} verify correctly, especially, the adversary will then have to make a guess at breaking the privacy without seeing the tally (Lines 12,19). The data needed for verification is stored in spsstate which in the definition has to be split into a pre- and post-tally part, see [10]. In the case of our Hyperion variant, the tally can update the post state to give the verification term g^{r_i} to the voter.

The main point of the malicious board ballot privacy definitions [5,10] is that they allow certain adversarial behaviour that obviously decreases privacy, but is seen as accepted or unavoidable behaviour, and then we require that there should be no further privacy leaks. In our case, we basically check that if we allow deletion and reordering of votes there will be no further leaks, e.g. no ballot copy attacks. This could, e.g., model an attacker that is able to block some ballots from reaching the authorities, which means less privacy for the remaining voters, but no further privacy attacks will be possible if the definitions are fulfilled. If we can somehow rule out the "allowed" adversarial behaviour, e.g. if the communication lines to the voters and the bulletin board itself are trusted, then we return to the standard ballot privacy definition. The allowed behaviour is defined by the recovery function Recover in Line 1 of the tally oracle $\mathcal{O}$tally, see [10] for details. Basically, this will look for unaltered ballots from the vote oracle on the $\beta = 1$ board and change it to the ballots output to the $\beta = 0$ board. Finally, there has to be a simulator Sim to simulate all the outputs of the tally procedure (mixing and proofs) in order for the adversary not to be able to distinguish the two worlds.

Definition 1. $\mathcal{V}$ satisfies du–mb–BPRIV with respect to Recover if there exists an efficient simulator Sim, such that for any efficient adversary $\mathcal{A}$, the advantage

$$\left| \mathsf{PrExp}_{\mathcal{A},\mathcal{V},\mathsf{Sim}}^{\mathsf{du-mb-BPRIV,Recover,0}}(\lambda) = 1 - \mathsf{PrExp}_{\mathcal{A},\mathcal{V},\mathsf{Sim}}^{\mathsf{du-mb-BPRIV,Recover,1}}(\lambda) = 1 \right| \text{ is negligible.}$$

Theorem 1. *Our everlasting version of Hyperion satisfies* du–mb–BPRIV *assuming that the proofs are zero-knowledge, correct and sound and the SXDH assumption holds.*

We here give a proof sketch.

Proof (sketch). We will prove the theorem using a number of game hopes starting from $\mathsf{Exp}_{\mathcal{A},\mathcal{V},\mathsf{Sim}}^{\mathsf{du-mb-BPRIV,Recover,0}}(\lambda)$. Without loss of generality we can assume that the board output by the adversary validates (Line 10) and even further that the tally is verified correctly, the latter since it is always possible for the adversary to create a verifying tally (Line 14), the latter following from the perfect correctness of the encryption schemes and zero-knowledge proofs.

In the first hop we simulate all zero-knowledge proofs (which is possible since they are all verified by the argument above). This follows from the zero-knowledge property of the proofs.

Since the decryption proofs are now also simulated and thanks to the soundness of the mixnet (due to verification of the shuffle proofs), along with the perfect correctness of the ElGamal encryption schemes and of the openings of PPATC, the set of votes opened from ballots which are output from the vote oracle will match the set of input votes. For the ballots which have not been changed from the oracles, we can thus stop decrypting the opening and just output the opening output from the oracle and use the vote input to the oracle as the plaintext vote. This game hop does not change the advantage. The ballots output by the adversary are processed as normal in the tally.

In the third hop we use the DDH assumption to change all cryptographic groups elements in the mixnet to random elements, except the input elements and except the output elements not coming the vote oracle calls. This is $2n \cdot N$ uses of DDH coming from the ElGamal encryption of the α terms and of the openings (per voter, per mix node) (all the remaining terms are uniformly random under the rerandomizations). We don't need to change the Hyperion terms pk^i in this process since we exponentiate these during the randomization procedure and they are hence perfectly uniform. We can thus preserve the set of correctly verifying voters here and there will be no leaks to the adversary from this. Note also that the voters always verify according to the $\beta = 0$ plaintext votes, hence there is no leak on β from who verifies correctly, see also [10].

In the fourth hop we use that the PPATC scheme is NM-CPA secure (see [7]) and we change the $\beta = 0$ output PPATC ballots to the ones from BB_1. Note that the adversary can track his own ballots using the Hyperion mechanism for the dishonest voters, but this is unproblematic for this game. Note that in the game, the voters always verify according to the $\beta = 0$ votes (Line 4 in the voting oracle) so this is still consistent. The tally result is still consistent with the tally result for $\beta = 0$ since the recovery function undoes exactly this change in the tally oracle for $\beta = 1$.

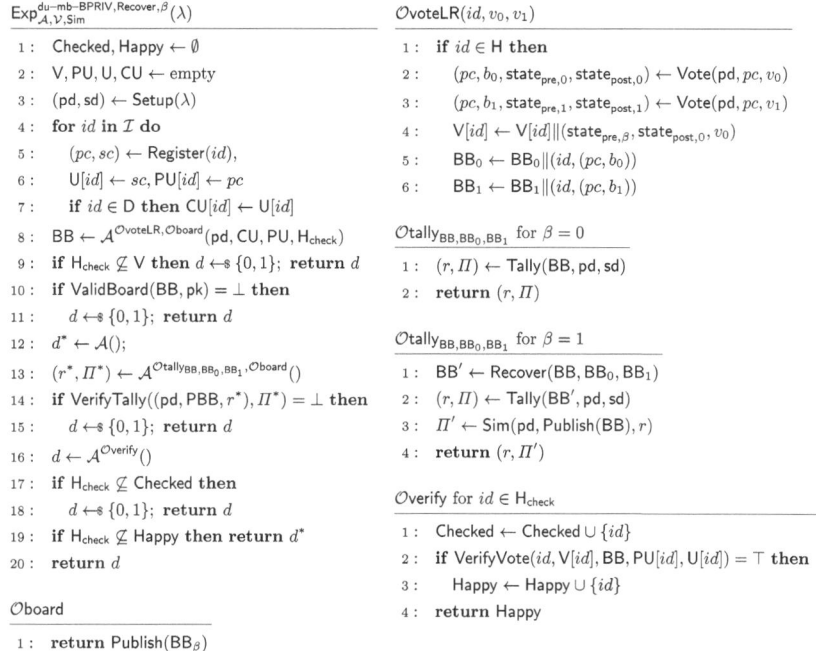

Fig. 1. du–mb–BPRIV ballot privacy against a dishonest ballot box from [10].

In the fifth and sixth hop we restore the mixnet using the DDH assumption, and we again do decryption of the vote oracle ballots.

In the final game we move back from simulated proofs to real proofs and we have reached $\mathsf{Exp}^{\mathsf{du-mb-BPRIV,Recover},0}_{\mathcal{A},\mathcal{V},\mathsf{Sim}}(\lambda)$ as desired. □

We note that whereas the definition only has one trusted (tally) authority, our protocol contains zero-knowledge proofs to ensure that it is only secure if there is at least one honest tallier (or a threshold set of talliers) and one honest mix server.

Another technical note is that in the proof, we assumed that the adversary gets the verification terms from the Hyperion mechanism. Contrary to Selene [10] this cannot simply be given in the secret data of the voter, but we can allow the adversary to have states for all the dishonest voters which get updated at the tally time. Even simpler, we could allow the tally to also output the decryptions of E_i for all voters, and this would still be secure under the DDH assumption. We leave it for future work to capture privacy leaks from whether the verifications are successful or not, as this is not captured using the current definition [10].

5.3 Everlasting Privacy

For everlasting privacy we do not consider an attacker controlling the board, but rather go for an updated version of the BPRIV [2] definition assuming secure and perfectly secret delivery of ballots. This is both because we would not be able to get privacy against an unbounded attacker acting at ballot casting time, since we relied on the (computational) soundness of the zero-knowledge proofs, but also because what we want protect against a future unbounded adversary, e.g. also if some of the crypto primitives should be broken e.g. using quantum computers. However, this doesn't mean that the attacker is not present during the election, and hence our Everlasting–BPRIV experiment in Fig. 2, $\mathsf{Exp}_{\mathcal{A},\mathcal{V},\mathsf{Sim}}^{\mathsf{Everlasting-BPRIV},\beta}(\lambda)$, allows for the adversary to control some voters and getting their credentials (and their verifications as in the last section). Compared to du–mb–BPRIV the adversary now only gets access the public parts of the ballots and the proof Π' in $\mathcal{O}$tally Line 2 will only contain the output to PBB. With access to the internal board an unbounded adversary could easily break privacy.

The definition of Everlasting–BPRIV is then as follows.

Definition 2. We say that $\mathcal{V}$ satisfies Everlasting–BPRIV if there exists an efficient simulator Sim, such that for any unbounded adversary $\mathcal{A}$, the advantage $\left| \mathsf{PrExp}_{\mathcal{A},\mathcal{V},\mathsf{Sim}}^{\mathsf{Everlasting-BPRIV},0}(\lambda) = 1 - \mathsf{PrExp}_{\mathcal{A},\mathcal{V},\mathsf{Sim}}^{\mathsf{Everlasting-BPRIV},1}(\lambda) = 1 \right|$ is zero (or bounded by some small probabiilty).

Theorem 2. *Our everlasting version of Hyperion satisfies* Everlasting–BPRIV *assuming the public proofs have perfect zero-knowledge.*

Proof (Sketch). We here only give a sketch of the proof. The proof is shorter than the proof of theorem 1 since the board and the tally are now honestly created. In the first hop, we simulate the proofs on PBB. Since these are perfect zero-knowledge by assumption, there is no advantage for the adversary in this hop. Secondly, all rerandomization of the commitment terms and the Hyperion public keys are uniformly random and can be replaced with random values and hence the permutation of votes is information-theoretically hidden. Third, we can replace the first commitments with the commitments coming from the $\beta = 1$ voting oracle, still keeping the final commitments and the corresponding $\beta = 0$ tally. Since the commitments are uniformly random, the advantage in this hop is also zero. Especially, the ballots submitted by the cast oracle do not help the adversary (who could in principle decrypt them on its own using the unbounded computational power). We have now arrived at the $\beta = 1$ game. □

5.4 Everlasting Receipt-Freeness

We now consider receipt-freeness of voting protocols, specifically against computationally unbounded attackers. We write this in terms of the experiment $\mathsf{Exp}_{\mathcal{A},\mathcal{V},\mathsf{Sim}}^{\mathsf{Everlasting-RF},\beta}(\lambda)$, shown in Fig. 3. This experiment is close to Everlasting–BPRIV. The different is that the adversary has to point out two honest voters id_1, id_2 and two vote choices v_a, v_b. The voter id_1 will vote for v_a for $\beta = 0$ and for v_b in $\beta = 1$, while id_2 votes oppositely (Line 8-9). The latter ensures that the adversary cannot directly win the game by just looking at the

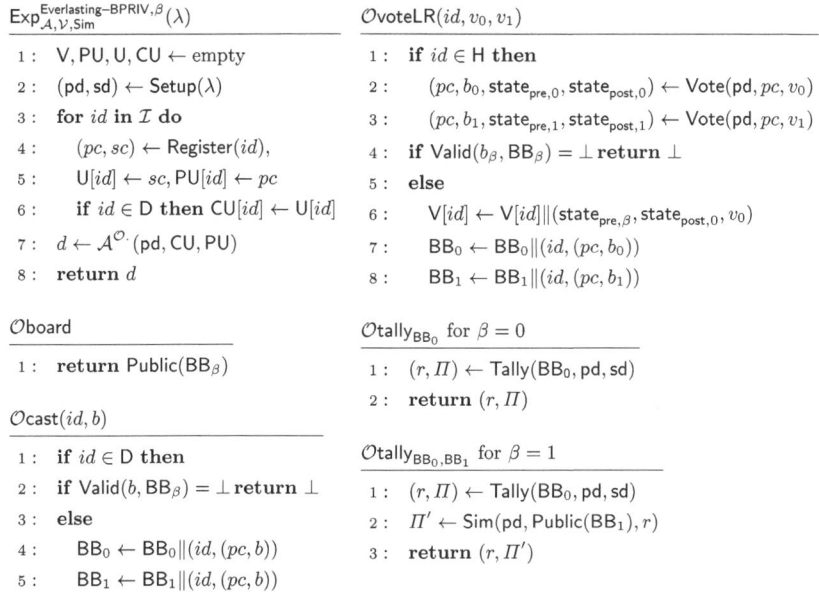

Fig. 2. Everlasting–BPRIV: Everlasting ballot privacy.

result. Further, the adversary can ask for a receipt from id_1 using the oracle $\mathcal{O}\mathsf{getReceipt}$. For $\beta = 0$ he gets the secret credential and the states of the voter. We will here assume he holds all possible random coins and data that the voter has access to. He also holds whatever material the authorities give to the voter, in our case the Hyperion term after mixing. For $\beta = 1$ this material is, however, manipulated using a faking algorithm Fake. In our case this fakes the Hyperion term to point to a vote for v_b. The definition is then

Definition 3. We say that $\mathcal{V}$ satisfies Everlasting–RF if there exists an efficient simulator Sim and faking algorithm Fake, such that for any unbounded adversary $\mathcal{A}$, the advantage $\left| \mathrm{PrExp}_{\mathcal{A},\mathcal{V},\mathsf{Sim}}^{\text{Everlasting–RF},0}(\lambda) = 1 - \mathrm{PrExp}_{\mathcal{A},\mathcal{V},\mathsf{Sim}}^{\text{Everlasting–RF},1}(\lambda) = 1 \right|$ is zero (or bounded by some small probability).

We note that this is a weaker definition than e.g. [4] which allows the adversary against receipt-freeness to cast a ballot on behalf of the voter. However, in our case we have individual plaintext verification which can create new attacks in such a case. The definition from [4] can still be fulfilled by our scheme, if adapted to our setup, especially taking into account the proof of plaintext knowledge at vote casting. We leave the comparison as future work.

Theorem 3. *Our everlasting version of Hyperion satisfies* Everlasting–RF *assuming the public proofs have perfect zero-knowledge.*

Proof (Sketch). The proof follows as for Everlasting–BPRIV. The only point is that voter id_1 might pick a vote from a dishonest voter revealing that she is

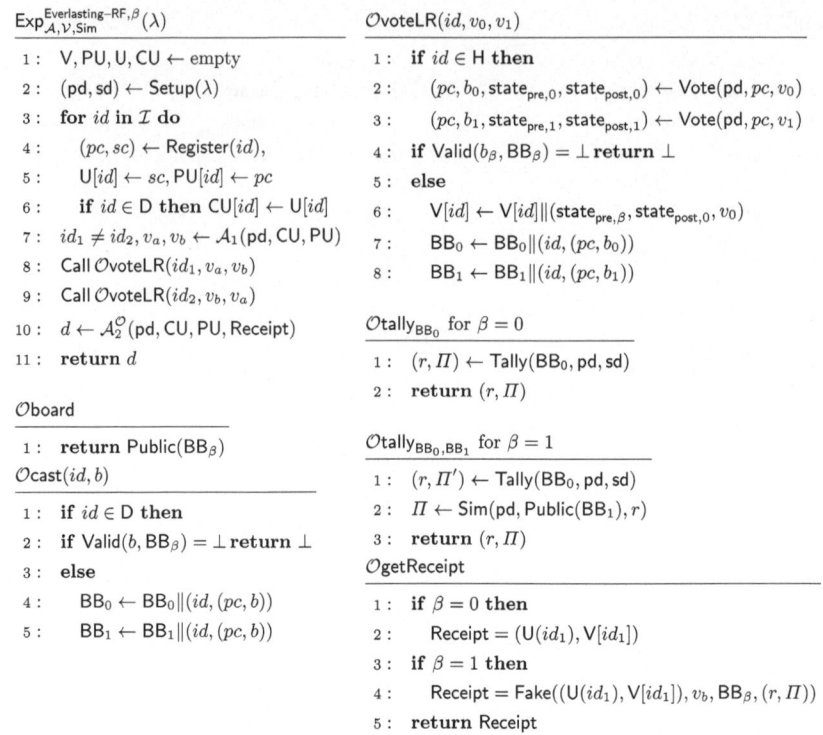

Fig. 3. Everlasting–RF: Everlasting Receipt-Freeness.

faking and letting the adversary win the experiment. Thus the probability of winning will depend on how many dishonest voters voted for v_b. The advantage of the adversary can thus be bounded by $d/(d+1)$.

Acknowledgements. This paper was partly supported by the Luxembourg National Research Fund (FNR) under the CORE project EquiVox (C19/IS/13643617/EquiVox/Ryan).

References

1. Arapinis, M., Cortier, V., Kremer, S., Ryan, M.: Practical everlasting privacy. In: Basin, D., Mitchell, J.C. (eds.) Principles of Security and Trust, pp. 21–40. Springer, Berlin Heidelberg, Berlin, Heidelberg (2013)
2. Bernhard, D., Cortier, V., Galindo, D., Pereira, O., Warinschi, B.: Sok: a comprehensive analysis of game-based ballot privacy definitions. In: Symposium on Security and Privacy, pp. 499–516. IEEE (2015)
3. Bernhard, D., Pereira, O., Warinschi, B.: How not to prove yourself: pitfalls of the fiat-shamir heuristic and applications to helios. In: Wang, X., Sako, K. (eds.) Advances in Cryptology – ASIACRYPT 2012, pp. 626–643. Springer Berlin Heidelberg, Berlin, Heidelberg (2012). https://doi.org/10.1007/978-3-642-34961-4_38

4. Cortier, V., Fuchsbauer, G., Galindo, D.: Beleniosrf: a strongly receipt-free electronic voting scheme. IACR Cryptol. ePrint Arch. **2015**, 629 (2015)
5. Cortier, V., Lallemand, J., Warinschi, B.: Fifty shades of ballot privacy: privacy against a malicious board. In: 33rd Computer Security Foundations Symposium (CSF), pp. 17–32. IEEE (2020)
6. Cramer, R., Gennaro, R., Schoenmakers, B.: A secure and optimally efficient multi-authority election scheme. Eur. Trans. Telecommun. **8**(5), 481–490 (1997)
7. Cuvelier, É., Pereira, O., Peters, T.: Election verifiability or ballot privacy: do we need to choose? In: Crampton, J., Jajodia, S., Mayes, K. (eds.) Computer Security – ESORICS 2013: 18th European Symposium on Research in Computer Security, Egham, UK, September 9-13, 2013. Proceedings, pp. 481–498. Springer Berlin Heidelberg, Berlin, Heidelberg (2013). https://doi.org/10.1007/978-3-642-40203-6_27
8. Damodaran, A., Rastikian, S., Rønne, P.B., Ryan, P.Y.A.: Hyperion: transparent end-to-end verifiable voting with coercion mitigation. Cryptology ePrint Archive, Paper 2024/1182 (2024)
9. Doan, T.V.T., Pereira, O., Peters, T.: Encryption mechanisms for receipt-free and perfectly private verifiable elections. In: Pöpper, C., Batina, L. (eds.) Applied Cryptography and Network Security: 22nd International Conference, ACNS 2024, Abu Dhabi, United Arab Emirates, March 5–8, 2024, Proceedings, Part I, pp. 257–287. Springer Nature Switzerland, Cham (2024). https://doi.org/10.1007/978-3-031-54770-6_11
10. Dragan, C.C., et al.: Machine-checked proofs of privacy against malicious boards for Selene and co. In: 35th Computer Security Foundations Symposium (CSF), pp. 335–347. IEEE (2022)
11. Fouque, P.-A., Pointcheval, D.: Threshold cryptosystems secure against chosen-ciphertext attacks. In: Boyd, C. (ed.) ASIACRYPT 2001. LNCS, vol. 2248, pp. 351–368. Springer, Heidelberg (2001). https://doi.org/10.1007/3-540-45682-1_21
12. Gjøsteen, K., Haines, T., Solberg, M.R.: Efficient mixing of arbitrary ballots with everlasting privacy: how to verifiably mix the PPATC scheme. In: Asplund, M., Nadjm-Tehrani, S. (eds.) Secure IT Systems: 25th Nordic Conference, NordSec 2020, Virtual Event, November 23–24, 2020, Proceedings, pp. 92–107. Springer International Publishing, Cham (2021). https://doi.org/10.1007/978-3-030-70852-8_6
13. Haines, T., Mueller, J., Mosaheb, R., Pryvalov, I.: Sok: secure e-voting with everlasting privacy. In: Proceedings on Privacy Enhancing Technologies (PoPETs) (2023)
14. Moran, T., Naor, M.: Receipt-free universally-verifiable voting with everlasting privacy. In: Dwork, C. (ed.) CRYPTO 2006. LNCS, vol. 4117, pp. 373–392. Springer, Heidelberg (2006). https://doi.org/10.1007/11818175_22
15. Schnorr, C.P.: Efficient signature generation by smart cards. J. Cryptol. **4**, 161–174 (1991)

Expanding the Toolbox: Coercion and Vote-Selling at Vote-Casting Revisited

Peter B. Rønne[1,2], Tamara Finogina[3], and Javier Herranz[4(✉)]

[1] SnT, University of Luxembourg, Esch-sur-Alzette, Luxembourg
[2] CNRS, LORIA, Université De Lorraine, Nancy, France
[3] Internxt, Valencia, Spain
`tamara@internxt.com`
[4] Department Matemàtiques, Universitat Politècnica de Catalunya, Barcelona, Spain
`javier.herranz@upc.edu`

Abstract. Coercion and vote-buying are challenging and multi-faceted threats that prevent people from expressing their will freely. Even though there are known techniques to resist or partially mitigate coercion and vote-buying, we explicitly demonstrate that they generally underestimate the power of malicious actors by not accounting for current technological tools that could support coercion and vote-selling. In this paper, we give several examples of how a coercer can force voters to comply with his demands or how voters can prove how they voted. To do so, we use tools like blockchains, delay encryption, privacy-preserving smart contracts, or trusted hardware. Since some of the successful coercion attacks occur on voting schemes that were supposed/claimed/proven to be coercion-resistant or receipt-free, the main conclusion of this work is that the coercion models should be re-evaluated, and new definitions of coercion and receipt-freeness are necessary. We propose such new definitions as part of this paper and investigate their implications.

1 Introduction

Coercion is one of those notions that is easier to understand than formally define, as it comes in many different shapes and forms. Generally, coercion incorporates all kinds of duress that can prevent people from voting freely while minimizing the possibility of undetected disobedience.

The threat is especially relevant for remote electronic voting, which happens in an uncontrolled and potentially coercive environment, but we also demonstrate attacks for the in-booth setting. Even though there are many distinct proposals for resisting, mitigating, or hampering the coercion threat, all of them require that the coercer cannot constantly control the voter nor intercept information sent over secure channels.

T. Finogina—Most of the work was done while the author worked at Scytl Election Technologies.

© The Author(s) 2025
D. Duenas-Cid et al. (Eds.): E-Vote-ID 2024, LNCS 15014, pp. 141–157, 2025.
https://doi.org/10.1007/978-3-031-72244-8_9

However, new tools like immutable blockchains, delay functions, time-based encryption, secret-input MPC smart contracts, trusted hardware, etc., have been developed to enforce certain types of honest behavior of participants. In this paper, we demonstrate how such tools in the hands of a coercer, in turn, can be used to ensure that the coerced voter follows the instructions of the coercer and cannot evade via anti-coercion strategies. Going further, these new tools can also be used by a voter to enable vote-selling.

The main difficulty in designing coercion-resistant or receipt-free verifiable voting protocols lies in combining those properties with the assurance that the voting device has not altered a voter's vote – a check known as cast-as-intended (CAI) verification. To get cast-as-intended verification we can use tracking numbers, return codes, QR codes containing encryption randomness, zero-knowledge proofs of plaintext correctness, or other techniques. However, they all need to convince the voter only, not a coercer or a vote-buyer, e.g. be deniable. This implies that any potential coercion-resistant and cast-as-intended verification should provide correctness proof for a final cast vote and a simulation strategy.

Several studies focus on the contradiction between coercion-resistance and cast-as-intended verification and offer potential solutions, see, e.g., [16] and references therein. However, to our knowledge, no paper has thoroughly studied the possibility of the coercer utilizing new cryptographic tools - blockchain, delay functions, etc. - to prevent the voter from simulating an alternative proof.

For example, a coercer can use blockchain to force voters to vote for a specific candidate in a voting system that relies on so-called Benaloh challenges [4]: A voter enters her choice into the voting device, which then prepares a ballot, commits to it, and asks the voter whether to cast it or audit it. In case of an audit, the encryption randomness is revealed so the voter can verify the ballot on another device. Otherwise, the vote is submitted. Since the voter never holds the randomness of the submitted ballot, there is no receipt. Note that the number of audits should be unpredictable to prevent the voting device from cheating.

With the aid of a blockchain, a remote coercer can always force voters to cast a ballot for a given option. To do so, the coercer tells voters to post the ballot's commitment on the blockchain, e.g., Bitcoin, before deciding whether to audit or cast the vote. If the next block starts with a bit 0, the voter must press audit and post the corresponding randomness on the blockchain. Otherwise, the voter casts the ballot. Since the coercer can see everything posted on the blockchain, he can always check if the voter behaved. Theoretically, the voter can disobey and commit to a ballot with a different candidate from the coercer's preference. However, with the probability of $1/2$, the disobedience would get caught.

Blockchain enforces the order of commitments and gives unpredictable randomness. Delay functions and time-lock encryption can ensure that a voter does not learn a secret until after some time, which can prevent the simulation of proofs. Privacy-preserving smart contracts, e.g., MPC-based [3,30], Trusted Execution Environments, and other trusted hardware can ensure the voter never knows a secret key required for coercion mitigation. These tools can act in place of the coercer and interact with the voter during the vote-casting phase, while the coercer or vote-buyer only verifies all the evidence at the end of the election.

Since the new tools allow an adversary to control the voter without observing her continuously, coercion can be done at a large scale without substantial costs. Hence, it is critical to evaluate and discuss these new attack vectors.

1.1   Related Work

Exploiting ballot verification mechanisms for coercion is not new, and we here present related work. An attack similar to the attack mentioned in the introduction on Benaloh challenges was presented in [10], without using blockchain technology. We give the details in Sect. 3.1, and explain how the attack can be mitigated (i.e., the voter can disobey and conceal this fact), whereas our attack is not repaired.

An interesting coercion attack utilizing scratch-off cards was proposed in [21] against the Punchscan [29] two-part ballots. The number revealed after scratching will force the voter to reveal a certain ballot part - much like the attack on Benaloh challenges. However, scratch-off cards require a physical delivery and support only a limited range of options. Thus, it would be infeasible for many digital ballots. Going further, our attack also works against receipt-freeness, as we explain below, whereas for the code sheets this would require a voter to obliviously create scratch codes on behalf of a vote-buyer, which seems hard to achieve in practice.

Many voting schemes have been proposed using various blockchain primitives to achieve different forms of security, perhaps most famously [23] used smart-contracts to prevent denial-of-service to a decentralized voting scheme, and in [7] smart contracts were used to disincentivize vote-selling.

On the other hand, many schemes have been proposed that naively implement blockchain technology and claim security without properly understanding possible pitfalls and the alignment of incentives [25,26].

Also note that parallel to our contribution is a blog post on vote buying in special DAOs [1] using SGX.

Finally, we note that we only consider coercion- and vote-buying rising from the vote-casting procedure. There has recently been improvements on the state-of-the-art for definitions of covering the full election, especially coercion attacks during the tally phase of JCJ [14]. See also [19] for recent definitions of receipt-freeness. However, this is out of scope for this paper.

1.2   Contribution and Organization of the Paper

We study unexplored coercion and vote-buying attacks based on new cryptographic primitives such as blockchain, delay function, time-lock encryption, privacy-preserving smart contracts, trusted hardware, etc. We give examples of new tools usage by showing how they help the coercer to force voters to comply or the voter to obtain a (probabilistic) receipt for vote selling. We will also present some attacks inspired by these, which will work even without these tools. Our last contribution will be the proposal of new security definitions for coercion-resistance and receipt-freeness that take into account the possibility that both the coercer and the voter can use such new tools.

We start by stating our model and trust assumptions in Sect. 2.1. First, we describe and list expectations for the new tools available to the coercer in Sect. 2.2 and categorize the coercion attack types in Sect. 2.3. Then, in Sect. 3, we proceed with attacks on the known e-voting verification methods and schemes. Section 4 contains new security definitions for the notions of coercion-resistance and receipt-freeness, and some relations between them. Finally, in Sect. 5, we summarize our observations and we briefly state some impossibility results we encountered and should be considered in future work.

2 Voter and Adversary Model

2.1 Parties and Communication Model

The parties involved in our protocol are the following. $\mathcal{EA}$ is the election authority, which is trusted for privacy and hence for coercion-resistance. $\mathcal{BB}$ denotes the bulletin board, which collects ballots and verifiably derives the tally result. $\mathcal{V}$ denotes the (single) voter; we consider only a single voter in this work because we are only concerned about the verifiability and coercion-resistance of the vote-casting procedure. $\mathcal{C}$ is the adversary against coercion-resistance. $\mathcal{VD}$ denotes the voting device, which helps the voter to prepare the ballot and sends it to $\mathcal{BB}$; it is assumed to not be colluding with $\mathcal{C}$.

In our model, we consider a voter without any knowledge pre-shared with $\mathcal{EA}$ except public election parameters available on $\mathcal{BB}$. We assume $\mathcal{C}$ can observe the ballot that $\mathcal{V}$ sends to $\mathcal{EA}$, e.g., because it is directly published on $\mathcal{BB}$. We will assume that $\mathcal{C}$ is not present during the vote casting since otherwise the voter would not be able to fake her view, but $\mathcal{C}$ can give instructions before and get information after the session to verify if the voter followed instructions.

2.2 The Coercer's Toolbox

We consider different cryptographic means that the coercer or vote buyer can use to control the voter without being present in the vote-casting situation. We assume the voter wants to vote for $\mathsf{Cand}_\mathcal{V}$ and the coercer expects $\mathsf{Cand}_\mathcal{C}$.

- Instr: Instructions that $\mathcal{C}$ gives to $\mathcal{V}$ before voting. We assume $\mathcal{V}$ already knows the preferred candidate of $\mathcal{C}$, but Instr will provide more details.
- CC: Chain of commitments. The committed values are add-only and immutable. This can be done, for example, via a blockchain or a hardware device that stores input from the voters.
- CC − PRF: Chain of commitments with (pseudo-)random output between commitments. One example could be Bitcoin, with the hash pointers treated as pseudorandom output. Another option is a hardware device taking inputs

x_i and returning $y_i = \mathsf{H}(x_i || y_{i-1} || \mathsf{sk})$, where H is a cryptographic hash function, and sk is a secret key only known to $\mathcal{C}$. Knowing the last output and inputs, $\mathcal{C}$ can verify the entire transcript without asking the hardware token back.

- Timed $-$ CC, Timed $-$ CC $-$ PRF: Timed chain of commitments without/with pseudo-random output. Similar to CC and CC $-$ PRF, but also commitments are time-stamped. A blockchain or a hardware token with timings would suffice.
- Timed $-$ Enc: Timed release of secrets. It can be done via Time-Lock-Puzzles [31], Delay Encryption [8], Homomorphic Time-Lock Puzzles [22], etc.
- Token: Tamper-proof hardware token. It gets inputs from the voter and can give outputs, record timings, store secret values known only by the coercer, and generate public keys while keeping private keys safe in the module. The coercer can ask the voter for the full transcript of inputs and outputs from the device and verify everything without receiving the token back. This can be done, via a Trusted Platform Module (available on most modern laptops, PCs, and smartphones), a Trusted Execution Environment, general trusted hardware, or privacy-preserving smart contracts (e.g., MPC-based versions).

We do not claim this to be an exhaustive list of tools, and would expect new tools to emerge in the future, but our methodology in selecting these, has been to look for methods used to enforce certain honest behaviours.

2.3 Coercion Attack-Types

We also classify different typ es of attacks according to their severity and difficulty

- Attack:Precision: An attack we can carry out with a probability that can be made close to 1.
- Attack:Probabilistic: An attack where the coercer has a certain probability to carry it out, but this probability is not close to 1.
- Attack:Complex: An attack where the coercer has to estimate a bound on the computational power of $\mathcal{V}$, e.g., for the delay time in the primitives in Timed $-$ Enc or the number of devices that $\mathcal{V}$ has.

3 Attacks

We the above tools at hand, we investigated how a coercer could use these to attack CAI mechanisms found in the e-voting literature. The attack impact varies from completely breaking privacy to computationally penalizing voters for using disobedience strategies. The attacks are categorized based on the type and the coercer's tools.

3.1 Benaloh Challenges

As mentioned in the introduction, the Benaloh challenges are a perfect example to demonstrate the different coercer tools and estimate how easily a coercer can attack multiple voters. For a detailed description please refer to [2,28].

Whereas Benaloh challenges were never claimed to be coercion-resistant[1] these attacks were not considered earlier. Even further, it is generally believed that Helios is receipt-free if the software does not leak the random coins, see e.g. page 3 of [9], which could e.g. be enforced using a hardware root of trust.

(Attack:Complex; Instr). An attack fitting our narratives was proposed for a polling booth-Helios [10]. We believe it would work for remote voting: $\mathcal{C}$ tells the voter to vote only if the receipt hash h fulfills some predicate $P(h)$ (e.g., the number of leading null bits which happens with some probability p) and audit otherwise. Then $\mathcal{C}$ demands to see all audited receipts and random coins. The attack can be avoided but requires double effort: the voter first uses the coercer's choice to obtain verification data, then (instead of casting the vote when receipt permits it) switches to the preferred option and re-runs the voting process until receipt allows vote-casting. Of course, all audit material corresponding to the voter's choice must be destroyed.

(Attack:Precision; Instr, CC − PRF) The coercer instructs the voter to use the $Cand_{\mathcal{C}}$, then add a commitment to the ballot that the voting device shows to CC − PRF and only cast if the CC − PRF output starts with 1 (alternatively: 0 or more complex predicate). The expectation is that the voter cannot predict when the CC − PRF will allow casting the ballot; thus, she does not know when it's safe to misbehave and use her preference. The coercer can always check that the commitment of the casting vote was added to the CC − PRF and resulted in the output indicating the case. Therefore, the voter has a high risk of being caught in the case of disobedience. In case of just checking the first bit this probability is $p = 1/2$, but the coercer can increase this to a general probability p the cost of the voter having to do $1/(1 - p)$ vote cast attempts on average.

Note that a voter with a CC − PRF, e.g. access to Bitcoin, also can use this to get a receipt of the vote, i.e. Helios is not receipt-free even with trusted software.

On a high level, the first previous attack (suggested in [10]) looks very similar to the second one (proposed by ourselves), with the only distinction being the use of blockchain. However, we claim this is not the case. To see why, one should observe that in the polling-booth-Helios the voter receives an electronic hash of her receipt as a commitment from the machine. This commitment is not publicly posted or stored anywhere. It is given to the voter in the privacy of the voting booth. Therefore, a realistic coercer (i.e. one who cannot compute the exact amount of time spent by the voter during vote casting) would have no way of knowing exactly how many hash commitments the voter received and would not notice if a few were not used. Thus, the voter can destroy receipts indicating audit and only show the coercer the receipt that allows casting. Unfortunately,

---

[1] An early version of Helios had a "coerce-me" button to point to the danger of coercion in remote e-voting which handed out the random coin.

omitting some of the receipts would be impossible with the blockchain attack as it is specifically designed to preserve the immutability of records.

3.2 STAR-Vote

For CAI verification, STAR-Vote [5] offers a novel variant of Benaloh's challenge: the voter either deposits the ballot in the ballot box or not. First, the voter makes selections on a terminal, which prints the paper ballot in human-readable form with a random serial number and a corresponding receipt that the voter might take home. The voting terminal also sends the encrypted vote and the receipt to the judge station and publishes the commitment to the ballot on a publicly bulletin board. If the voter chooses to cast the vote, she takes the paper ballot to the ballot scanner, which reads the ballot's serial number and marks it as complete. If the voter decides to spoil the vote, she should return to a poll worker, who scans the vote and indicates it is spoiled. Such a vote would be decrypted during the tally. The verification mechanism works like the original Benaloh challenge: the voting terminal commits to the ballot before it knows whether the voter decides to cast or spoil it.

(Attack:Probabilistic; Instr) The coercer tells the voter to cast their ballot only if the printed receipt starts with some predicate, say a bit'0'. Otherwise, the voter must spoil the vote and give the receipt to the coercer. For our example, the chance of an audit is $1/2$, but it can vary depending on the complexity of the predicate. Regardless, the voter cannot predict when the vote-casting happens and thus must take a risk or obey. However, if the voter disobeys and the receipt indicates spoiling the ballot, the coercer can trivially detect misbehavior by checking the decrypted spoiled ballot.

3.3 Belenios-CAI

Belenios [13] is built upon the Helios and recently obtained CAI verifiability [12]. After the voter selects a vote v, she receives two random integers a and b such that $b = v + a(\text{mod}\mu)$ for some positive μ larger than the biggest possible v. Then, the ballot is formed as three ciphertexts encrypting values v, a, and b, plus a zero-knowledge proof that $b = v + a(\bmod \mu)$. After that, the voting device commits to the ballot and asks the voter to choose if the ciphertext encrypting b or a should be opened. The selected ciphertext is publicly opened. To modify v and create a convincing zero-knowledge proof, one has to change both v and one of the values a or b; therefore, the voter will detect it with probability $1/2$. For a detailed description please refer to [12].

We stress that, as far as we know, Belenios-CAI has never claimed to enjoy receipt-freeness. It only highlights that revealing only one of two values does not affect the privacy of the vote but says nothing about vote-selling or coercion. Mostly, this is because the Belenios voting family defines receipt-freeness in the strong sense, where the voter can forcefully extract randomness from the voting device to facilitate vote-selling. However, in our model, we trust $\mathcal{VD}$.

(Attack:Probabilistic; Instr, CC − PRF) The coercer $\mathcal{C}$ instructs the voter $\mathcal{V}$ to use the $v = \mathsf{Cand}_{\mathcal{C}}$, commit all values generated by $\mathcal{VD}$ to CC − PRF, and choose between a or b based on the CC − PRF's output. Theoretically, voter can receive (c_v, c_a, c_b, a, b) corresponding to Cand, then set $b^* = (\mathsf{Cand}_{\mathcal{C}} - a)$ and post $(c_v, c_a, c_b, a, b*)$ on the CC − PRF. However, if the output of the CC − PRF indicates to open c_b, then the coercer would notice the disobedience. Again this attack can also means there is no receipt-freeness for a voter with access to CC − PRF.

3.4   Themis

Closely related to Belenios-CAI is the in-person voting scheme Themis [6], which uses the same idea of splitting the candidate number v, which is always odd, into randoms a and b, ensuring that $v = a + b$ mod $2n$ (n is the number of candidates) and verifying the encryption of one of the numbers. However, the voter gets this splitting on a printed ballot and chooses which side to audit.

(Attack:Probabilistic; Instr) Assume the voter can compute a boolean function f in the head. The voter in the booth computes $f(a, b)$ in the head and audits the left or right side according to the value. For example, assume that $f = 0$ indicates opening a while $f = 1$ says audit b. If the voter votes for $v = \mathsf{Cand}_{\mathcal{V}}$ and gets a and b such that $v \equiv a + b$ but then claims to have selected $v^* = \mathsf{Cand}_{\mathcal{C}}$, she needs to fake a and make sure that $f(a, v^* - b) = 0$ or fake b and ensure that $f(v^* - b, b) = 1$. If f is random, then it can happen with probability $1/4$. It might not be high, but it is an interesting observation and could be enough to have a monetary incentive for a vote buyer.

(Attack:Probabilistic; Instr) A better and easier attack is as follows. The possibilities for a and b such that $a + b = v$ mod $2n$ are depending on v. Consider a simple case of $n = 2$ candidates (e.g., "A" and "B") with assigned numbers 1 and 3. Then for the candidate A the possible codes are $(0, 1)$ and $(2, 3)$, and for B – $(0, 3)$ and $(2, 1)$. If the coercer demands the audited number to be 0 or 1, voting for B always allows compliance with the demand. However, voting for A would result in $(a, b) = (0, 1)$ only in $1/2$ of cases. Thus, if the voter votes for A, the coercer will find out with the probability of $1/2$. Note that the attack can scale to more candidates if the coercer demands computing numbers modulo 4.

3.5   Proof of Correct (Re-)Encryption

Voting schemes often offer the voter a proof of correct encryption or re-encryption (of the ciphertext that contains the chosen option) as a CAI verification method. Of course, such proof should be interactive, or else the coercer can demand to see it. Moreover, the proof should have full zero-knowledge and not merely honest-verifier zero-knowledge if one wants to avoid coercion. We have identified three different proposals for verification based on (re-)encryption correctness that can be attacked by a coercer with new tools: two protocols in [17] and one protocol in [24]. The three attacks are described in the long version [18] of this work; here we describe the first one.

Authors of [17] analyze a Σ-protocol for proving encryption correctness with an initial commitment to the challenge (so, four rounds of communication in total) and conclude it is both coercion-resistant and CAI. However, we will show how such a scheme can be attacked using new coercion tools.

The public parameters of the election system must contain elements (q, G, g, h) such that $G = \langle g \rangle = \langle h \rangle$ has prime order q. To commit to the challenge, the perfectly hiding Pedersen commitment scheme [27] is used. In Step 1, voter samples $e, \hat{r} \xleftarrow{R} \mathbb{Z}_q$, computes $Z = g^e \cdot h^{\hat{r}}$ and sends (Z, Cand) to $\mathcal{VD}$. In Step 2, $\mathcal{VD}$ samples $r, t \xleftarrow{R} \mathbb{Z}_q$, computes $\mathsf{C} = (c_1, c_2) = (g^r, \mathsf{Cand} \cdot \mathsf{pk}^r)$ and $a = (A_1, A_2) = (g^t, \mathsf{pk}^t)$, so that values (C, a) are sent back to $\mathcal{V}$. In Step 3, $\mathcal{V}$ replies with $(e, \hat{r})$. Finally, $\mathcal{VD}$ checks that $Z = g^e \cdot h^{\hat{r}}$, computes $z = t + e \cdot r \mod q$ and sends z to $\mathcal{V}$, who can verify that both $g^z = A_1 \cdot c_1^e$ and $\mathsf{pk}^z = A_2 \cdot \left(\frac{c_2}{\mathsf{Cand}}\right)^e$ hold.

(Attack:Complex; Instr, Timed − CC − PRF, Timed − Enc) Shortly before the voting phase, the coercer $\mathcal{C}$ gives the voter $\mathcal{V}$ commitments $Z = g^e h^{\hat{r}}$ and the corresponding openings under delay encryption $X = \mathsf{Delay}(\hat{r}||e)$, which can be opened only after time $\mathcal{T}$. The voter is ordered to commit to the ciphertext $\mathsf{C} = (c_1, c_2)$ and the first move of the sigma protocol $a = (A_1, A_2)$ using timed commitment chain of the coercer's choice Timed − CC before time $\mathcal{T}$. We note that to prevent pre-computation by the voter, the coercer could use timed encryption like [15] to release the puzzle at a precise time.

One can consider a modified protocol (with five rounds, started by $\mathcal{VD}$) where (i) the generator h for Pedersen commitments is not fixed in the public parameters, but instead chosen by $\mathcal{VD}$ in step 1 of the protocol, and (ii) the commitment sent by $\mathcal{V}$ in step 2 is defined as $Z = g^{\hat{r}} \cdot h^e$ instead. This is actually the specific instantiation of the protocol proposed in the Appendix of [24]. The coercion strategy based on combining a blockchain and a delay function does not seem to work against this modified protocol; giving some formal proof of the security of this protocol is left as future work.

3.6   Civitas

Civitas [11] is a modification of the JCJ electronic voting protocol proposed by Juels, Catalano, and Jakobsson [20]. They are considered two of the voting schemes enjoying the strongest level of coercion-resistance. The coercion-evading strategy is based on the fact that a voter can compute and show fake credentials to the coercer, whereas he uses real credentials for the desired vote casting. Fake and real credentials are indistinguishable because real credentials are verified using a designated verifier technique, which takes as input an ElGamal public designation key K_{V_E} of the voter (different from the voter's registration key used, among others, for authentication purposes). The voter can use the secret key k_{V_E} to compute the (indistinguishable from real) fake credentials. However, if a coercer can force a voter to use a specific public key K_{V_E} without knowing the matching secret trapdoor k_{V_E}, then the voter cannot resist coercion.

Even a modification of Civitas where the voter is requested to prove, in zero-knowledge, that he knows the trapdoor k_{V_E} could be vulnerable to our new coercion tools. Moreover, these attacks do not seem to contradict Trust Assumption 1 of Civitas: *The adversary cannot simulate a voter during Registration.* On the one hand, the attacks we propose are off-line: the coercer gives K_{V_E} to the voter before Registration starts. On the other hand, coercion involves only the designation keys and not the registration keys (which are the focus of all the discussion about this Assumption 1 in [11]).

3.7   Voting Based on Trusted Computing

Smart and Ritter proposed a coercion-resistant protocol [33] based on trusted computations (specifically, the TPM and Direct Anonymous Attestation protocol). It consists of three phases: registration, where the voter has to prove their identity in person; joining, where the voter uses a trusted TPM to receive a certificate confirming eligibility; and signing, where the trusted TPM signs the vote. The authorities re-encrypt the ballot before publishing and send the voter a designated proof of re-encryption. If the voter is coerced and does not want to send the coercer's ballot, she can send a different ballot instead and use her designated key to simulate the re-encryption proof for the coercer.
(Attack:Complex; Instr, Timed − CC − PRF, Timed − Enc) As a part of the protocol, the voter (not a trusted TPM!) is supposed to generate a fresh Elgamal key pair $(s_v, h_v = g^{s_v})$, which is her designated key. Without s_v, the voter cannot simulate a re-encryption proof, which is why it is a crucial component of the coercion-resistance strategy. However, with the new tools, the coercer can give the voter a pre-generated pair $(\mathsf{Delay}(s_v), h_v)$, hidden by the delay function Delay that cannot be opened before time T, and demand the re-encryption proof before time T. The voter will have no choice but to obey.

A similar attack applies to a version of BeleniosRF [9] where voters generate their signing keys and register the public part with the registrar. As a side observation, we think an untrusted election authority generating public parameters pp can undetectably modify ballots of this particular version of BeleniosRF.[2]

4   New Security Definitions

The attacks presented in this paper have demonstrated that it is necessary to make a more general definition of receipt-freeness and coercion-resistance for the vote-casting phase to take into account the new tools for coercers and vote-buyers. We will first give a game-based definition without the new tools and then introduce these as oracles that can be used by the coercer and voter. A formal definition of the of cast-as-intended verifiability can be found in [32] and the long version of this paper [18].

---

[2] A dishonest election authority, instead of selecting z randomly from G_1, sets $z = g_1^v$ for some v in $\mathsf{Setup}(1^\lambda, 1^k)$. Now, the re-randomization server can compute $X_1^v = (g_1^x)^v = (g_1^v)^x = z^x = Y$ (i.e., the voter's private signing key) and sign any ballot.

We now note that most systems either can be analyzed in our setting or will have CAI verifiability based on the assumption that a secret key, e.g. a signing kay, is not being leaked to $\mathcal{A}_{ver}$ or using some trusted party.

Our settings also include schemes that achieve receipt-freeness or some coercion-resistance using deniable re-voting or vote updates, e.g., re-randomization as in Belenios-RF [9]. To see how our definition can be extended to cover those cases, please refer to the long version of this paper [18].

4.1   Vote Casting Phase Coercion-Resistance

We consider Coercion-Resistance for the Vote Casting Phase, $\mathsf{VC} - \mathsf{CR}$, which is a necessary condition for achieving coercion-resistance for the full voting system considering vote submissions from all voters and information leaks from the tally.

The definition is in terms of an experiment $\mathsf{Exp}_{\mathcal{A},\mathcal{V}}^{\mathsf{VC}-\mathsf{CR},1}(\lambda)$ given in Fig. 1, where the coercer, $\mathcal{A}$, can give instructions, Instr, to the voter before vote-casting. Vote-casting is done using a vote-device $\mathcal{VD}$. To be general, this is modeled as an oracle $\mathcal{O}_{\mathsf{state}_{\mathcal{VD}}}\mathcal{VD}$ with a state $\mathsf{state}_{\mathcal{VD}}$ which is updated during the interaction between the voter and device. We assume that the instruction Instr uniquely defines an algorithm $\mathcal{V}_{\mathsf{Instr}}^{\mathcal{O}_{\mathsf{state}_{\mathcal{VD}}}\mathcal{VD}}$ which models what the voter does when following the instructions of the adversary. The adversary has to distinguish the output from this compared to the case where the voter casts her own vote using some coercion-evasion strategy, denoted $\mathcal{V}$, which we will assume is public, normally given as part of the voting scheme. In both cases, the voter can output a message msg to the coercer, which can include the (faked) View between the voter and the voting device plus auxiliary information such as random coins.

We have kept Instr and msg abstract since they depend on the voting protocol and values obtained when accessing the new tools. When proving a specific protocol secure they should be made specific to facilitate the security proof.

As mentioned above, the coercer will get access to the ballot ballot produced by $\mathcal{VD}$ in the end. We get this ballot from the final state of $\mathcal{VD}$ using the algorithm Vote. Finally, we extract the underlying vote enclosed in the ballot using the algorithm $\mathsf{Extract}$. We use this to ensure that the voter following the coercion-evasion strategy really casts the preferred vote $\mathsf{Vote}_{\mathcal{V}}$, and we require that the voter following instructions casts the coercer's choice $\mathsf{Vote}_{\mathsf{coerc}}$, i.e., we do not consider randomisation attacks or forced abstention. The latter is impossible to protect against when the coercer sees the output ballot. The ballot randomisation attacks are interesting but outside the scope of this paper, but could be modelled using a similar type of definition allowing $\mathsf{Vote}_{\mathsf{coerc}} \neq \mathsf{Vote}_{\mathcal{V}}$.

We use abbreviations for the constraints in the game code on the vote choices using $\mathsf{Require} \cdot$ which stands for ' if not $\cdot$ then Stop with $\perp$ ' and $\mathsf{Promise} \cdot$ which stands for ' if not $\cdot$ then Stop with $\top$ '.

Definition 1. (Vote Casting Phase Coercion-Resistance) The protocol Vote enjoys Coercion-Resistance for the Vote Casting Phase, $\mathsf{VC} - \mathsf{CR}$, if there exists a PPT voter algorithm $\mathcal{V}$ such that for all vote choices $\mathsf{Vote}_{\mathcal{V}} \neq \mathsf{Vote}_{\mathcal{C}}$ and for any

$\mathsf{Exp}_{\mathcal{A},\mathcal{V}}^{\mathsf{VC-CR},b}(\lambda)$

1 : $(\mathsf{sk},\mathsf{pk}) \leftarrow \mathsf{Setup}(\lambda)$

2 : $\mathsf{state}_{\mathcal{V}\mathcal{D}} \leftarrow \mathsf{empty}$

3 : $(\mathsf{Instr},\mathsf{state}_{\mathcal{A}}) \leftarrow \mathcal{A}_1(\mathsf{pk},\mathsf{Vote}_{\mathcal{V}},\mathsf{Vote}_{\mathcal{C}})$

4 : if $b = 0$

5 : $\mathsf{msg} \leftarrow \mathcal{V}^{\mathcal{O}_{\mathsf{state}_{\mathcal{V}\mathcal{D}}}\mathcal{V}\mathcal{D}}(\mathsf{pk},\mathsf{Instr},\mathsf{Vote}_{\mathcal{V}})$

6 : $\mathsf{ballot} \leftarrow \mathsf{Vote}(\mathsf{state}_{\mathcal{V}\mathcal{D}})$

7 :   Promise $\mathsf{Extract}(\mathsf{ballot},\mathsf{sk}) = \mathsf{Vote}_{\mathcal{V}}$

8 : if $b = 1$

9 : $\mathsf{msg} \leftarrow \mathcal{V}_{\mathsf{Instr}}^{\mathcal{O}_{\mathsf{state}_{\mathcal{V}\mathcal{D}}}\mathcal{V}\mathcal{D}}(\mathsf{pk})$

10 : $\mathsf{ballot} \leftarrow \mathsf{Vote}(\mathsf{state}_{\mathcal{V}\mathcal{D}})$

11 :   Require $\mathsf{Extract}(\mathsf{ballot},\mathsf{sk}) = \mathsf{Vote}_{\mathcal{C}}$

12 : $b' \leftarrow \mathcal{A}_2(\mathsf{pk},\mathsf{msg},\mathsf{ballot},\mathsf{state}_{\mathcal{A}},\mathsf{Vote}_{\mathcal{V}},\mathsf{Vote}_{\mathcal{C}})$

13 : return $b' = b$

$\mathsf{Exp}_{\mathcal{A},\mathcal{V},\mathsf{Sim}}^{\mathsf{VC-RF},b}(\lambda)$

1 : $(\mathsf{sk},\mathsf{pk}) \leftarrow \mathsf{Setup}(\lambda)$

2 : $\mathsf{state}_{\mathcal{V}\mathcal{D}} \leftarrow \mathsf{empty}$

3 : if $b = 0$

4 : $\mathsf{msg} \leftarrow \mathcal{V}^{\mathcal{O}_{\mathsf{state}_{\mathcal{V}\mathcal{D}}}\mathcal{V}\mathcal{D}}(\mathsf{pk},\mathsf{Vote}_{\mathsf{sell}})$

5 : $\mathsf{ballot} \leftarrow \mathsf{Vote}(\mathsf{state}_{\mathcal{V}\mathcal{D}})$

6 :   Require $\mathsf{Extract}(\mathsf{ballot},\mathsf{sk}) = \mathsf{Vote}_{\mathsf{sell}}$

7 : if $b = 1$

8 : $\mathsf{msg} \leftarrow \mathsf{Sim}_{\mathcal{V}}^{\mathcal{O}_{\mathsf{state}_{\mathcal{V}\mathcal{D}}}\mathcal{V}\mathcal{D}}(\mathsf{pk},\mathsf{Vote}_{\mathsf{own}},\mathsf{Vote}_{\mathsf{sell}})$

9 : $\mathsf{ballot} \leftarrow \mathsf{Vote}(\mathsf{state}_{\mathcal{V}\mathcal{D}})$

10 :   Promise $\mathsf{Extract}(\mathsf{ballot},\mathsf{sk}) = \mathsf{Vote}_{\mathsf{own}}$

11 : $b' \leftarrow \mathcal{A}(\mathsf{pk},\mathsf{msg},\mathsf{ballot},\mathsf{Vote}_{\mathsf{own}},\mathsf{Vote}_{\mathsf{sell}})$

12 : return $b' = b$

$\mathcal{O}_{\mathsf{state}_{\mathcal{V}\mathcal{D}}}\mathcal{V}\mathcal{D}(m)$

1 : $(\mathsf{state}_{\mathcal{V}\mathcal{D}},m_{out}) \leftarrow \mathsf{VoteDev}(\mathsf{pk},\mathsf{state}_{\mathcal{V}\mathcal{D}},m)$

2 : return m_{out}

Fig. 1. On the left, the experiment for Coercion-Resistance for the Vote Casting Phase, VC − CR, and on the right, for Receipt-Freeness, VC − RF. Below the vote-device oracle.

polynomial-time adversary $\mathcal{A}$ we have that $\mathsf{Adv}_{\mathcal{A}}^{\mathsf{vc-cr}}(\lambda) = \left| \Pr\left[\mathsf{Exp}_{\mathcal{A},\mathcal{V}}^{\mathsf{VC-CR},0}(\lambda)\right] - \Pr\left[\mathsf{Exp}_{\mathcal{A},\mathcal{V}}^{\mathsf{VC-CR},1}(\lambda)\right] \right|$ is a negligible function of the security parameter λ.

There are many variations of this definition, see [18] for a more exhaustive list,

- Minimal Instructions, VC − CR(Min − Instr): Here the coercer just needs to output the desired vote $\mathsf{Vote}_{\mathcal{C}}$ as instruction.
- Known coerced vote, VC − CR(Known − Vote): Note that $\mathsf{Vote}_{\mathsf{coerc}}$ is not explicitly given to the voter algorithm $\mathcal{V}$ to model that the voter might just get some instructions without knowing what the desired vote of the coercer is. A weaker definition can be made where $\mathsf{Vote}_{\mathsf{coerc}}$ is known to the voter.
- No secret in instruction, VC − CR(No − Secret − in − Instr): In this case it is not necessary for the coercer to keep secrets from the coerced voter. We model this as $\mathcal{A}_1$ being a deterministic algorithm using some random tape r and which is included as part of the instructions Instr together with the algorithm $\mathcal{A}_1$. In this case $\mathsf{state}_{\mathcal{A}}$ used by $\mathcal{A}_2$ can just be Instr.
- No secret for classifier, VC − CR(No − Secret − in − Classifier): We can make a weaker definition where the coercer does not need to remember a secret used in the instructions to classify whether the coerced voter follows instructions or not. We model this by not giving the $\mathsf{state}_{\mathcal{A}}$ to the algorithm $\mathcal{A}_2$ where adversary decides which world he is in, but only the instructions Instr. This means the verification could be done by any party just knowing the instructions from the coercer. We denote this VC − CR(No − Secret − in − Classifier).

– Finally, we note that we can combine the above definitions. E.g. we can have VC − CR(Known − Vote, No − Secret − in − Instr, Minimal − Classifier) for the case where the voter knows the coercer's vote choice, there are no secrets in the instruction, and no secret or instructions used in the classifier.

Oracles for the Coercer's Toolbox. To model coercion via the new tools, we slightly modify the security game by giving the coercer and the voter access to extra oracles. For space reasons, we only mention two oracles, see [18] for a long list. An oracle $\mathcal{O}_{\text{Timed}-\text{CC}}$ captures an append-only immutable chain of commitments with time stamps. It starts with an empty list $\textbf{List}_0$ and supports two functions **TimedCommit**(x) and **Return**. Upon being called an i-th time, **TimedCommit**(x) calls **RequestTime** from a global time oracle to get current time t and updates the internal list $\textbf{List}_i \leftarrow \textbf{List}_{i-1}||(x||t)$. **Return**, upon being called an i-th time, outputs the list $\textbf{List}_i$. The oracle $\mathcal{O}_{\text{TPM}}$ captures the functionality of a trusted platform module. The exact interface can depend on the particular emulated module, but it can run a program determined by the coercer without leaking internal secrets, and it allows the voter to make inputs to this program and get the outputs.

4.2   Receipt-Freeness

Receipt-freeness for vote-casting phase VC − RF is defined much like corcion-resistance using the experiment $\mathsf{Exp}_{\mathcal{A},\mathcal{V},\text{Sim}}^{\text{VC}-\text{RF},b}(\lambda)$ in Fig. 1. The point of our defini-tion is that for any (malicious) voter algorithm $\mathcal{V}$ trying to obtain a receipt in the form of some information msg for her vote $\mathsf{Vote}_{\text{sell}}$, there exists a simulator that casts a vote for another choice $\mathsf{Vote}_{\text{own}}$ but gives information msg which is indistinguishable from the claimed receipt. It models that the voter tries to cheat a coercer or vote buyer by voting for another vote option.

Definition 2. (Vote Casting Phase Receipt-Freness) The protocol Vote enjoys Receipt-Freeness for the Vote Casting Phase, VC − RF, if there exists a simulator Sim such that for all vote choices $\mathsf{Vote}_{\text{sell}} \neq \mathsf{Vote}_{\text{own}}$, for all PPT algorithms $\mathcal{V}$ (corresponding to a malicious voter trying to obtain an receipt) and for all polynomial-time adversaries $\mathcal{A}$ we have that $\mathsf{Adv}_{\mathcal{A}}^{\text{vc}-\text{rf}}(\lambda) = \left| \Pr\left[\mathsf{Exp}_{\mathcal{A},\mathcal{V}}^{\text{VC}-\text{RF},0}(\lambda)\right] - \Pr\left[\mathsf{Exp}_{\mathcal{A},\mathcal{V}}^{\text{VC}-\text{RF},1}(\lambda)\right] \right|$ is a negligible function of the security parameter λ.

Again we can define variants of this definition, see [18].

Implications and Separations Between Definitions. In the long version of this paper [18] we show relations between the different flavour of definitions and give separating examples. Especially we give an (informal) proof of the following theorem, which demonstrates the usefulness of the definitions.

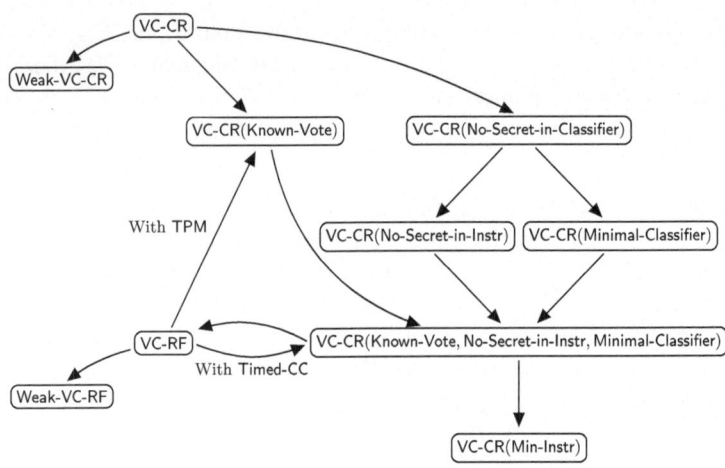

Fig. 2. Implications between the new security definitions

Theorem 1. *Receipt-freeness* $\mathsf{VC-RF}$ *implies the constrained coercion-resistance* $\mathsf{VC-CR(Known-Vote, No-Secret-in-Instr, Minimal-Classifier)}$ *and with access to a timed commitment oracle* $\mathcal{O}_{\mathsf{Timed-CC}}$ *(see Section 4.1) they are equivalent.*

The proof follows by relating the simulator, Sim, in $\mathsf{VC-RF}$ to the coercion-mitigation algorithm $\mathcal{V}$ in $\mathsf{VC-CR}$, and correspondingly relate the voter algorithm $\mathcal{V}$ in $\mathsf{VC-RF}$ to $\mathcal{V}_{\mathsf{Instr}}$ in $\mathsf{VC-CR}$. We need the timed commitment oracle since in the coercion game, the adversary gives instructions before voting. However, in the vote-seller experiment the output message is produced after voting which could allow the vote-seller to choose a favourable coercion instruction after voting which fits with the view of the voter interaction.

We also conjecture that $\mathsf{VC-RF}$ implies $\mathsf{VC-CR(Known-Vote)}$ with access to the trusted hardware module $\mathcal{O}_{\mathsf{TPM}}$, since the vote seller can commit to a coercion instruction, let the module output the coercer instructions and in the end output all secrets to the distinguisher including an attestation of what it was running.

In Fig. 2 we present some of the relations between the security definitions.

5   Conclusion and Future Work

We studied previously unexplored coercion and vote-selling attacks based on new cryptographic primitives such as blockchains, delay functions, time-lock encryption, etc. Our investigation showed many examples of how the coercer can force voters to comply with his demands by relying on those new tools. We described some of the possible attacks and sketched others. Since some successful coercion attacks occur on voting schemes that were supposed/claimed/proved to be coercion resistance or receipt-free, the main conclusion of the first part of the work was that the coercion models should be re-evaluated, and new definitions were required. Such definitions, that are presented in Sect. 4, lead to some interesting lines of future work. For example, it would be interesting to prove that no scheme can be coercion-resistant if the coercer uses Token, or that a trusted $\mathcal{VD}$ is essential in our model, or that no voter interacting with the coercer $\mathcal{C}$ directly can enjoy CAI and coercion-resistant at the same time.

Acknowldgements. This work received funding from the France 2030 program managed by the French National Research Agency under grant agreement No. ANR-22-PECY-0006. PBR also received support from the Luxembourg National Research Fund (FNR) under the CORE project (C21/IS/16221219/ImPAKT).

References

1. On-chain vote buying and the rise of dark DAOs. https://hackingdistributed.com/2018/07/02/on-chain-vote-buying/. Accessed 13 Dec 2023
2. Adida, B.: Helios: Web-based Open-Audit Voting. In: USENIX Security'0817th USENIX Security Symposium, pp. 335–348 (2008)
3. Baum, C., Chiang, J.H., David, B., Frederiksen, T.K.: Eagle: efficient privacy preserving smart contracts. In: Baldimtsi, F., Cachin, C. (eds.) Financial Cryptography and Data Security: 27th International Conference, FC 2023, Bol, Brač, Croatia, May 1–5, 2023, Revised Selected Papers, Part I, pp. 270–288. Springer Nature Switzerland, Cham (2024). https://doi.org/10.1007/978-3-031-47754-6_16
4. Benaloh, J.: Simple verifiable elections. In: EVT'06 Electronic Voting Technology Workshop (2006)
5. Benaloh, J., et al.: Star-vote: a secure, transparent, auditable, and reliable voting system. arXiv preprint arXiv:1211.1904 (2012)
6. Bougon, M., et al.: Themis: an on-site voting system with systematic cast-as-intended verification and partial accountability. In: Proceedings of the 2022 ACM SIGSAC Conference on Computer and Communications Security, pp. 397–410 (2022)
7. Boyd, C., Haines, T., Rønne, P.B.: Vote selling resistant voting. In: Bernhard, M., Bracciali, A., Camp, L.J., Matsuo, S., Maurushat, A., Rønne, P.B., Sala, M. (eds.) Financial Cryptography and Data Security: FC 2020 International Workshops, AsiaUSEC, CoDeFi, VOTING, and WTSC, Kota Kinabalu, Malaysia, February 14, 2020, Revised Selected Papers, pp. 345–359. Springer International Publishing, Cham (2020). https://doi.org/10.1007/978-3-030-54455-3_25
8. Burdges, J., De Feo, L.: Delay encryption. In: Canteaut, A., Standaert, F.-X. (eds.) Advances in Cryptology – EUROCRYPT 2021: 40th Annual International Conference on the Theory and Applications of Cryptographic Techniques, Zagreb, Croatia, October 17–21, 2021, Proceedings, Part I, pp. 302–326. Springer International Publishing, Cham (2021). https://doi.org/10.1007/978-3-030-77870-5_11
9. Chaidos, P., Cortier, V., Fuchsbauer, G., Galindo, D.: BeleniosRF: A non-interactive receipt-free electronic voting scheme. In: Proceedings of CCS'2016, pp. 1614–1625 (2016)
10. Chaum, D., et al.: Paperless independently-verifiable voting. In: Kiayias, A., Lipmaa, H. (eds.) E-Voting and Identity, pp. 140–157. Springer Berlin Heidelberg, Berlin, Heidelberg (2012). https://doi.org/10.1007/978-3-642-32747-6_9

11. Clarkson, M.R., Chong, S., Myers, A.C.: Civitas: toward a secure voting system. In: 2008 IEEE Symposium on Security and Privacy (S&P 2008), 18–21 May 2008, Oakland, California, USA, pp. 354–368. IEEE Computer Society (2008)

12. Cortier, V., Debant, A., Gaudry, P., Glondu, S.: Belenios with cast as intended. In: Essex, A., et al. (eds.) Financial Cryptography and Data Security. FC 2023 International Workshops: Voting, CoDecFin, DeFi, WTSC, Bol, Brač, Croatia, May 5, 2023, Revised Selected Papers, pp. 3–18. Springer Nature Switzerland, Cham (2024). https://doi.org/10.1007/978-3-031-48806-1_1

13. Cortier, V., Gaudry, P., Glondu, S.: Belenios: a simple private and verifiable electronic voting system. Foundations of Security, Protocols, and Equational Reasoning: Essays Dedicated to Catherine A. Meadows, pp. 214–238 (2019)

14. Cortier, V., Gaudry, P., Yang, Q.: Is the JCJ voting system really coercion-resistant? Cryptology ePrint Archive (2022)

15. Döttling, N., Hanzlik, L., Magri, B., Wohnig, S.: McFly: verifiable encryption to the future made practical. In: Baldimtsi, F., Cachin, C. (eds.) Financial Cryptography and Data Security: 27th International Conference, FC 2023, Bol, Brač, Croatia, May 1–5, 2023, Revised Selected Papers, Part I, pp. 252–269. Springer Nature Switzerland, Cham (2024). https://doi.org/10.1007/978-3-031-47754-6_15

16. Finogina, T., Herranz, J.: On remote electronic voting with both coercion resistance and cast-as-intended verifiability. J. Inform. Security Appl. **76**, 103554 (2023)

17. Finogina, T., Herranz, J., Larraia, E.: How (not) to achieve both coercion resistance and cast as intended verifiability in remote evoting. In: Conti, M., Stevens, M., Krenn, S. (eds.) Cryptology and Network Security: 20th International Conference, CANS 2021, Vienna, Austria, December 13-15, 2021, Proceedings, pp. 483–491. Springer International Publishing, Cham (2021). https://doi.org/10.1007/978-3-030-92548-2_25

18. Finogina, T., Herranz, J., Roenne, P.B.: Expanding the toolbox: coercion and vote-selling at vote-casting revisited. Cryptology ePrint Archive, Paper 2024/1167 (2024)

19. Fraser, A., Quaglia, E.A., Smyth, B.: A critique of game-based definitions of receipt-freeness for voting. In: Steinfeld, R., Yuen, T.H. (eds.) Provable Security: 13th International Conference, ProvSec 2019, Cairns, QLD, Australia, October 1–4, 2019, Proceedings, pp. 189–205. Springer International Publishing, Cham (2019). https://doi.org/10.1007/978-3-030-31919-9_11

20. Juels, A., Catalano, D., Jakobsson, M.: Coercion-resistant electronic elections. In: Proceedings of the 2005 ACM workshop on Privacy in the electronic society, pp. 61–70 (2005)

21. Kelsey, J., Regenscheid, A., Moran, T., Chaum, D.: Attacking paper-based e2e voting systems. In: Chaum, D., Jakobsson, M., Rivest, R.L., Ryan, P.Y.A., Benaloh, J., Kutylowski, M., Adida, B. (eds.) Towards Trustworthy Elections, pp. 370–387. Springer Berlin Heidelberg, Berlin, Heidelberg (2010). https://doi.org/10.1007/978-3-642-12980-3_23

22. Malavolta, G., Thyagarajan, S.A.K.: Homomorphic time-lock puzzles and applications. In: Boldyreva, A., Micciancio, D. (eds.) Advances in Cryptology – CRYPTO 2019: 39th Annual International Cryptology Conference, Santa Barbara, CA, USA, August 18–22, 2019, Proceedings, Part I, pp. 620–649. Springer International Publishing, Cham (2019). https://doi.org/10.1007/978-3-030-26948-7_22

23. McCorry, P., Shahandashti, S.F., Hao, F.: A smart contract for boardroom voting with maximum voter privacy. In: Kiayias, A. (ed.) FC 2017. LNCS, vol. 10322, pp. 357–375. Springer, Cham (2017). https://doi.org/10.1007/978-3-319-70972-7_20

24. Müller, J., Truderung, T.: CAISED: a protocol for cast-as-intended verifiability with a second device. In: Volkamer, M., et al. (eds.) Electronic Voting: 8th International Joint Conference, E-Vote-ID 2023, Luxembourg City, Luxembourg, October 3–6, 2023, Proceedings, pp. 123–139. Springer Nature Switzerland, Cham (2023). https://doi.org/10.1007/978-3-031-43756-4_8

25. Nasser, Y., Okoye, C., Clark, J., Ryan, P.Y.: Blockchains and voting: Somewhere between hype and a panacea. White Paper (2018)

26. Park, S., Specter, M., Narula, N., Rivest, R.L.: Going from bad to worse: from internet voting to blockchain voting. J. Cybersecurity **7**(1) (2021)

27. Pedersen, T.P.: Non-interactive and information-theoretic secure verifiable secret sharing. In: Proceedings of CRYPTO (1991)

28. Pereira, O., Adida, B., de Marneffe, O.: Bringing open audit elections into practice: Real world uses of Helios. In: swiss e-voting workshop (2010)

29. Popoveniuc, S., Hosp, B.: An introduction to punchscan. In: Chaum, D., et al. (eds.) Towards Trustworthy Elections, pp. 242–259. Springer Berlin Heidelberg, Berlin, Heidelberg (2010). https://doi.org/10.1007/978-3-642-12980-3_15

30. Qi, H., Xu, M., Yu, D., Cheng, X.: Sok: privacy-preserving smart contract. High-Confidence Computing, p. 100183 (2023)

31. Rivest, R.L., Shamir, A., Wagner, D.A.: Time-lock puzzles and timed-release crypto (1996)

32. Rønne, P.B., Ryan, P.Y.A., Smyth, B.: Cast-as-intended: a formal definition and case studies. In: Bernhard, M., et al. (eds.) Financial Cryptography and Data Security. FC 2021 International Workshops: CoDecFin, DeFi, VOTING, and WTSC, Virtual Event, March 5, 2021, Revised Selected Papers, pp. 251–262. Springer Berlin Heidelberg, Berlin, Heidelberg (2021). https://doi.org/10.1007/978-3-662-63958-0_22

33. Smart, M., Ritter, E.: True trustworthy elections: remote electronic voting using trusted computing. In: Calero, J.M.A., Yang, L.T., Mármol, F.G., García Villalba, L.J., Li, A.X., Wang, Y. (eds.) Autonomic and Trusted Computing, pp. 187–202. Springer Berlin Heidelberg, Berlin, Heidelberg (2011). https://doi.org/10.1007/978-3-642-23496-5_14

Intelligo Ut Confido: Understanding, Trust and User Experience in Verifiable Receipt-Free E-Voting

Marie-Laure Zollinger[1], Peter B. Rønne[1], Steve Schneider[2($\boxtimes$)],
Peter Y. A. Ryan[1], and Wojciech Jamroga[3]

[1] Interdisciplinary Centre for Security, Reliability and Trust, University of
Luxembourg,Esch-sur-Alzette, Luxembourg
`zollinger.marielaure@gmail.com`, {`peter.roenne,peter.ryan`}`@uni.lu`
[2] Surrey Centre for Cyber Security, University of Surrey, Guildford, UK
`s.schneider@surrey.ac.uk`
[3] Institute of Computer Science, Polish Academy of Sciences, Warszawa, Poland
`wojciech.jamroga@ipipan.waw.pl`

Abstract. Voting protocols seek to provide integrity and vote privacy in elections. To achieve integrity, procedures have been proposed allowing voters to verify that their vote is correctly counted– however this impacts both the user experience and privacy. In particular, vote verification can lead to vote-buying or coercion, if an attacker can obtain a proof of the cast vote. Thus, some voting protocols provide mechanisms to prevent such receipts.To be effective, such *receipt-freeness* depends on voters being able to understand and use these mechanisms.In this paper, we present a study with 300 participants to evaluate the voters' experience and understanding of the receipt-freeness procedures in the Selene scheme in the context of vote-buying. This is the first user study dealing with vote-buying in e-voting. While the usability and trust factors were rated low in the experiments, we found a positive correlation between trust and understanding.

1 Introduction

Voting and elections are a prime example of socio-techncial systems where humans interact in a technological environment [6]. This applies even more obviously to electronic voting [11]. *Voting protocols* are designed to satisfy certain important properties, in particular Privacy and Integrity. Privacy is often defined by three sub-properties: Ballot-Secrecy, Receipt-Freeness and Coercion-Resistance. Ballot-Secrecy ensures that the protocol does not reveal the voter's choice. Receipt-Freeness says that the system will not provide any evidence enabling a voter to prove how they voted. Finally, Coercion-Resistance anables the voter to pretend to cooperate actively with a coercer [8], but still cast their intended vote. When interacting with a vote-buyer, a voter has an economical incentive to obtain a receipt of the vote. A vote buyer offers a voter money for a vote cast a particular vote, but the money is only paid upon receiving "proof"

© The Author(s) 2025
D. Duenas-Cid et al. (Eds.): E-Vote-ID 2024, LNCS 15014, pp. 158–174, 2025.
https://doi.org/10.1007/978-3-031-72244-8_10

of the vote. However, if the "proof" can be faked, the vote buyer cannot trust the receipt and hence vote buying should be disincentivised.

Integrity means that the announced outcome of the election is correct. Verifiable schemes demand more: the system should also deliver a proof that the result is correct. *End-to-end verifiable voting protocols* [28], entail two complementary procedures: firstly, universal verifiability means that anyone can check that the vote count is correctly computed from the submitted ballots, secondly, individual verifiability means that each voter can check that their vote intent was correctly captured in the submitted ballot. The latter is most interesting from a user perspective since it inherently involves user interaction.

In the Selene e-voting protocol [27] voters receive a tracking number which points to their vote in plaintext in the tally. Voters can present a fake tracking number to a vote-buyer, providing a *receipt-free mechanism*. A vote buyer cannot determine whether the presented tracker is real or fake, and hence has no proof of how the voter actually voted. The voter's understanding and the user experience of the verifiability procedures in Selene were explored in several papers [9,22, 34,35]. However those studies did not include the receipt-free mechanism which introduce additional trust issues.

Receipt-Free or Coercion-Resistance mechanisms have rarely been tested with end-users; to our knowledge, only [23] explored a Coercion-Resistance mechanism for the JCJ e-voting protocol [12], and Receipt-Freeness in the context of Vote-Buying has not been investigated. This is a gap in the assessment of practical security of voting procedures. For an overview, see [14].

In this paper, we present the first large scale study of the receipt-free mechanism iof the Selene voting protocol. The study is based on experiments with 300 human participants recruited through the platform Prolific. We evaluated the user experience (UX), trust, and understanding of the voting procedure, and formulated three hypotheses to be tested:

H1 The voting application and its receipt-free feature provide a positive user experience to the participants.
H2 The application and receipt-free mechanism are trusted by the participants.
H3 Participants who understand the receipt-free mechanism have increased trust in the application.

To evaluate the UX, we use the user experience questionnaire (UEQ). At the time of the user experiment there was no standard questionnaire to assess this metric in the voting context (Ref. [1] appeared later). Therefore, we defined trust for voting and proposed a new questionnaire assessing the voters' trust in the protocol, see Sect. 4. Correct understanding of the receipt-free mechanism was evaluated by observing the steps performed by participants. To evaluate understanding, we designed game inspired by [18] for privacy in voting. Correct understanding of the mechanism leads to a specific workflow, see Sect. 5.

Finally, participants were invited to tell us why they made their choice in the game, and how they felt. We categorized their answers in a qualitative analysis and correlated this with the participants' understanding (Sect. 6.2).

To summarize, our contributions are:

- A questionnaire to evaluate trust in the context of voting,
- A unique game design to assess the voters' understanding of a system,
- An evaluation of the relationship between understanding and trust,
- A qualitative analysis of user feedback on receipt-freeness and vote-buying,
- A list of recommendations for future voting systems and user studies.

2   Related Work

Our experiment is inspired by [18] where a game approach was used to evaluate the understanding of the privacy mechanisms in the e-voting protocol Prêt-à-Voter (PaV) [26]. In PaV voters get receipts, but with their votes in encrypted form. In the game the 12 participants tried to guess each other's votes and had the choice between publishing their receipt or not. They were rewarded for revealing it. Hence, participants who understood that receipts did not reveal their vote should choose to reveal the receipt as the most profitable strategy. Thus understanding could be measured, but with so few participants a conclusion was hard to draw. We improve on this with a large number of participants.

Until now, most studies focused on the usability and appreciation of voters for a given system, but an evaluation of their understanding is rarely performed. Also, it has been been evaluated with reference to predefined mental models of the participants. In [2], the authors let voters draw their mental models for three voting schemes. This study reveals that voters focused much more on the voting phase in all three protocols, as the verification features remained unclear to them. In the case of Selene, two studies have looked at mental models of participants [34,35]. It appears that the understanding of verification was better when the participants have seen a possible threat, e.g. a vote manipulation [35]. The verification mechanisms of Selene were implemented without the receipt-free mechanism [29], augmenting an existing voting system. The user experience was evaluated [4] showing satisfaction and a higher confidence in the system. The evaluation of coercion-mitigation features have rarely been performed, except for the protocol JCJ [12] in [23].

3   The Selene Protocol

Selene is an e-voting protocol designed to make the individual verification more usable and intuitive for voters. Verification procedures can be categorized into four types, [22]: audit-or-cast, verification device, code sheets and tracker-based. Selene belongs to the last category, the other categories require the voters to either handle ciphertexts, or to verify codes. Tracker based protocols allow voters to verify the presence of their vote in plaintext in the final tally using a (private, deniable) tracking number. The special feature of Selene is that this tracker is only delivered to the voter *after* the tally is published to allow the coercion evasion strategy described below.

The complete description of the protocol is available at [27]. Each voter has a pair of public and private keys that are used in the verification phase. The election keys are also generated and the election public key is distributed to voters. A public bulletin board (BB) is used to display the public data.

1) Setup. The election authorities generate the list of tracking numbers. These are encrypted under the election public key, then shuffled and associated with the voters. A trapdoor commitment to each tracker is created and published on the bulletin board, sealing the relation between a tracker and a voter. To open a commitment and see the tracker, one needs the voter's private key and a secret (dual key) which is revealed later to the voter by the authorities.

2) Voting. When the setup phase is over, voters can cast a vote encrypted with the election public key. The encrypted vote is published on BB.

3) Tally. After voting, the authorities retrieve the pairs of encrypted tracking numbers and encrypted votes, shuffle the pairs and decrypt them to obtain and publish the pairs of plaintext tracking numbers and votes.

4a) Verifying. Some time after the tally is published, the secret dual key associated to each commitment is delivered to the voter. Combining the dual key, the commitment and their private key, each voter can retrieve the tracking number, and verify the associated plaintext vote.

4b) Faking. If a voter is interacting with a vote-buyer or being coerced , the voter can choose an alternative tracker, showing a plaintext vote that corresponds to the adversary's request. From this tracker and the commitment, a fake dual key is computed by the voter using her private key. This can be done after the tally phase. The combination of this fake dual key with the commitment and private key of the voter will open to the selected fake tracking number.

In the trial, participants could verify their own vote and later request that an alternative tracker be displayed to mislead the vote-buyer. This results in a more complex experience compared to what most voters would encounter in normal elections.

Web Application For the experiment, we implemented a web app reflecting the user steps described above. The voter can access the following pages through a menu, after login:

- *Home:* this page explains the purpose of the web app and the different pages.
- *Voting:* the voting question is displayed with the possible vote choices.
- *Verification:* this page presents the election result as vote/tracker pairs. The voter can retrieve the tracking number to verify the vote, or choose a fake tracking number.
- *About:* information about Selene and its features is displayed here.
- *Contact:* a link to our email is provided in case of questions.
- *Logout:* used to log out from the study.

A default workflow is proposed once the voter is connected. In the voting section, after selecting the candidate, a confirmation page is displayed. The voter can the click on a button "Encrypt and send my vote". As shown in [22,35], such an interaction does not require any skill, but increases the security perception. On the verification page, the tally is displayed and the voter is offered two choices: fake the tracking number in case of coercion or vote-buying, or go for verification directly. To fake the tracking number, a new page is displayed where the voter can access the bulletin board and type the chosen tracking number. The voter is warned that it is not possible to retrieve the real tracking number after this request. After validating, the voter is redirected to the main verification page. If the voter chooses to verify , the app computes the (real or fake) tracking number and the voter can connect to the bulletin board to verify the vote.

In previous implementations of Selene [9,22,34,35], the authors decided to highlight the tracking number and corresponding vote directly in the application to increase usability, with the risk of lowering privacy and the security perception. In this version, we provide the tracking number and the user has to display the bulletin board and look for the tracker to verify the vote. This is more faithful to the original protocol design but less usable.

4   Trust

Trust features in many studies about voting [3,7,15,21,30,33,34]. It is rather complex to evaluate, as trust has many aspects: trust in politics, trust in digital technologies, understanding of the app, etc.

There is no standard questionnaire available to evaluate trust of users for voting systems. The UEQ+ questionnaire [32] proposes little related to trust. To close this gap and explore the relation between understanding and trust, we designed a more specific questionnaire for the e-voting context. We now discuss trust and the design of the questionnaire. After our experiment was done another trust measure for voting was proposed [1]. However, with 44 questions this is not suitable for our online experiment where participants have limited patience.

In [19], Luhmann differentiates trust and confidence. Confidence can be obtained without any additional explanation, in particular security does not need to be perceived to be acknowledged while trust requires an evaluation from the users' of their security perception to be granted.

In [24], Pieters observes that a voting system can obtain the voters' *confidence* if it works correctly. A system that guarantees a correct result should not worry the voters. But, when a new system implementing new procedures, such as verifiability features, is comparised to the old system which has the confidence of voters, *trust* may be impacted. The author also mentions the relationship between trust and explanation. The voters need to *understand* verifiability in a new system to convince them to use it. Previous works have already mentioned the relationship between trust and the explanations [10], and in voting [34,35].

We aimed to provide a reasonable amount of information about the protocol, to support a good trust rating. However, the participants have limited time to evaluate the app, so we should not provide too much information that could overwhelm them.

4.1   Our Metric

Our voting-oriented trust questionnaire contains eight questions. From the studies and literature cited above, we see that trust depends on a positive evaluation of the security. In our questionnaire, we evaluate the feeling of security on one hand; and the acceptance of the system on the other, to see if trust is engendered. The questions, labelled by topic, are 1) [Acceptance] "I trust the system and I would use it in a real election". 2) [Security] "I believe that the personal information (vote included) is kept private". 3) [Security] "I think that the system ensures the integrity of the elections". 4) [Security] "I think that the system is transparent and lets me know everything about its behaviour". 5) [Acceptance] "I think that the verification phase is important". 6) [Security] "I was convinced by the verification phase that my vote was correctly recorded". 7) [Acceptance] "I would use such a verification system if it was available". 8) [Security] "I think that the result of the election can be changed by an attacker". Answers were given on a Likert scale with 6 choices from strongly disagree to strongly agree. The results were scaled so that each question gives 0–10 points, with 10 indicating maximal trust. We used the following classification: High trust for a score > 64, moderate trust $48 - 63$, low trust $32 - 47$ and very low trust < 32.

5   User Protocol

For the experiment we used the crowd-sourcing platform Prolific [25]. The context provided to the participants was the following: the city council is organising local elections to request its citizens' opinion on several society subjects. To cast their vote, the participants used our online application.

Trust and UX were evaluated in the standard way: after having interacted with the application, the participants were given questionnaires. We used the System Usability Scale, the User Experience questionnaire [31] and our trust questionnaire. Then, to evaluate the understanding, we designed a user game inspired by the game theoretic experiment in [18]. The participants interact once more with the application but we provided an additional scenario: the participant had to interact with a vote buyer[1]. The instructions from the vote buyer were displayed in a box next to the web page: the vote-buyer asks for a different vote than the choice made by the voter (we configured the game by asking in advance the voter's opinion, see below). Our evaluation consists in looking at the participant's behaviour in such a scenario. Our assumption is that a correct understanding will lead the participants to vote for their candidate and use the receipt-free mechanism to provide a fake tracker to the vote buyer.

Pilot studies. We ran two pilot studies with five participants in each. In the first pilot, none of the five participants watched the video nor tried the receipt-free mechanism (even with the vote-buying scenario) and they finished the study in less than five minutes (while 20 min. were given). This rush bias is well known and called "satisficing" in Prolific's terms of use. To ensure the participants use the

---

[1] With Selene, countering vote buying and coercion involves the same user steps.

app fully, we introduced a workflow: they could not access the questionnaires and continue the study before they used the mechanism to get a new tracking number. Guidance was provided as side notes on the website. Also, some attention checks were added to the questionnaires as recommended by Prolific. We further discuss the limitations in sect. 5.1 below.

Participants were paid 2.5£ for the study (20 min) which was evaluated as a *Good* hourly rate by Prolific, and we added an extra 1£ as a bonus payment for having played the game.

After a consent form, the user experiment had the following steps

Demographics. We recruited 300 participants on the crowd-sourcing website Prolific [25]. We used the pre-screening feature to select participants: to ensure that they have a similar experience in voting, we chose UK citizens living in UK. The average age was 33 years (Min=18, Max=73, SD=11). They come from various backgrounds, the education level differed: No diploma (0,67%), A-Levels (13,33%), College Level (19,33%), Bachelor (42,33%), Master Degree (20%), PhD (1,33%) and other (3%). Finally, regarding their attitude toward online voting, 2,33% were negative, 7% were rather negative, 39,67% were neutral, 35,67% were rather positive and 14,67% were positive.

Configuration. In the end of the demographics' questionnaire, we asked the participants to answer the voting question used in the game, to configure the vote buyer's instruction. The question was about the COVID-19 crisis:

Regarding the recent events related to the COVID-19 pandemic, according to you, what would be the best policy to adopt at the beginning of the epidemic?
- A strict confinement for all
- No confinement but detection tests available for everyone

We configured the game by changing the vote buyer's instructions according to their opinion. If they chose "A strict opinion for all", the vote buyer asks for "No confinement but detection tests available for everyone" and vice versa.

Video. explaining the protocol: We describe the Selene protocol in a 4-minute video that the voter was invited to watch.

A Tutorial to Demonstrate the Receipt-free Mechanism. First, we let the participants use the application through a tutorial. As mentioned above, the first pilot study has shown that participants were rushing to end the study as fast as possible. The tutorial ensures that they see and test all available features in the application, a specific workflow was forced with guidance, given as side notes. Therefore, participants were able to verify their vote and then fake their tracking number. We wanted to show that they can see their plaintext vote, but also have the ability to change their tracking number to show another vote to a coercer or vote-buyer.

Questionnaires. We evaluated the usability, user experience and trust after this tutorial phase. The reason was that we did not want to influence their trust rating by going through a coercive scenario, but obtain their general impression of the app. Also, we put a few attention checks (through questions about the app) at the beginning of our questionnaire. The checks were announced in the study description on Prolific. Our goal was to increase the attention given to the explanations in the app. Of course there is a possibility that the participant did not understand the protocol and provide wrong answers. We did not exclude such participants, our goal was to help them to focus on the information rather than skipping it as in the pilot study.

Vote-Buying Game. We introduced the game by telling the participants that they will receive instructions from a vote buyer. The rules were given as:

A vote buyer wants to buy your vote by giving you a vote instruction. He may ask you how you voted and to reveal your tracking code, in which case you can give an alternate code.

If you send a tracking code for the requested candidate, you will receive 70 pence from the vote buyer.

If you want to keep your vote intention, you will receive 30 pence.

These incentives will be provided as bonus payment after the study.[2]

When participants start, they were asked to vote as they did in the tutorial but additional instructions given by the vote buyer on the left side of the screen. The participants van choose whether or not to follow the vote buyer's instructions. Our idea was to determine whether the participants understood that they can keep their vote while convincing the vote buyer that they follow his choice. Indeed, the dominant strategy for a player, given the possibilities offered by the application, is to cast the intended vote while selling a fake tracker to the vote buyer.[3] After computing the tracking number, the participant could choose to send it to the vote buyer or not by clicking on a button.

End of Study. To finish the study, the participants were asked to tell which choice they made - keep their vote intention or follow the vote buyer's instructions - and why. Our last question was about how they felt during the game.

Ethical approval. We obtained ethical approval from our institution's Ethics Panel. Our work is compliant with GDPR and the research terms of Prolific.

---

[2] In the end we provided both incentives as bonus payment to all participants regardless of their choice, for fairness.

[3] Note that the instructions were formulated without directly revealing this optimal strategy, but the participants should deduce it if they understood the introduction to the study and the explanatory video.

5.1   Limitations

While Prolific brought many advantages, including reaching many participants rapidly, and good demographic samples, we found some limitations.

Regarding our trust questionnaire, even though we built the questionnaire to answer specific needs, we are aware that the questionnaire needs further testing to be validated by the community. This first study using it is an attempt to grasp insights on trust with a specific approach of security perception and acceptance.

Correlations were shown between our measurements (see the next section): some items have been assessed *before* the vote-buying game (trust, usability), while others have been asked *after* the vote buying game (feelings). The correlations found between those measurements could be altered by the game.

Our first pilot study showed that participants are rushing, likely to increase their reward per hour. Without any guidance, we could not hope that participants will visit all pages in our app, forcing us to make them first test the app through a tutorial rather than exploration. This is known as "satisficing bias" and is acknowledged by Prolific [25]. To counter this, we asked the participants to answer questions regarding their understanding in the app: these "attention checks" are recommended by Prolific and helped us to lower this bias.

Another limitation concerns our scenario with vote-buying. As for studies in the lab, participants might have a bias to give a good image of themselves, hence answering what would be ethically acceptable [16,17]. In this study, some participants justified themselves for having followed the vote buyer because "this is just a game", or mentioned their integrity for not having followed him.

Finally, we ask participants to understand new features in a limited amount of time. More time would be necessary to understand the features.

6   Results: Evaluation of Understanding of Receipt-Freeness

6.1   Quantitative Results

Usability and User Experience. In this section we will explore the results obtained for the user experience and the usability questionnaires. Following to the UX handbook [31], a result above 0.8 for the UEQ categories would be considered as positive.

We obtained the following results with the UEQ: Attractiveness obtained -0.1 (SD=0.08), Perspecuity obtained -0.41 (SD=0.09), Efficiency obtained 0.31 (SD=0.09), Dependability obtained 0.6 (SD=0.06), Stimulation obtained 0.12 (SD=0.07), Novelty obtained 0.55 (SD=0.07).

Compared to the previous studies on Selene measuring the user experience through a mobile application [9,22], we can see that the web application performed poorly. The attractiveness has been rated as -0.1 (SD=0.08), the usability aspects received the score of 0.16 (SD=0.08) and the hedonic aspects received the score of 0.33 (SD=0.06). At a subscale level, dependability received the higher score with 0.6 (SD=0.06).

Where perspicuity (difficult to learn/easy to learn) was the highest score in [9] (with 2.16 and 1.90), we obtained the lower score with -0.41 (SD=0.09). We will discuss the possible reasons in the discussion.

We summarise the SUS (System Usability Scale) results. We measured effectiveness by asking the participants to give a self assessment of their individual verification step: we asked if they found their tracking code on the bulletin board. Only 86% of the participants answered that they found their vote, even though we know that all participants have computed their tracking number.

Efficiency was measured through the time taken by the participants to vote and to compute their tracking code after having logged in to the application. The mean time is 57 s (median=45.5, SD=39.65, min=17, max=324).

Compared to [22], again, the web application performed poorly on the satisfaction scale (mean=48.67, median=45, SD=22.81, min=0, max=100) with a mean score below 51, considered as "unacceptable" in [5]. We can also note that participants were on average six times faster to vote and verify compared to the lab study in [22], while the minimum time to cast a vote is almost twelve times faster with the web app, questioning the participants' commitment to the test.

In conclusion, the hypothesis **H1** is not supported by the experiments: our web app did not provide a positive user experience (scores below 0.8) nor an acceptable usability.

Trust. As mentioned above, the questionnaires were filled after the tutorial phase and before the game. This was to let the participants give an evaluation of the app and of its features before we collect the data regarding their understanding. We did not want a specific threat scenario to influence their opinion on the protocol itself.

Overall, trust received an evaluation of 46.81 ($SD = 16.132, Min = 4, Max = 78$). On the subscale level, the acceptance (over 30) was rated 18.59 ($SD = 7.264, Min = 0, Max = 30$) and the feeling of security (over 50) was rated 28 ($SD = 20.093, Min = 0, Max = 48$).

Regarding the grading proposed in Sect. 4, the trust has been evaluated as low by the participants. We can conclude from this result that our hypothesis **H2** is not supported by our results.

Understanding. As a reminder, we evaluate the understanding of the receipt-free mechanism as correct when participants kept their vote intention while faking their tracker for the vote-buyer. In total, 54 of 300 participants chose this dominant strategy, and *correctly* understood the faking mechanism.

6.2   Qualitative Results and Relations Between Variables

We have done a qualitative analysis of the answers from the game and the feedback from our two last questions. The details are included in the full version of the paper[4]. Especially we categorise the answer to the question "Why have you

---

[4] https://arxiv.org/abs/2407.13240.

made this choice in the game?" in terms of the labels money, integrity, understanding, experimenting (wanting to experiment) and miscellaneous. And for the question "How did you feel during the study" we use the labels overwhelmed, stressed, offended, good, interested, confident, confused and observed.

While the questionnaires were filled after the first phase (tutorial) of the user study, the understanding of participants and the qualitative data were collected after the second phase (game). In particular, the vote-buying scenario might have impacted some participants' feedback especially their feeling regarding the study. The following correlations should be considered under this limitation.

Trust and Understanding: When defining trust, our questionnaire was built with the idea that the explanations provided were important to give transparency and to increase the voters' understanding in the application. During the study, we gave explanations through video and text, participants followed a tutorial before playing a game designed to evaluate their understanding of the features. This study design allows us to check the correlation between the Trust results and the voters' Understanding, measured by observing their decisions.

Understanding was measured by looking at the capacity of a participant to vote as intended while faking the tracker for the vote buyer. We obtained one group of 54 participants out of 300 who understood. To measure the correlation between trust and understanding, we performed an independent t-test. The participants who understood the concealing feature gave a statistically higher evaluation of trust ($Mean = 51.22$, $SD = 15.372$) compared to participants who did not understand it ($Mean = 45.84$, $SD = 16.163$), $t(298) = 2.236$, $p = 0.026$. Further, Cohen's effect size value ($d = 0.34$) suggested a small to moderate practical significance. We conclude the evidence was in favour of hypothesis **H3**.

Trust and Satisfaction Measures: We computed the Pearson correlation coefficient $r = 0.561$ ($p = 0.01$) between our trust and satisfaction measures, implying a moderate positive correlation between trust and usability. Similarly, the coefficients between Trust and the UEQ's scale are: Attractiveness 0.14 (p=0.05); Perspicuity 0.135 (p=0.05); Efficiency 0.149 (p=0.01); Dependability 0.151 (p=0.01); Stimulation 0.173 (p=0.01); Novelty 0.063. The values for r are below 0.2 indicating a weak positive relation.

Understanding and Time Spent in the Study: 47 participants finished in less than 20 min (which was the planned time), whereas the mean was 35 min and 55 sec. Participants took more time than planned, probably because of our attention checks, added after the pilot studies where participants rushed through within five minutes. We ran a one-way ANOVA test, which showed no significant difference between those who understood the game and the others.

Self-explanation/Feeling and Understanding: Of the 54 participants who faked their tracking code to send to the vote buyer, 26 mentioned integrity, 3 money, 17 gave an explanation about their understanding. Conversely, 2 participants explained correctly how the system works, but did not fake their tracking code for the vote buyer. Regarding feelings, 22 participants of the 54 said that they were confused, 25 that they were felt good, confident or interested in the system, the remaining 7 were felt observed, stressed, overwhelmed or frustrated.

A Welch ANOVA test between the decision categorization and the understanding shows no significant differences between the five groups ($p > 0.05$). Hence in our sample, we cannot conclude on the relation of the understanding of participants to the reason for following the vote buyer or not. Similarly, we found no significant differences between the 8 groups of feelings ($p > 0.05$). Thus the understanding of participants might not be related to the feelings of participants.

Self-explanation/Feeling and Trust: The relation between the decision's categories and the trust assessments is analyzed with a 1-way ANOVA. The ANOVA test shows a significant difference between the five categories ($F(4, 295) = 2.872, p = 0.023$). A post-hoc Tukey is run to locate differences between categories, and found that participants who mentioned integrity rated trust better (8 points) than those interested in money ($p = 0.016$). On the other hand, there was no significant difference between the 8 groups of feelings ($p > 0.05$). Hence, the participants' trust (evaluated after the tutorial) was not influenced by their feelings (evaluated after the game).

Self-explanation/Feeling and Usability: We run a 1-way ANOVA test to investigate a relation between the SUS assessments and the self-explanation provided. The test shows a significant difference between the five categories ($F(4, 295) = 2, 729, p = 0.029$). A post-hoc Tukey found that participants who mentioned an experimentation gave a better evaluation than those doing the test for money ($p = 0.049$).

We also run a 1-way ANOVA test to find a relation between the feeling's categories and the SUS assessments. The ANOVA test shows a significant difference between the 8 categories ($F(7, 292) = 3.446, p = 0.001$). A post-hoc Tukey found that participants who felt interested rated better than those feeling overwhelmed or stressed (for reference here $p < 0.05$). The details of the analysis are as follows (we report those with a significant difference only):

	Difference between the means	P value
Experimenting over Money	15.48	0.049
Interested over Overwhelmed	21.34	0.039
Interested over Stressed	21.34	0.009

Similarly, we run a 1-way ANOVA to find relations between the UEQ items and the categories for self-explanation and feelings. For self-explanation, no relation was found ($p > 0.05$). We found a relation between the feelings' groups and the UEQ items with statistical significance ($p < 0.001$). Overall, participants having a positive feeling regarding the app rated it better than the other participants with $p < 0.05$.

6.3   Analysis and Discussion

No relation was found between the understanding of participants and their self-explanation or feeling regarding the application. However, we have seen that trust and understanding are correlated, which supports our hypothesis.

We see that the user experience and usability were poorly rated. Here we found a moderate correlation between satisfaction and trust, but only a small correlation between UEQ items and trust. In the SUS questionnaire, some items concern the acceptance of the tested application, which is one aspect of our trust questionnaire, and might explain the stronger correlation. However, we argue that a good user interface will benefit a voting application. In [13,20], the authors mention the signals impacting trust, including usability. We had good results regarding effectiveness and the efficiency, but we failed at convincing the participants that our application was easy to use and enjoyable.

To explain this, we look at the feelings formulated by the participants. The most expressed feeling was *confusion*: with participants unsure about the steps to follow. A highlighted reason was the complexity of the study, while Prolific's users are used to surveys, which are linear and require less commitment (in the sense of direct interactions influencing the behaviour of the app) from the user. Other feelings expressed by participants were *stress* and *frustration*.

However, we also found that 128 participants had a positive feeling about the study (feeling *good*, *interested*, or *confident*), mentioning their curiosity for online voting or their satisfaction regarding the security of the app. Those participants also rated the usability and UX of the application better than the others, supporting our previous idea of the benefits of a good interface.

We also note that in previous studies using the Selene protocol, for example [9,22], the usability and user experience of Selene obtained higher scores. In these studies, Selene was implemented as a mobile app with a linear workflow, and without the faking mechanism. As a result, participants just cast their vote and verify that it was correctly recorded. In our study, all participants had to go through the faking feature, which might be a reason for participants' confusion. Further, participants could navigate through the pages without a unique workflow. The lack of linearity and the faking mechanism could also have lowered the usability score. This low score should be seen in the context of the study : we wanted to evaluate the full implementation with all participants testing the faking mechanism. In a real election it is unlikely that all voters need this feature. verification phases would probably increase the satisfaction of voters.

Finally, we hypothesize that the vote buying scenario could have led to lower trust: the qualitative feedback has shown that several people were shocked by the possibility of showing their vote to a coercer/vote buyer, and was sometimes seen as vote selling. In fact, the mechanism is designed to prevent vote buying, since a vote buyer cannot detect if it is a fake tracker. The security feature and the exacerbation of a possible threat has possibly decreased the trust from the participants, when being misunderstood. We can also note that around 50% of participants were positive to online voting and more than 90% did not have negative opinion about it before the study, adding credence to this assumption.

6.4 Recommendations

Here we provide a list of recommendations: four concern the development of future voting systems (VS), and two are about the design of user studies (US).

[VS] Focus on understandability. We found that participants who understood our security features rated trust higher than other participants. However, we saw that our application was confusing and tasks too complex. When providing a new security feature one must ensure it is correctly understood to obtain an increase of trust. It is crucial to provide a transparent interface, with understandable features, to increase trust and acceptance.

[VS] Provide an easy-to-use interface. While we must provide understandable and transparent information to participants, it also remains important to keep the interface as simple as possible. People who got stressed and overwhelmed by the application were less satisfied. Indeed, we found that the participants who rated the application better had a positive feeling during the study. Hence, we recommend remaining simple and straightforward, keep the workflow as linear and guiding as possible.

[VS] Raise awareness and improve education. Many participants highlighted the illegality of vote buying. To them, the fact that the law is already designed to counter some threats is sufficient to trust the system. However, if a voting system is not trustworthy opens a door to attackers. We recommend communicating good practices in security and risks that could arise from a misuse of the procedure. Good education, as highlighted in previous work on mental models [34,35] and in [13], is key to trusted applications.

[VS] Adapt the interface to the voters' profile. Many participants did not see the need for a receipt-free feature (in the context of the participants' country). For future implementations, we suggest adapting the interface that will be more realistic to a targeted audience, making receipt-free aspects optional.

[US] Reduce the complexity and simplify (online) user studies. We have discussed that many participants were confused during the test. We know from previous studies [21,34] that the concept of Verifiability is hard to understand. The receipt-free feature increased the complexity. We learned that Prolific's participants need guidance to follow a study correctly, as they won't take time to explore an application. We recommend simplifying such user studies.

[US] Use the right tool. In relation to limitations observed with Prolific, we further recommend in-person interviews for studies about understanding. The bias of satisficing does not help participants to focus and take time to understand the features and new concepts provided. In this study, we had a small number of participants who clearly understood the features, and we saw a correlation between their understanding and trust in the system. For an evaluation of voters' understanding and of the user experience, in-person studies with focus groups and/or interviews will bring better insights.

7   Conclusion and Future Work

In this paper, we defined trust in a voting system, and proposed a new questionnaire to assess it. We also designed and conducted a user study to evaluated the Selene voting system, including its receipt-free mechanism. Our application was tested by 300 participants; we evaluated their experience by measuring their understanding through a unique game design, and assessed their trust in the system using the new questionnaire. While the usability and trust factors were rated low in the experiments, the results supported a positive relation between trust and understanding. This let to recommendations to increase trust and usability in voting applications and to improve future user studies. Our recommendations are: 1) Focus on the understandability, 2) Provide an easy-to-use-interface, 3) Raise awareness and improve education, 4) Adapt the scenario to the audience, 5) Reduce the complexity and 6) Use the right tool. The first four apply to any (verifiable) voting system, the two last concern the execution of such trials.

For future research, it would be interesting to compare the feedback from another country, where our scenario is more common. We could set up a two-players game where one participant plays the role of a coercer or vote buyer and another plays the role of the voter, to see if the mechanism is better understood by the participants. We plan to apply and validate our trust questionnaire for other e-voting protocols and compare to [1].

Acknowldgements. The research was supported by Luxembourg National Research Fund FNR C21/IS/16221219/ImPAKT and C22/IS/ 17232062/SpaceVote, and NCBR Poland under the project SpaceVote POLLUX-XI/14/SpaceVote/2023.

References

1. Acemyan, C.Z., Kortum, P., Oswald, F.L.: The trust in voting systems (TVS) measure. Int. J. Technol. Hum. Interact. (IJTHI) **18**(1), 1–23 (2022)
2. Acemyan, C.Z., Kortum, P., Byrne, M.D., Wallach, D.S.: Users' mental models for three end-to-end voting systems: helios, Prêt à voter, and scantegrity II. In: Tryfonas, T., Askoxylakis, I. (eds.) HAS 2015. LNCS, vol. 9190, pp. 463–474. Springer, Cham (2015). https://doi.org/10.1007/978-3-319-20376-8_41
3. Agbesi, S., Dalela, A., Budurushi, J., and Kulyk, O.: What will make me trust or not trust will depend upon how secure the technology is: factors influencing trust perceptions of the use of election technologies. In: Proceedings of Seventh International Joint Conference on Electronic Voting, p. 1 (2022). University of Tartu

4. Alsadi, M., and Schneider, S.: Verify my vote: voter experience. In: Electronic Voting - E-Vote-ID 2020 (TalTech Proceedings), p. 280 (2020)
5. Bangor, A., Kortum, P.T., Miller, J.T.: An empirical evaluation of the system usability scale. Int. J. Hum. Comput. Interact. **24**(6), 574–594 (2008)
6. Bella, G., Curzon, P., Giustolisi, R., and Lenzini, G.: A socio-technical methodology for the security and privacy analysis of services. In: COMPSAC Workshops, IEEE Computer Society, pp. 401–406 (2014)
7. Chiang, L.: Trust and security in the e-voting system. Electron. Gov. Int. J. **6**(4), 343–360 (2009)
8. Delaune, S., Kremer, S., and Ryan, M.: Coercion-resistance and receipt-freeness in electronic voting. In: 19th IEEE Computer Security Foundations Workshop, (CSFW-19), pp. 28–42 (2006). IEEE Computer Society
9. Distler, V., Zollinger, M.L., Lallemand, C., Rønne, P.B., Ryan, P.Y., Koenig, V.: Security-visible, yet unseen? how displaying security mechanisms impacts user experience and perceived security. In: CHI Conference on Human Factors in Computing Systems (CHI 2019) (2019)
10. Glass, A., McGuinness, D.L., Wolverton, M.: Toward establishing trust in adaptive agents. In: Proceedings of the 13th International Conference on Intelligent User Interfaces, pp. 227–236(2008)
11. Hao, F., Ryan, P.: Real-World Electronic Voting: Design. Auerbach Publications, Analysis and Deployment (2016)
12. Juels, A., Catalano, D., Jakobsson, M.: Coercion-resistant electronic elections. In: ACM Workshop on Privacy in the Electronic Society, pp. 61–70 (2005)
13. Kirlappos, I., Sasse, M.A.: What usable security really means: trusting and engaging users. In: Human Aspects of Information Security, Privacy, and Trust, vol. 8533 of Lecture Notes in Computer Science, Springer, pp. 69–78 (2014)
14. Kulyk, O., Neumann, S.: Human factors in coercion resistant internet voting – a review of existing solutions and open challenges. In: E-Vote-ID (2020)
15. Kulyk, O., Neumann, S., Budurushi, J., Volkamer, M.: Nothing comes for free: how much usability can you sacrifice for security? IEEE S&P **15**(3), 24–29 (2017)
16. Lallemand, C., Koenig, V.: Lab testing beyond usability: challenges and recommendations for assessing user experiences. J. Usability Stud. **12**(3) (2017)
17. Levitt, S.D., List, J.A.: What do laboratory experiments tell us about the real world. J. Econ. Perspect. 153–174 (2007)
18. Llewellyn, M., et al.: Testing voters' understanding of a security mechanism used in verifiable voting. In: 2013 Electronic Voting Technology Workshop/Workshop on Trustworthy Elections (EVT/WOTE 13) (2013)
19. Luhmann, N.: Trust and Power, 3 ed. Polity Press (2017)
20. Malheiros, M., Jennett, C., Seager, W., Sasse, M.A.: Trusting to learn: trust and privacy issues in serious games. In: McCune, J.M., Balacheff, B., Perrig, A., Sadeghi, A.-R., Sasse, A., Beres, Y. (eds.) Trust 2011. LNCS, vol. 6740, pp. 116–130. Springer, Heidelberg (2011). https://doi.org/10.1007/978-3-642-21599-5_9
21. Marky, K., Kulyk, O., Renaud, K., Volkamer, M.: What did I really vote for? On the usability of verifiable e-voting schemes. In: Proceedings of the Conference on Human Factors in Computing Systems (CHI), pp. 1–13 (2018). ACM
22. Marky, K., Zollinger, M.-L., Roenne, P.B., Ryan, P.Y.A., Grube, T., Kunze, K.: Investigating usability and user experience of individually verifiable internet voting schemes. ACM Trans. CHI **28**, 5 (2021)
23. Neto, A.S., Leite, M., Araújo, R., Mota, M.P., Neto, N.C.S., Traoré, J.: Usability considerations for coercion-resistant election systems. In: 17th Brazilian Symposium on Human Factors in Computing Systems, pp. 1–10 (2018)

24. Pieters, W.: Explanation and trust: what to tell the user in security and AI? Ethics Inf. Technol. **13**(1), 53–64 (2010)
25. Prolific: Prolific. https://www.prolific.co/
26. Ryan, P.Y., Bismark, D., Heather, J., Schneider, S., Xia, Z.: Prêt à voter: a voter-verifiable voting system. IEEE Trans. Inf. Forensics Secur. **4**(4), 662–673 (2009)
27. Ryan, P.Y.A., Rønne, P.B. Iovino, V.: Voting with transparent verifiability and coercion-mitigation. In Financial Crypto, Selene (2016)
28. Ryan, P.Y.A., Schneider, S.A., Teague, V.: End-to-end verifiability in voting systems, from theory to practice. IEEE S&P **13**(3), 59–62 (2015)
29. Sallal, M., et al.: VMV: Augmenting an internet voting system with Selene verifiability 2019. arXiv:1912.00288
30. Schneider, S., Llewellyn, M., Culnane, C., Heather, J., Srinivasan, S., Xia, Z.: Focus group views on Prêt à Voter 1.0. In: 2011 International Workshop on Requirements Engineering for Electronic Voting Systems, pp. 56–65 (2011)
31. Schrepp, M.: User experience questionnaire handbook (2018). https://www.ueq-online.org/
32. Schrepp, M.: The extended user experience questionnaire (2019). http://ueqplus.ueq-research.org/
33. Schürmann, C.: Electronic elections: trust through engineering. In: First International Workshop on Requirements Engineering for e-Voting Systems, pp. 38–46 (2009)
34. Zollinger, M., Distler, V., Rønne, P.B., Ryan, P.Y., Lallemand, C., Koenig, V.: User experience design for E-voting: how mental models align with security mechanisms. In: E-Vote-ID 2019, TalTech Proceedings (2019)
35. Zollinger, M.L., Estaji, E., Ryan, P.Y., Marky, K.: Just for the sake for transparency: exploring voter mental models of verifiability. In: Electronic Voting - Sixth International Joint Conference, E-Vote-ID 2021 (2021)

Author Index

© The Editor(s) (if applicable) and The Author(s) 2025
D. Duenas-Cid et al. (Eds.): E-Vote-ID 2024, LNCS 15014, p. 175, 2025.
https://doi.org/10.1007/978-3-031-72244-8